Andrea Pető
The Forgotten Massacre

Andrea Pető
The Forgotten Massacre

—

Budapest in 1944

The writing of this book was possible because of research leave granted from the Central European University between 2017 and 2019, and the distinguished fellowship of the Institut für Zeitgeschichte Zentrum für Holocaust-Studien (München) in 2019.

ISBN 978-3-11-109509-7
e-ISBN (PDF) 978-3-11-068755-2
e-ISBN (EPUB) 978-3-11-068759-0

Library of Congress Control Number: 2020952344

Bibliographic information published by the Deutsche Nationalbibliothek
The Deutsche Nationalbibliothek lists this publication in the Deutsche Nationalbibliografie; detailed bibliographic data are available on the Internet at http://dnb.dnb.de.

© 2022 Walter de Gruyter GmbH, Berlin/Boston
This volume is text- and page-identical with the hardback published in 2021.
Cover Image: Entrance of Csengery utca 64, Budapest. Photograph by Andrea Pető. Printing and binding: CPI books GmbH, Leck

www.degruyter.com

Acknowledgements

In 2003 I became acquainted with a group of the survivors of the Csengery Street massacre who for decades fought for a dignified remembrance of the bloody events. I thank them for helping in my research and I dedicate this book to them.

This volume is based on my research on far-right women's politics, which started in 2002, on my dissertation for the Hungarian Academy of Sciences (MTA) submitted in 2012 and defended in 2015, and on my book *Láthatatlan elkövetők* (Invisible Perpetrators. Budapest, Jaffa 2019). I received much help during this time, especially from Barna Ildikó, Bárd Károly, Gyáni Gábor, Kovács András, Örkény Antal and Sipos Balázs, as well as from Klaartje Schrijvers, Selma Leydesdorff, Eleonore Lappin, Ayşe Gül Altınay, Patricia Chiantera-Stutte, and Zonneke Matthée. I am grateful to the defenders of my MTA dissertation, Mezey Barna, Standeisky Éva and Kozáry Andrea, for their meticulous work. I also would like to thank to the publisher for the very helpful anonymus review and for all the support received during the publishing process and when I had to move with the Central European University to Vienna.

I am especially grateful to the different archives and their achivists supporting my work in *Állambiztonsági Szolgálatok Történeti Levéltára* (Historical Archive of State Security Services), *Budapest Főváros Levéltára* (Budapest City Archives), *Magyar Fotográfiai Múzeum* (Hungarian Museum of Photography), *Magyar Nemzeti Múzeum Történeti Fényképtára* (Hungarian National Museum's Historical Photo Department), *Nyílt Társadalom Alapítvány Archívuma* (Open Society Archives), *Budapesti Ügyvédi Kamara Irattára* (Archive of the Budapest Bar Association), *Magyar Nemzeti Levéltár* (National Archives of Hungary), *Politikatudományi Intézet Levéltára* (Archive of the Institute of Political History), *Országos Széchényi Könyvtár* (National Széchényi Library), *Rendőr Múzeum Fotóarchívuma* (Photoarchive of the Police Museum), *MTVA Nemzeti Fotótára* (Photoarchive of the National Broadcasting Foundation), and the CEU Library.

The writing of this book was possible because of research leave granted from the Central European University between 2017 and 2019, and the distinguished fellowship of the Institut für Zeitgeschichte Zentrum für Holocaust-Studien (München) in 2019.

Thanks to Petra Bakos for her work translating and supporting this publication.

Contents

List of Acronyms —— XI

1	**Introduction —— 1**	
1.1	The reasons for forgetting —— 7	

2 What makes Csengery 64 important? —— 13

3 The House —— 20

4 Piroska Dely in Budapest —— 26
4.1   Her biography —— 27
4.2   Her trial —— 28
4.2.1   The People's Tribunals —— 28
4.2.2   Between sloppiness and rigor: The People's Tribunals' activity —— 33
4.2.3   Piroska Dely in front of the People's Tribunal —— 35
4.2.4   Was she present at all? —— 38
4.2.5   Changing explanations —— 40
4.2.6   The power objects: The Arrow Cross armband and the weapon —— 46
4.2.7   The power of "executive power" —— 47
4.2.8   The endgame —— 49

5 Death and the Maiden —— 51
5.1   Those who speak for the dead —— 53
5.1.1   Why were they killed? The "Jewish resistance" version —— 55
5.1.2   Why were they killed? The Széplaki version —— 57
5.2   Murders at night —— 58
5.2.1   The Strucky version —— 59
5.2.2   The Steiner version —— 61
5.3   What happened to the dead? —— 63

6 The Perpetrators —— 65
6.1   The janitors' greed —— 66
6.2   The collaborating projectionist, translator, courier, driver, SS-soldier, and father —— 69
6.3   The verdict —— 73

6.4	The truth of the perpetrators' memories —— 76	
6.5	The Szamocseta story – As told by them —— 78	

7	**The Greed** —— 82	
7.1	The birth of wealth —— 83	
7.2	The loss of wealth —— 87	

8	**Revenge and Forgiveness** —— 90	
8.1	The frameworks of justice —— 90	
8.2	Moral witness or political witness? —— 92	
8.3	The affect of testimony —— 94	

9	**The Survivors and the Surviving Memories** —— 98	
9.1	Taking an inventory —— 99	
9.2	In defense of the right to memory —— 101	
9.3	The missing dialogic collective memory —— 104	
9.4	Csengery Street 64: A memorial or a monument? —— 109	

10	**Conclusion** —— 111	

References —— 118

Archival Sources —— 128
        List of Interviews —— 128
        Manuscripts —— 129

Appendix 1 The chronology of Piroska Dely's trial, its background and afterlife —— 130

Appendix 2 The Chronology of the Szamocseta Case —— 139

Appendix 3 The story of the Csengery Street massacre —— 148

Appendix 4 *Persilschein* —— 159

Appendix 5 Tenant registry —— 161

Appendix 6 The text of the memory plaque —— 170

Appendix 7 The victims of the Csengery Street massacre —— 171

Appendix 8 Petition for the Csengery Street commemorative plaque —— 174

Appendix 9 Interview with the son of Nándor Szamocseta —— 176

Appendix 10 List of illustrations —— 178

Index of Names —— 179

Index of Subjects —— 182

List of Acronyms

ÁBTL	Állambiztonsági Szolgálatok Történeti Levéltára / Historical Archives of the Hungarian State Security Services
ÁVO	Államvédelmi Osztály / Department of State Protection
BFL	Budapest Főváros Levéltára / Budapest City Archives
BÜKI	Budapesti Ügyvédi Kamara Archívuma / Archives of the Budapest Bar Association
MÁR	Magyar Állami Rendőrség / Hungarian State Police
MOL	Magyar Országos Levéltár / Hungarian National Archives
NOT	Népbíróságok Országos Tanácsa / National Council of People's Tribunals
SZEB	Szövetséges Ellenőrző Bizottság / Allied Commission

1 Introduction

In 2003 I held a public lecture in Budapest on the history of the Arrow Cross women's movement. At the end of the lecture an elderly grey-haired man approached me with a question: "Have you heard about Piroska Dely?" "Of course – I answered self-assuredly –, the literature on the people's tribunals mention her name. She was the bloodthirsty Arrow Cross woman who was executed after her people's tribunal trial." My colleagues in Hungary never exhibited much enthusiasm when I told them about my research on women in the Arrow Cross Party.[1] Still, everyone knew Dely's name, because every volume on post-Second World War justice listed the names of those female war criminals, among them Piroska Dely, who were sentenced to death and executed.[2] The elderly man with impeccable silver hair nodded and said: "I met her." This is how I met a group of the Csengery Street massacre's survivors who for decades fought for a dignified remembrance of the bloody events. János Kun's sentence gave an entirely new dimension to my research, which led to my Hungarian Academy of Sciences doctoral dissertation and to the writing of this book. I thank them for helping in my research and I dedicate this book to them.

During the Second World War Hungary was Germany's loyal foreign ally. From 1938 four Anti-Jewish Laws were put in effect, that is laws that limited the employment, marriage, and property rights of Jewish Hungarian citizens. On April 11, 1941 Hungary's armed forces participated in the German invasion of Yugoslavia with the aim of returning territories lost at the end of the First World War. For these territorial gains Hungary paid a huge price: the Hungarian economy was sacrificed to Germany's war goals. In the meantime, Hungarian propaganda machinery emphasized the Hungarian government's independence and its national commitment, but the country's territorial demands and geopolitical realities tied Hungary to Nazi Germany, while Germany increasingly expected commitment and support from its allies.

In popular memory it seems as though Hungary only entered the Second World War in 1944. Newspapers and newsreels were full of military propaganda and, due to effective censorship, the military success of Germany and of course Hungary. The strategy of the Hungarian political elite was framed by the devastating experience of the First World War when Hungary was expected to sign a peace treaty without a functioning army. That explains the reluctance of Hungary

---

1 Andrea Pető, *Invisible Women in the Arrow Cross Party* (London: Palgrave Macmillan, 2020).
2 Ákos Major, *Népbíráskodás, forradalmi törvényesség* [People's Tribunals, revolutionary justice] (Budapest: Minerva, 1988), 123.

as an ally of Nazi Germany to send troops to Yugoslavia in 1941 and to the Soviet Union. The fact that hundreds of thousands of soldiers were on the front did not have an impact on the 'business as usual' attitude of civilian life back in Hungary. Somehow that was also the case with Jewish citizens of the country, as the fact that the increasing deprivation of their rights by Anti-Jewish legislation, with Jewish men drafted in to do labour, was considered the 'new normal' by the gentile population. In oral history interviews, however, the starting point of the Second World War is usually only 1944, when the war moved inside the territory of the Kingdom of Hungary.

Aware of Hungary's faltering loyalty, Germany occupied Hungary on March 19, 1944. This date marked the beginning of the Second World War for Hungarian Jewry because soon after, and without direct German orders, Hungary commenced the mass deportation of Hungarian Jews based on the April 4, 1944 6136/1944 No. VII decree of the Ministry of Internal Affairs. Between April 28 and July 8, 1944 more than 435,000 Jewish Hungarian citizens were deported to German concentration and annihiliation camps with the Hungarian administration's active participation. For non-Jewish Hungarians only the threat of the approaching Red Army and the Allied bombings marked the beginning of the war. On October 15, 1944 the Hungarian far-right seized power and thus began the short but bloody and chaotic rule of the Arrow Cross Party.

After the mass deportations of Jewish people from the Hungarian countryside the fate of the largest Hungarian Jewish community, the Budapest Jewry was increasingly unpredictable. On June 16, 1944 a mayoral decree was issued for the forcible relocation of the Jewish citizens of Budapest into approximately 2,600 designated yellow Star of David houses. The deadline for the move was midnight June 24, 1944. About 12,000 Christians remained in the yellow star houses, among them the Strucky-Szamocseta family of the janitors of Csengery Street 64, the site of the events central to this book.[3]

October 15, 1944 was a nice sunny day. People listened to Regent Horthy's radio speech in which he proclaimed that Germany had lost the war and Hungary was ready to sign an armistice with the Allied Powers. In Budapest's Csengery Street, 64 yellow star-wearing people gathered on the courtyard to listen to Horthy's historic declaration. This radio earlier belonged to one of the Jewish tenants of the house, but as the Anti-Jewish Laws came in effect, which prohibited Jews from owning a radio, it came into the possession of the only Christian fam-

---

3 Dezső Laky, "A háztulajdon alakulása Budapesten" [State of Household Ownership in Budapest]. *Statisztikai Közlemények* 66.1 (1932): 89–99.

ily that remained in the house, the janitors.⁴ The janitor put it on the windowsill so the Jewish tenants could also listen to the news while standing in the courtyard.

Horthy's radio proclamation had a very different effect on the tenants and the janitors. The Jews thought that the war was indeed over and they took the yellow star off the gate.⁵ At the same time the janitors felt rather sorry at losing their lucrative position: since June 1944 they had had full authority over the building's Jewish tenants including the building's former owner, which helped them secure considerable financial gains. The janitors requested money for all their otherwise free services, thus the yellow star houses were turned into "private prisons" where the tenants lived according to rules set by the Christian janitors.

A few hours later the radio announced that the Arrow Cross Party had come to power. The janitors celebrated their regaining of authority, while the elderly men and young boys who gathered on the courtyard decided to keep guard at the gateway. The night that followed the coup by Ferenc Szálasi, leader of the Arrow Corss Party, marked the lives of several dozen families in Csengery 64. This book is about them and about that night.

During that night of October 15, 1944 armed people intruded into the yellow star house and after a bloody massacre left 19 dead behind. Why this house? Perhaps they were there to break down alleged Jewish resistance, or maybe they were there to rob the jeweler living on the first floor; there is no way to know. The final resting place of the tenants is also unknown. It is certain though that the intruders, with the active collaboration of the Christian janitor family, robbed the tenants, murdered probably 18 of them although the numbers, as I will argue in the book, are uncertain. The armed intruders also forcibly took away all the other Jews hoping that they would never return from deportation and so their crime would remain unnoticed. However, most of the tenants returned during the next few days because the deportations were temporarily halted. There was another wave of deportations in November this time organized by the Arrow Cross Party, but some tenants returned after liberation, and with that the battle for justice and the dignified remembrance of the Csengery 64 victims began.

Piroska Dely's case was among the first trials of the newly established people's tribunals in Budapest. The massacre was also covered extensively by a

---

4 For more on the janitors, see Ádám Pál István, *Budapest Building Managers and the Holocaust in Hungary* (London: Palgrave, 2017).
5 On yellow star houses, see Randolph L. Braham, *A Magyar Holocaust* (Budapest: Gondolat, 1988), 124–129.

press hungry for new stories of the first atrocity committed by the Arrow Cross after the takeover. In the daily press, Piroska Dely was portrayed as the "Beast" of the Arrow Cross, a woman responsible for the gravest wartime massacre of civilians in Budapest. The people's tribunal exposed the image of Hungarian women, alleged members of the Arrow Cross Party, who had used violence while looting. This was the first time female perpetrators were portrayed in public, and explains why, even today, the name Piroska Dely is associated with the "Women of the Arrow Cross" – even though, as I show below, she was never a member of the Arrow Cross Party.

The survivors' testimonies were central to the trial process during the Dely case in 1945 as well as during the people's tribunal trial of the Strucky–Szamocseta janitor family in 1947. On March 23, 1946 Piroska Dely was executed, although as this book shows the people's tribunal trial could not quite confirm whether she participated or that she was at all present at the massacre. Still she became "the" Piroska Dely, the embodiment of the bloodthirsty Arrow Cross woman.

Based on the story of the armed robbery in Csengery 64, I will examine the so far neglected intersection of perpetrator research, political radicalism, memory politics and gender studies to reveal why some female perpetrators of the Hungarian Holocaust became overly visible while others remained invisible. A certain version of Piroska Dely's story has become the part of the historical canon about the Holocaust in Hungary. But, as I will argue here, exactly how this integration into official historiography happened made the most important elements of this story invisible. Unlike mainstream Holocaust research on Hungary, which until recently has focused on political history, this book shows the disturbingly human dimension of collaborators and perpetrators that were so far "invisible" to history, and also examines the factors which contributed to their invisibility.

After the Second World War their battle for remembrance took place on different levels. The book uses several sources to map those levels. The transcripts of the people's trubunals have been used before. This book will show the process of how testimonies in the people's tribunals shaped multicolored and multilayered memories, or using Assmann's words, moved from communicative memory into collective memory.[6] Based on records of police hearings, people's tribunal documents, and the contemporary press, I will analyze how the testimonies changed over time and also reflect on the phenomenon that they were different

---

6 Jan Assmann, *Das Kulturelle Gedächtnis: Schrift, Erinnerung und Politische Identität in frühen Hochkulturen* (Münich: C.H. Beck, 1992).

depending on the audiences, because the witnesses appropriated the language that seemed the most effective in a given situation to achieve the aims of punishing the perpetrators.

I also conducted interviews with the survivors and with the perpetrator family. The interviewing process with the survivors was another space where memory was shaped. My research was primarily inspired by my conversations with the survivors. They honored me with their trust. They shared with me their family stories and the story of the battle they have been fighting with various institutions including the people's tribunals and with the Jewish congregation to keep the memory of the massacre alive. Csengery Street 64 is the setting of what was probably the very first privately erected Hungarian Holocaust memorial. One of the survivors had enough of waiting for unresponsive institutions and made a memorial plaque from his marble kitchen counter. The plaque was installed on the first anniversary of the massacre, October 15, 1945, still, it never became the space for official commemorations, although it adapted the anti-fascist terminology and never mentioned that the victims were Jews. Then after 1989, another fight began as the survivors had to protect the plaque from those tenants who, in fear of rekindled anti-Semitism, wanted to remove it. The survivors also hoped that the municipal district would protect this commemorative plaque. The complicated story of the plaque demonstrates how the framework within which the Holocaust could be discussed in inner city Budapest has changed with time.

I also conducted an interview with the family of perpetrators, the Strucky-Szamocseta family who resided as janitors in the house. It is a specificity of Hungarian memory politics that it has developed in a parallel, unconnected and polarized manner. The interviews with the survivors required different methodological preparation than the interview with the perpetrators' relative. For the survivors, the story that they told me multiple times during our meetings represented the genuine truth, the only possible narrative of the events. I had to be exceptionally careful so that they would not feel as if the analytical methods I used, such as source criticism and discourse analysis, in any ways questioned their authenticity and legitimacy as witnesses and survivors. During the perpetrator interview the challenge was to not judge the interviewee's narrative, which was handed down in his family through generations and had obviously nothing to do with the real events.

The historiography of Holocaust is defined by the dynamics of closures and openings: monuments, schoolbooks and commemorations ritualize and thereby provide a closure for happenings, while the survivors' remembrance as well as the newly discovered private open new possibilities for interpretation. The Csengery Street story demonstrates how the story of a murder gets ritualized through a process during which various institutions (such as the people's tribunal), media (photographs, movies), the survivors, the perpetrators and the historians' works transform communicative memory into collective memory.

Hungarian Holocaust research has mainly focused on deportation and the descriptions of concentration and death camps.[7] Hungarian perpetrator research started only recently and thus far it has focused solely on the stories of politically important men. The Dely case is an atypical Holocaust story as it does not cover a history of deportations. This is an example of intimate violence when in inner city Budapest armed Hungarians killed Hungarians in their own apartments, when the Hungarian state still attributed to German or Hungarian occupied territories. Furthermore, the people's tribunal sentenced a woman to death as the main culprit, which is again not typical in the history of the Hungarian Holocaust. The figure of the far-right's "new man" has only recently become the subject of scientific research and thus far researchers have not had much more to say about the "new woman" other than she was the "new man's" companion.[8] That the Csengery case is not only an atypical event but has contributed to its own selective forgetting is a central concept of this book.

The analysis of the sources unwrapped the history of emotions – resentment, hatred, violence, envy, greed – in a very challenging historical period. This book will not discuss whether the operation of the people's tribunals fell within the existing legal framework or not, or how the trials constructed the remembrance of the Shoah (although I will necessarily touch upon these). Rather this book focuses on the ways survivors and perpetrators constructed memory of the events to create legal meaning and emotional content. It also shows how the perpetrators' stories became simplified and untellable due to the people's tribunals, which necessarily led to a polarized memory culture of the Second World War. I aim at a multifocal reconstruction of the events in order to explore the various perspectives which led to forgetting, invisibility and divided memory in relation to this event, but also in relation to our current battles within memory politics.

In the past decade Hungary has made headlines with its historical revisionism actively supported by the government.[9] This revisionism has not come out of thin air but, as this book argues, it has a long and often forgotten history.

---

[7] Andrea Pető, "'Non-Remembering' the Holocaust in Hungary and Poland," in *Polin: Studies in Polish Jewry. Poland and Hungary Jewish Realities Compared*, volume 31, ed. Francois Guesnet, Howard Lupovitch, Antony Polonsky, 471–480 (The Littman Library of Jewish Civilization/ Liverpool University Press, 2019).

[8] Jorge Dagnino, Matthew Feldman, Paul Stocke, eds. *The "New Man" in Radical Right Ideology and Practice, 1919-1945* (London: Bloomsbury, 2018), 2.

[9] Andrea Pető, "Revisionist Histories, 'Future Memories': Far-Right Memorialization Practices in Hungary," *European Politics and Society* 1.18 (2017): 41–51.

In pre-1989 anti-fascist rhetoric, the perpetrators were labelled as social outcasts and criminal, successfully hiding the structural continuity of racist discrimination in Hungary. After 1989, along with the revision of progressive political traditions, anti-communism, fuelled by the persecutions which took place during the Soviet occupation, became the foundation of the emerging political discourses within the former Eastern Bloc countries and in Hungary. In 2011, the Hungarian Parliament accepted the Fundamental Law of Hungary replacing the Constitution. The Preamble (the National Avowal, in the English translation) states: "We date the restoration of our country's self-determination, lost on the nineteenth day of March 1944, from the second day of May 1990, when the first freely elected organ of popular representation was formed."[10] With this, Hungary caught up with other former communist states that after the end of the Cold War had started to promote the memory of a "double occupation," and to increasingly rely on the concept of victimhood in their memory politics.[11]

The Hungarian Holocaust memorialization is challenged by two thorny political issues. The first one is the chronology: when did the persecution of Jews start? Before the German occupation with the *numerus clausus* law in 1920 and the anti-Jewish legislation of 1938,[12] or just after the German occupation of 19 March, 1944? And when did the persecution end? In 1945, as the anti-fascist narratives states, or in 1948 as the revisionist rhetoric claims, when the communist Hungarian state persecuted Jews while fighting against religion? The question of chronology is also related to the second question about the responsibility of the Hungarian state in the persecutions. The massacre analysed in this book contributes to a long overdue discussion about the responsibility of Hungarian citizens in the Holocaust in Hungary.

1.1 The reasons for forgetting

This volume aims to analyze the memory of Hungarian Holocaust through the concept of forgetting. This is especially exciting since my case study, the Csen-

---

[10] Https://www.kormany.hu/download/f/3e/61000/TheFundamentalLawofHungary_20180629_FIN.pdf, accessed 26 August, 2019.
[11] Lim Jie-Hyun, "Afterword: Entangled Memories of the Second World War," in *Remembering the Second World War*, ed. Patrick Finney (London, New York: Routledge, 2018), 249-256.
[12] Mária M. Kovács, "The Numerus Clausus in Hungary, 1920-1945," in *Alma mater antisemitica: Akademisches Milieu, Juden und Antisemitismus an den Universitäten Europas zwischen 1918 und 1939*, ed. Regina Fritz, Grzegorz Rossoliński-Liebe, Jana Starek, 85-112 (Vienna: New Academic Press, 2016).

gery Street massacre has been listed in most of the relevant scholarly works about the people's tribunals and Arrow Cross rule in Hungary as the most prominent example of women of the Arrow Cross committing violent crimes. The way it is remembered has contributed to the forgetting and, I argue, to pollarized memory cultures about the Second World War.

In this volume, memory and forgetting are not used as descriptive categories for mapping, rather as processes created by those who remember. Those who remember select, cover up, silence, invisibilize, change, exaggerate, simplify, glorify and demonize during the process of remembrance. This volume belongs with the genre of "intimate history" and through the analysis of an atypical Holocaust story it aims to show how remembrance is shaped by those who remember, i.e. how memory grants agency to the protagonists of this story. I use the concept of agency according to Saba Mahmood, for whom agency is "a capacity for action that historically specific relations of subordination enable and create."[13]

Memory is often criticized from the perspective of objective, factual history. In this book, I contrast the processes through which the witnesses filtered, left out and invisibilized certain events and actors with every accessible document.

Lack of acknowledgement means forgetting. The Jewish victims of the Csengery Street massacre first failed to secure their rightful place in the anti-fascist memory canon, before the post-1989 turn in memory politics with its emphasis on Hungarian losses and the myth of the "double occupation" invisibilized Hungarian perpetrators. Women perpetrators have not been the focus of Hungarian perpetrator research, while in recent years several books were published about this new field of study internationally.

Recent research on women in the Ukrainian underground movement, together with research on women working in the occupying Nazi administration there have dismantled a number of taboos including a simple dichotomy of victim and perpetrator.[14] Studies of women's participation in the different far right move-

---

13 Saba Mahmood: "Feminist Theory, Agency, and the Liberatory Subject: Some Reflections on the Islamic Revival in Egypt," *Temenos* 42.1 (2006): 34.
14 Oksana Kis, "National Femininity Used and Contested: Women's Participation in the Nationalist Underground in Western Ukraine during the 1940s–50s," *East/West: Journal of Ukrainian Studies* 2.2 (2015): 53–82; Olena Petrenko, "Frauen als 'Verräterinnen.' Ukrainische Nationalistinnen im Konflikt mit den kommunistischen Sicherheitsorganen und dem eigenen Geheimdienst" [Women as Perpetrators. Ukrainian Nationalist in Conflict with the Communist Security Organizations and their own Security Services], in *"Frauen im Kommunismus." Jahrbuch für Historische Kommunismusforschung*, [Women in Communism. Yearbook of Research on Communism], ed. Ulrich Mählert, Jörg Baberowski, Bernhard H. Bayerlein et al, 57–74 (Berlin: Metropol Verlag, 2015); Wendy Lower, *Hitler's Furies. German Women at the Nazi Killing Fields* (Boston, Mass.: Houghton Mifflin Harcourt, 2013).

ments in Croatia,[15] in the Hlinka guard in Slovakia,[16] in Estonia,[17] in Romania,[18] in Italian Republic of Salò's[19] contributed to a more complex understanding of gender relations in perpetrator research.

As part of research in women's history, this work focuses on exemplary women and shunned mass murderers. Firstly, the main protagonist of this book is, in Christopher Browning's term, an "ordinary perpetrator."[20] Secondly, the perpetrator is a woman, which enables the examination of the gendered aspect of the story.

Forgetting is also connected to the conscious destruction of relevant documents. Lichter, one of the main protagonists of the story after October 23, 1956, on the first day of the Hungarian revolution against communism, called his relatives who had a tile stove in their apartments and asked them to burn his entire correspondence concerning the Dely case. His relatives carried the correspondence in briefcases through the city and burned them – to the great regret of the historian.[21]

Two books were the primary inspiration for this volume. Hannah Arendt's *Eichmann in Jerusalem* offers a still valid analysis of the banality of evil and how legal process frames the ways in which past events can be retold.[22] The lit-

---

15 Rory Yeomans, "Militant Women, Warrior Men and Revolutionary Personae: The New Ustasha Man and Woman," *The Slavonic and East European Review* 4.83 (2005):720–721; Martina Bitunjac, *Verwicklung. Beteiligung. Unrecht. Frauen und die Ustaša-Bewegung* [Involvement, Participation, Injustice. Women in the Ustasha Movement] (Berlin: Duncker&Humblot, 2018).
16 Marína Zavacká, "Crossing Sisters: Patterns of Protest in the Journal of the Catholic Union of Slovak Women during the Second World War," *Social History* 4.37 (2012): 425–451, DOI: 10.1080/03071022.2012.733509.
17 Andres Kasekamp, "Radical Right-Wing Movements in the North-East Baltic," *Journal of Contemporary History* 4.34 (1999): 587–600.
18 Valentin Sandulescu, "Fascism and its Quest for the 'New Man.' The Case of the Romanian Legionary Movement," *Studia Hebraica* 4 (2004): 349–361.
19 Gianluca Schiavo, "The Italian Civil War in the Memoirs of Female Fascist Soldiers," in *Gendered Wars, Gendered Memories. Feminist Conversations on War, Genocide and Political Violence*, ed. Ayşe Gül Altınay and Andrea Pető, 135–145 (London: Routledge, 2016).
20 Christopher R. Browning, *Ordinary Men. Reserve Police Battalion 101 and the Final Solution in Poland* (New York: HarperCollins, 1992).
21 Interview, (April 1, 2005). (See list of interviews).
22 Hannah Arendt, *Eichmann in Jerusalem. A Report on the Banality of Evil* (London/New York: Penguin Books/Viking Press, 1994). On the debate about the book, see Shoshana Felman, *Theater of Justice*, 201–238; Richard J. Bernstein, *Hannah Arendt and the Jewish Question* (Cambridge, Polity Press, 1996); Devin O. Pendas, "Eichmann in Jerusalem, Arendt in Frankfurt. The Eichmann Trial, the Auschwitz Trial, and the Banality of Justice," *New German Critique Winter* 34.1 (2007): 77–109.

erature analyzing the Eichmann trial emphasizes the paradigm change in how the role of the witness has changed. Arendt's statement that Eichmann did not hate Jews and that he was – together with his companions – a "normal" human being was one that stirred passionate debates back in the day.

My other inspiration was Erzsébet Balla's novel, *József körút 79*. [23] (József Boulevard 79). The novel takes place in a Budapest apartment building in 1944, and shows how anyone can turn into a perpetrator and how a house's Jewish community experienced the effects of the Jewish Acts and the battle of Budapest. In the introduction of the novel the author says:

> I strived for truth. I wanted to face the past without bias. This is why I put a non-Jewish person in the focus of the story, to show the happenings from the other side that is filtered through their anti-Semitic sentiment. Most novels on their first page emphasize that it is all the author's imagination and any resemblance to reality is purely coincidental. However, my novel is not the work of imagination, it is reality. More accurately, it is a fragment of reality in a nutshell. Characters are actual people, or they were actual people.[24]

This book is about a case that also represents "a fragment of reality in a nutshell." But, as I have already stated, this case is not a "typical" Holocaust story: the site is not a concentration camp and the perpetrators are not Germans.[25] Hungarians killed Hungarian citizens in the middle of Budapest during peacetime but on the day of the Arrow Cross takeover. The volume tries to resolve the debate on whether the Holocaust is a part of Jewish or European history by claiming that it is part of both, and that the two are inseparable.[26]

My aim was to map various biases and silences within a historical framework. My method relied on a critical analysis and contrast of accessible sources. As a historian and as a privileged narrator, I certainly do not consider that my

---

23 Balla Erzsébet, *József körút 79* (Tel Aviv, Új Kelet Kiadás, 1964). I am grateful to Vasvári Lujza for this recommendation.
24 Ibid., 1.
25 For a synthesis, see Raul Hilberg, *The Destruction of the European Jewry* (Chicago, Quadrangle Books, 1961). Another atypical feature of the Hungarian case is that the executed German women were concentration camp guards or doctors. See Insa Eschebach, "Gespaltene Frauenbilder. Geschlechterdramaturgien im juristischen Diskurs ostdeutscher Gerichte," in *"Bestien" und "Befehlsempfänger". Frauen und Männer in NS-Prozessen nach 1945*, ed., Ulrike Weckel, Edgar Wolfrum (Göttingen: Vandedhoeck & Ruprecht, 2003), 96; Wendy Lower, "Male and Female Holocaust Perpetrators and the East German Approach to Justice 1949–1963," *Holocaust and Genocide Studies* 24.1 (2010): 56–84.
26 See David Engel, *Historians of the Jews and the Holocaust* (Stanford: Stanford University Press, 2010).

interpretation is the only "right" interpretation of the events, and that is why I try to show the events from all angles.

The title of the book claims that the massacre was forgotten. This forgetting marks the historiography as well as our collective and individual remembrance. The Dely case's analysis offers a perspective to map blind spots of post-war political justice and the consequences of this legal framing.

Both in the case of my Hungarian Academy of Science dissertation and the Hungarian edition of this book, I was driven by a sincere hope that the analysis of the Csengery Street case would contribute to the reevaluation and nuancing of Hungary's Second World War history, as well as to a necessary dialogue about the past.[27] The books' Hungarian edition sold many copies, and due to the way it presents a little known case in a crime fiction-like framework it was a professional and public success with wider audiences too. It proved that writing in a different, accessible language without hiding behind professional lingo can reach a wider audience on difficult and painful topics. My professional credo is that historians should move out from the ivory tower of scholarship while keeping all professional standards and requirements and communicate with the larger audience. While writing, my aim was to tell a story that is interesting, inviting and important. Therefore, the author reached her goal. However, some reviews and social media platforms celebrated the book as one that showed that the people's tribunals were politically controlled, and relatedly that Piroska Dely was sentenced to death for a crime that she did not commit. Both arguments fit the current revisionist tendencies of Hungarian historiography that invisibilizes, in other words it does not acknowledge crimes committed during Second World War in harmony with the government endorsed cult of "double occupation" set out in the Preamble of the Hungarian National Avowal (*Nemzeti Hitvallás*).[28] This new narrative framework acts as a tool of "repressive erasure"[29]

---

[27] The seminal volumes of Hungarian Holocaust research include the following: Randolph L. Braham: *A Magyar Holocaust* (Budapest: Gondolat, 1988); Randolph L. Braham, *The Politics of Genocide. The Holocaust in Hungary* (New York: Columbia University Press, 1981); David Cesarini, ed., *Genocide and Rescue. The Holocaust in Hungary* (London/New York: Berg, 1997); Randolph L. Braham, Pók Attila, ed., *The Holocaust in Hungary. Fifty Years Later* (New York: Columbia University Press, 1997); Tim Cole, "Constructing the 'Jew.' Writing the Holocaust. Hungary 1920–1945," *Patterns of Prejudice* 33.3 (1999): 19–27; Horváth Cecília, *A magyar zsidóság és a holokauszt* (Budapest: Új Palatinus, 2004); Karsai László, *Holocaust* (Budapest: Pannonica, 2001); Nathaniel Katzburg, *Zsidópolitika Magyarországon, 1919–1943* (Budapest: Bábel, 2002); Stark Tamás, *Zsidóság a vészkorszakban és a felszabadulás után (1935–1955)* (Budapest: MTA Történettudományi Intézet – História Alapítvány, 1995).
[28] Https://www.keh.hu/the_fundamental_law/1536-The_fundamental_law_of_Hungary*&pnr=1.
[29] Paul Connerton, "Seven Types of Forgetting," *Memory Studies* 1.1 (2008): 60–61.

and provides the theoretical and ideological foundation for the defensive remembrance strategy of contemporary Hungarian populist politics, which blames the Germans and the Soviets for all traumas of the twentieth century, completely dismissing Hungarian responsibility.[30]

Whether this book, which looks at past events through the dynamics and politics of forgetting, contributes to the revisionist process or, as the author hopes, to a battle against forgetting, time will show.

---

[30] Andrea Pető, "The Lost and Found Library," *Memory at Stake* 9 (2019): 72–82.

2 What makes Csengery 64 important?

> The hastily armed Arrow Cross militia immediately set upon the Jews. SS soldiers and armed Hungarians intruded into Csengery 64. A survivor, who played dead, said, that "in the apartments children, women, and men were shot haphazardly, altogether 21 of them."[31]

It is a fact that someone shot the unarmed tenants of Budapest's Csengery Street 64 on the night of October 15, 1944. It is also a fact that the Budapest People's Tribunal sentenced Piroska Dely, a notorious "Arrow Cross woman" to death for the massacre. The Budapest press covered the case as the first massacre committed by Arrow Cross Party members. The key questions however remain unresolved: whether Piroska Dely was the murderer and whether she was a member of the Arrow Cross. The people's tribunal trial did not identify the perpetrators with certainty; and since the analysis of witness statements leads to different conclusions this book will not offer definite answers either. Its aims are different.

Firstly, the examination of the Csengery Street massacre can shed light on a part of Hungarian past that is still a subject of political and scholarly debates. Doing so is particularly pertinent today. Since Hungary's recent populist turn, history writing increasingly focuses on simple people as central actors of history, while it simultaneously neglects methodological challenges in order to legitimize particular political goals and undermine the legitimacy of post-war political justice.[32]

The chronology of the October 15, 1944 events at Csengery 64 can be reconstructed fairly well, as there are many although often contradictory sources. The chronology in the appendix (see appendix 1, 2 and 3) provides a framework that makes the event straightforwardly narratable and hopefully relatable and understandable too. As Pierre Nora holds:

> [T]he event is always revolutionary, the grain of sand in the machine, the accident that shakes us up and takes us by surprise [....] It is best circumscribed from the outside:

---

31 The quote is from Pál Kádár's testimony to the Committee for the Investigation of Nazi and Arrow Cross Atrocities, February 24, 1945. http://konfliktuskutato.hu/index.php?option=com_content&view=article&id=328:nyilas-terror-budapesten-1944-1945&catid=39:dka-hatter&Itemid=203, last accessed January 23, 2019.
32 Pető Andrea, "Roots of Illiberal Memory Politics: Remembering Women in the 1956 Hungarian Revolution," *Baltic Worlds* 10.4 (2017): 42–58.

https://doi.org/10.1515/9783110687552-004

what is the event and for whom? For if there is no event without critical consciousness, there is an event only when, offered to everybody, it is not the same for all.[33]

The versatility of available sources on the Csengery 64 event make it possible to analyse the perspective of victims and perpetrators alike, with which the historian aims to avoid the simplification of the historical narrative. By asking with Nora: "what is the event and for whom?" the analysis strives to contribute to a much-needed multilayered dialogue about a controversial segment of Hungary's past.

The murders at Csengery 64 differed from other killings not only because of the site of the murder but also because of their intimacy and their timing. I call these murders intimate because neither the industrial killing mechanism of the concentration camps nor the disciplined behavior typical of the military was present in Csengery 64. In a sense these events were like the widely discussed events in Jedwabne.[34] Neighbors took part in killing and robbing their neighbors. The massacre's timing was also particular because it happened on the very day when the Arrow Cross Party seized power with the support of the occupying German troops. Previous research has already examined the October 15 and 16, 1944 actions of the Arrow Cross, when several thousand people were forcibly driven from the 8th district to Sebestyén Rumbach Street because of alleged armed resistance from forced laborers. After a swift protest from the side of neutral countries' representatives as well as some Hungarian notables, these people were let home in the middle of the night.[35] The Csengery 64 massacre had strong ties to this series of events on the dramatic night of 15 October, 1944 but the people's tribunal in 1945 could not see these connections. This connection between this massacre and the "Jewish resistance" was later integrated via the testimonies of survivors.

The people's tribunal's witnesses unanimously claimed that the armed intruders were led by a woman, Piroska Dely. Through the case therefore we can examine a rarely researched dimension of Second World War, that is female perpetrators. Data suggests that in Hungary seven women were sentenced to death

---

33 Quoted by Shoshana Felman, "Theaters of Justice. Arendt in Jerusalem, the Eichmann Trial, and the Redefinition of Legal Meaning in the Wake of the Holocaust," *Critical Inquiry* 27.2 (2001): 201–238, 210.
34 Jan Gross, *Neighbors: The Destruction of the Jewish Community in Jedwabne, Poland* (Princeton: Princeton University Press, 2001).
35 Randolph L. Braham, *Politics of Genocide: the Holocaust in Hungary* (Detroit: Wayne State University Press, 2000), 155–157.

as war criminals.[36] Piroska Dely is a good example for the independent, "new" working woman of the interwar times. Her story reveals the political and emotional consequences of women's non-elite paid employment. To be a wage earner in the city profoundly shaped the experiences and political motivations of this generation of women. Among them the largest and least organized group of employed women were the domestic servants, followed by women factory workers.[37] For these Hungarian women who, like Dely, experienced both the difficulties of gaining employment and discrimination against women in workplace, only the far right offered a viable political alternative. This was largely due to the fact that during Regent Horthy's decades long anti-communist governance the leftist alternatives – the trade unions and the social democratic party – got sidelined as the left was blamed for Hungary's devastating loss after the First World War. The literature about post-war political justice mentions Dely as a "woman with agency," who as an "Arrow Cross woman" uncritically embraced far right thoughts, discourse and actions; but it is still a question whether she had official ties to the Arrow Cross Party.[38]

The sources on Csengery 64 also allow for an in-depth analysis of systematic plundering of Hungarian Jewry. Hungarian Jews were first deprived of rights and dispossessed by way of bureaucratic decisions, then, after their deportation, as no one expected them to return, their belongings were considered free prey.[39] The systematic stripping of Jewish citizens of their money and assets was a part of their dehumanization.[40] Still, in comparison with Poland, where German

---

36 On uncertainties concerning the numbers, see Pető Andrea, "Problems of Transitional Justice in Hungary. An Analysis of the People's Tribunals in Post-War Hungary and the Treatment of Female Perpetrators," *Zeitgeschichte* 34 (November–December, 2007): 335–349; Karsai László, "The People's Court and Revolutionary Justice in Hungary, 1945–1946," in *The Politics of Retribution in Europe. World War II and Its Aftermath*, ed., Deák István, Jan T. Gross, and Tony Judt, 233–252 (Princeton: Princeton University Press, 2000).
37 Balázs Sipos, *Women and Politics: Nationalism and Femininity in Interwar Hungary* (Trondheim: Studies on East European Cultures & Societies, 2019).
38 It is crucial to separate the concepts "woman of the Arrow Cross" (*nyilasnő*) and "Arrow Cross woman" (*nyilas nő)*. "Woman of the Arrow Cross" signifies women with ties to the Hungarian far-right party, while "Arrow Cross woman" has been historically used for those women, who at the end of Second World War participated in violent actions, such as robbery, plunder, and even murder, but had no direct connection to the party.
39 On the institutionalized aspects of the dispossession of Hungarian Jewry, see Kádár Gábor, Vági Zoltán, *Hullarablás. A magyar zsidók gazdasági megsemmisítése* (Budapest: Jaffa, 2005).
40 On the situation of Jews who returned to Paris, see Leora Auslander, "Coming Home? Jews in Postwar Paris," *Journal of Contemporary History* 40.2 (2005): 237–259.

"cleansings" set an example,[41] in Budapest the shaming and plundering of Jews was not an inescapable historical reality, partly because of the brevity of German occupation, and partly because of the general chaos of Arrow Cross rule. There was room for individual negotiation, as we will see from the variegated stories of Csengery 64 tenants. In other words, in the fall of 1944, with the Red Army on its way to Budapest, pillaging by private individuals was not a "normalized" behavior in the Hungarian capital. Csengery 64 survivors claimed that before the armed people who wore some kind of a uniform entered the house there was a gunshot outside. The gunshot was probably the perpetrators' attempt at an alibi: they could claim that they entered the house to restore order after an assumed armed mutiny. This suggests that at that point maintaining some resemblance of legality still mattered.[42] The fact that police investigators came to examine the location after the massacre also offers evidence that it was an isolated action of crime and not a concerted effort by the collapsing Hungarian state administration.[43]

Most sources suggest that the Csengery massacre was primarily an armed robbery driven by greed and the belief that the perpetratrators could get away with the crime. After the building was officially marked as a yellow star house on June 21, 1944 its Christian janitors, József Strucky and his wife stayed in the house. The family safeguarded Jewish assets in exchange for money; they also hid Jews at great risk and for great monetary compensation, and lastly, they played a crucial role in the robbing of the Jewish tenants on October 15. After the next wave of deportations in November 1944, the janitors arbitrarily occupied the best apartment of the building. From February 1945, that is when some of the tenants returned from deportation, the janitors went on living among the people whom they robbed and betrayed but now back in their original apartment. After October 15, 1944 – and before the Soviet troops arrived – the janitors even had the presence of mind to collect the *Persilschein* (see appendix 4) that is a paper in which the Jewish tenants expressed gratitude for the protection they had allegedly received. Therefore, the story of Csengery 64 also contributes to the ever-richer rescuer literature, as it shows that the motivation

---

41 Tomasz Fryde, "The Pazifizierungsaktion as a Catalyst of Anti-Jewish Violence. A Study in the Social Dynamics of Fear," in *The Holocaust and European Societies, The Holocaust and its Contexts*, ed., Frank Bajohr and Andrea Löw, 144–166 (London: Palgrave, 2016).
42 Interview (April 1, 2005).
43 Állambiztonsági Szolgálatok Történeti Levéltára (ÁBTL - Historical Archives of the Hungarian State Security Services), V 48889, 17654/1949. 34. On the responsibility of Hungarian police organizations, see Veszprémy László Bernát "Népirtás és mozgástér. A Magyar közigazgatás felelőssége az 1944-es deportálásokban és a nyilasterrorban," *Archivnet* 18.2 (2018).

behind hiding Jews could have been driven by financial considerations besides empathy or morals. Motives are hard to reconstruct retrospectively, but in the case of Csengery 64 it was clear which tenants could and which could not remunerate the janitors' services, and there were survivors from both groups who later held the Struckys accountable for lack their of empathy and morals. Upon their return from deportation, the building's Jewish tenants were shocked to find their clothing and other personal items in the janitors' apartment. Through the microhistorical analysis of how wealth disappeared and how new wealth was born within one house, this book attempts to nuance the commonly perceived black and white image of perpetrators and rescuers in Hungarian historiography.[44]

I was able to personally meet the survivors of Csengery 64, and as they honored me with their trust, I listened to them recounting that fatal day. The juxtaposition of these interviews with other accessible sources (the people's tribunals' papers, contemporary press, photographs) created an idiosyncratic base of resources, which made possible the examination of connections between memory, trauma, and gender.[45] At the same time the most important sources, that is the interviews and the people's tribunal testimonies, posited a tremendous methodological challenge since these personal narratives represent a different temporality of interpretation and are subject to change. Just as important, the site of remembrance determines how remembrance is framed. The survivors and witnesses talked about the event differently on the house's corridor or during a family dinner, and again differently in their denunciation letters sent to the police, then during the police hearings, later as witnesses for the people's tribunal, and differently again during the oral history interviews. The audience and the circumstance determines what story is told and how it is being told.

As a first step I tried to establish who was where in the house, i.e. who could hear or see what happened during the night of October 15, 1944. I went around Csengery 64 several times and based on my knowledge of the premises I can claim that the testimonies do not fully reconstruct the story. By examining the testimonies, and the recordings of the preliminary police hearings, and the verdict, it is traceable how the narration of the events became "simplified." The parallel events were translated into legal terms which resisted complexities. The court wanted to establish a linear story about the event knowing what has happened, while the survivors wanted to tell their own, often different story. This

---

[44] For more on this, see Randolph Braham, "Rescue Operations in Hungary: Myths and Realities," *East European Quarterly* 38.2 (2004): 173–203.
[45] On the court trial as the space of memory production, see Inga Markovits, "How the Law Affects what we Remember and Forget about the Past: The Case of East Germany," *Law and Society Review* 35.3 (2001): 513–563.

process suited the political expectations and tendencies of the time. During the people's tribunals' trials, a ritualized language was developed through which the traumatic, unspeakable events of the Holocaust were translated into legal categories, which in turn made certain deeds punishable. This process evoked traumatic memories, or in Ross Chambers's words, "orphanated memories" that fundamentally determine the interpretation of events within the triangle of trauma, the trauma's community, and the audiences.[46] This is what Friedländer calls the "unease in historical interpretation," which is the "noncongruence of intellectual interpretation and blocking of intuitive comprehension."[47] This "unease" is also present in this volume: while I strive to establish the facts of what happened and I also try to describe the perspective of the actors, including survivors and perpetrators. This would be unimaginable had I insisted on using a positivist approach, i.e. if I had tried to figure what "objectively" happened. I certainly aimed at maximum objectivity, but I was also aware of my profession's boundaries.

The tenants of Csengery 64 were assimilated Jews, during the interviews no one claimed to have practiced their religion nor to have been exposed to anti-Semitic atrocities before the German occupation. Similarly, there was no mention of previous political involvement either. For them the politics of the Horthy regime was a farce concocted by the elites, which did not affect them until the Anti-Jewish Laws were introduced in 1938. I am of course aware that they must have had preliminary experiences of everyday anti-Semitism, but those were not central in the interviews because the life-threatening events of the German occupation overshadowed whatever happened earlier.

The case carries further moral lessons about the way the invisible tension between ethnicities exploded, and the way the Jewish tenants came to know the real Christian janitors. Ethnic cleansing is often accompanied by crimes against property, because the collapse of the state is an opportunity for murder, plunder and pillage with no consequences.[48] The violence against Jews in particular can be explained with a desire for revenge for earlier political decisions that were connected with Jewish interests, as well as by anti-Semitic hatred and eco-

---

46 From Ross Chambers, "Orphanated Memories, Phantom Pain. Towards Hauntology of Discourse," *Untimely Interventions*. Quoted in Thomas Treize, "Between History and Psychoanalyses. A Case Study in the Reception of Holocaust Survivor Testimony," *History and Memory* 1 (2008): 36.
47 Saul Friedländer, *Memory, History, and the Extermination of the Jews of Europe* (Bloomington: Indiana University Press, 1993), 111.
48 Norman Naimark, *Fires of Hatred. Ethnic Cleansing in Twentieth-Century Europe* (Cambridge, Mass.: Harvard University Press, 2001), 8.

nomic rivalry.⁴⁹ The Csengery Street event was most probably primarily a robbery with which the perpetrators tried to enhance their financial situation in the historical moment of the Arrow Cross coup. Piroska Dely lived on Dob Street 74, around the corner from Csengery Street, and was therefore close to the crime scene. She was also well acquainted with the wealth of the Jewish families in the neighborhood. Before October 15, 1944, she had already participated in the robbing of Jews forced to live in yellow star houses, i.e. independent of the Arrow Cross seizure of power. She was put on trial after the liberation of Budapest for one of these minor robberies, and it was during this trial that Andor Lichter, who lived in Csengery utca – who had lost his mother, father, and son during the massacre – identified her.

The survivors of the Csengery Street massacre erected the first privately funded Holocaust memorial in Budapest. The memory plaque (see appendix 6) exhibits the 19 names of people murdered in their homes on October 15, 1944.⁵⁰ The memory plaque was inaugurated on October 15, 1945, and is a homage to the resourcefulness and organization skills of survivors as it is there to this day (see appendix 8). The story of the plaque is paradigmatic of post-1945 memory culture: it shows how the spaces of remembrance were shaped and reshaped by subsequent regimes of memory. During my personal meetings with the survivors they shared their memories about the massacre, the erection of the plaque and its upkeep especially after 1989 when it became increasingly endangered.

The massacre in Csengery 64 qualifies as important due to the place, space, and timing of the events. The available archival sources press material together with interview material offer a unique insight into life and feelings of survivors and perpetrators together with its unique memorialization practice are important for understanding a new and rarely analyzed aspect of the Holocaust: a mass killing in Budapest committed very possibly by Hungarians allegedly led by a woman. The history of the post-1945 period is characterized by forgetting, as silencing and omission were parts of a strategy of survival. This case, which had been a high-profile court case right after the liberation, proves that the strategy of forgetting had no alternative when a narratable story needs to be constructed from different stories. On the other hand, even telling the story of this massacre during this high-profile court case contributed to a selective forgetting of some aspects of this event.

---

49 Jeffrey S. Kopstein and Jason Wittenberg, *Intimate Violence. Anti-Jewish Pogroms on the Eve of the Holocaust* (Ithaca, NY: Cornell University Press, 2018).
50 The issues concerning the number of victims will be discussed in a separate chapter. There are 19 names on the commemorative plaque.

3 The House

Located on the Pest side of the Danube, Csengery Street 64 is a typical Budapest apartment building through the micro-history of which we can shed light on a thus far unexamined, invisible slice of the Hungarian Holocaust.

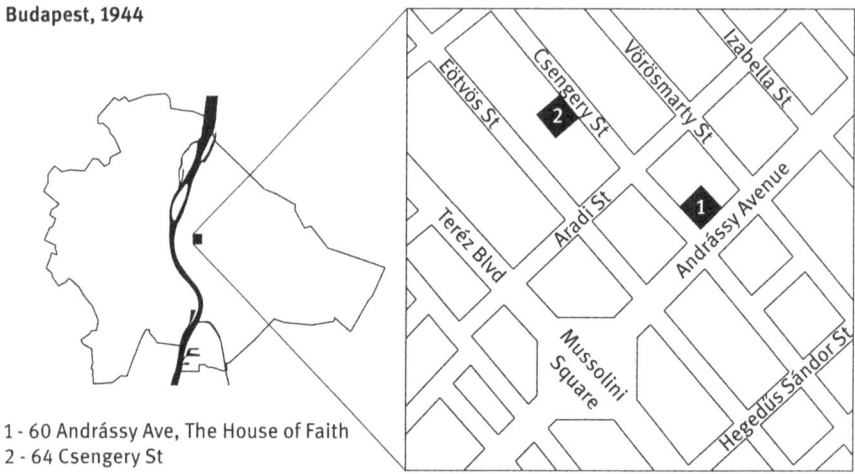

Budapest, 1944

1 - 60 Andrássy Ave, The House of Faith
2 - 64 Csengery St

Figure 1: Map of Budapest (Graphic by Balázs Egri).

There are several explanations for why the massacre happened in this particular house. One of those concerns its topographical position: Csengery 64 was very close to Andrássy Avenue 60, The House of Faith that was the main headquarters of the Arrow Cross, as well as to Hotel Royal on the Grand Boulevard (*Nagykörút*), where the occupying German forces' headquarter was established in October 1944. In June 1944, the house was designated as one of the yellow Star of David houses that were the compulsory residences of Budapest's Jewish citizens who had been expelled from their homes.[51]

In the following I shall introduce the architectural features of the house, as this is crucial for understanding the events.[52] Csengery 64 is a four-level apart-

---

51 Laky Dezső, "A háztulajdon alakulása Budapesten," *Statisztikai Közlemények* 66.1 (1932): 89–99.
52 To learn how the composition of tenants in Erzsébetváros has changed, see Erika Szívós, "Bonds Tried by Hard Times: Jews and Christians on Klauzál tér, Budapest, 1938–1945," *Hungarian Historical Review* 1.1–2 (2012): 166–199. Https://www.ceeol.com/search/article-detail?id=253807.

Figure 2: House (Photo by Andrea Pető).

ment building with one street entrance and a set of storefronts from the street side (see list of illustrations in appendix 10).

The builder and owner of the house, widow of Dr. Rubinyi Mózes, née Ilona Bodor, also lived in the building. She hired the Strucky family as janitors in 1929. The tailor shop of the janitors' relative, György Szamocseta was on the street front. An L-shaped cellar served as a bomb shelter and runs along under the whole building. This large cellar saved many lives as the Jewish tenants hid there during the raid. It was connected to the cellar of the next house with a wooden door, in case the sole staircase leading to the cellar collapsed.

The building encircled a large cobblestone yard. This is the yard where the tenants listened to Horthy's radio broadcast proclamation on October 15, 1944. This is also where, a few hours later, they were rounded up by the armed intruders. After liberation this was where the Jewish tenants gathered before they broke into the janitor family's home, as Strucky kept on postponing the return of their belongings.

Although the 1941 and 1945 tenant registries, officially required by the Municipal of Budapest, survived in the Budapest City Archives (BFL – *Budapest Főváros Levéltára*), it is hardly possible to accurately establish who lived in Csen-

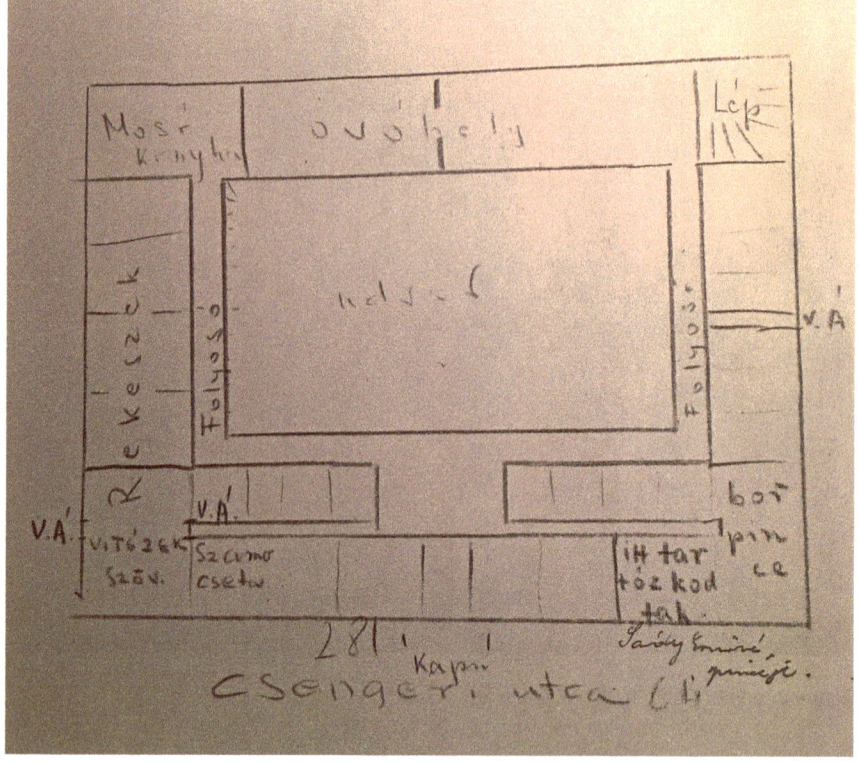

Figure 3: Map of the cellar (ÁBTL V 19273/1949. without page numbers).

gery 64 on October 15, 1944.[53] During the interviews, I asked the survivors to help me identify who was present in the building on that date. The survivors only remembered the tenants of their own floor or children of their own age because these were the people they had ties to fifty years ago. For the same reason it is also impossible to reconstruct which Jewish families moved in from June 1944 on. The mayor of Budapest issued a decree on the forcible relocation of Jews into the designated yellow Star of David houses on June 16, 1944 and all Jewish residents had to move by midnight June 24, 1944. This was a form of ghettoization and a preparation for deportation. It was expected that 220,000 individuals would move into 2,600 houses within this short period, which caused chaos

---

[53] Similar tendencies are described in Nagy Ágnes, "Hatalom – lakásrendszer – társadalom. Egy lipótvárosi bérház lakói 1941 és 1960 között," *Korall* 17 (2004): 138–166. For an interesting case study about the church, see Lugosi András: "'Sztálin főhercege': Kohn báró vacsorái a Falk Miksa utcában a fajgyalázási törvény idején," *Fons* 17.4 (2010): 527–576.

and uncertainty. In Csengery 64, not only the Jewish residents remained in the house but some other people moved in who only stayed for a day, others were on forced labor service but were allowed to sleep at home, and there were some whose names no survivor remembered. The chaotic circumstances are well exemplified by the fact that at one point 11 people lived in the jeweler Steiner's two-room apartment.[54]

Regulations prescribed that a tenant registry should be put together every two or three days. It had to be prepared in two copies, one for the authorities and one for the janitor. These documents disappeared and they were not part of the people's tribunal papers either. The Csengery 64 tenant registry was put together by János Kun, who offered his generous help throughout my research. "They wanted to make us feel monitored,"[55] said Kun about the lists. Upon my request he reconstructed the registry (see appendix 5 and 7) from which later another survivor found out that an uncle she had considered lost since October 1944 was still in Csengery 64 on the fifteenth of the month. It is possible that the list that the witnesses of the janitor family's 1947 trial remembered having seen in the hands of Piroska Dely on October 15, 1944 was a copy of the tenant registry that Strucky as janitor promptly handed to the intruders. This might have been the crucial moment discussed several times during the trial, when Piroska Dely, according to people's tribunal testimonies, might have asked who the Christians among the tenants were and who were not. During the time of legal uncertainties these lists held enormous power: many people died because the law was blindly followed, concomitantly many lives were saved because of "inventive" interpretations of law.

The first changes among the tenants of this house happened in June 1944, when the yellow star houses were established. As already stated, it is hard if not impossible to reconstruct who moved when into which apartment, and the same is true for the often improvised, life-saving escapes. In 1945, of the 33 apartments only 19 had the same tenants as in 1941. During June 1944, six new Jewish families moved in, and after the November deportations starting on the ninth and finished by the twentieth when all Jewish tenants were deported to participate in building a protecting wall around Budapest, and were forced into death marches to the West.[56] This was the time when nine Christian families came to

---

54 BFL 19273/1949. 191. Mrs. Andor Steiner's testimony January 24, 1946.
55 Interview, March 3, 2005.
56 For more, see Szita Szabolcs, *Haláleröd. A munkaszolgálat és a hadimunka történetéhez 1944-1945* [Death Fortress. To the History of labor service and military labor] (Budapest: Kossuth, 1989); Szita Szabolcs, *Utak a pokolból. Magyar deportáltak az annektált Ausztriában 1944-1945*

Figure 4: The janitor's apartment (Photo by Andrea Pető).

live in the building. These families that arrived between November 1944 and January 1945 had many children and were mainly clerks of the Beszkárt (*Budapesti Közlekedési Társaság* – Budapest Transportation Services) who were notorious for their support for the Arrow Cross Party.[57] They obtained the larger, nicer, more valuable apartments. From 1945, due to flat shortages and an increased influx of inhabitants from the rural areas, a system of joint tenants and lodgers was established. The Jewish families living in the house usually had an elderly relative or a solitary old Jewish woman share their apartment as a lodger. Among the Christian tenants there was no such system in place. The building itself was nationalized in 1952 and its Jewish owner received no compensation. The family left the country after the 1956 revolution and the relatives now live in Israel.

The German occupation of Hungary on March 19, 1944 was a moral test for all. From June 1944 some were willing to help, and some were willing to take ad-

---

[Roads from Hell. Hungarian deportees in occupied Austria] (Budapest: Metalon Manager Iroda KFT, 1991).
57 Andrea Pető, *Women of the Arrow Cross Party* (London: Palgrave MacMillan, 2020).

vantage of their position. The Strucky janitor family had a close relationship to the house's Jewish owner who considered them to be reliable safeguards of her assets, for which she also offered monetary compensation. On the other hand, the Strucky family, as the sole Christian family that remained in a yellow star house, conceptualized their role as prison guards. For the Struckys the chance of quick financial gain was probably too much of a temptation, although they could have gained a substantial sum of money had they "only" used legal means, such as performing paid services for the Jewish tenants. In the power vacuum of the night of the Arrow Cross takeover they reverted to autocratic methods and charged money for services that were their duty to perform. They were probably aware that they might be held accountable, so they worked alone and "only" used their strong ties with Arrow Cross to blackmail the tenants.

It should be emphasized that though the janitors unscrupulously robbed the Jewish tenants of the house, some still owed their life to them. They hid them during the raids and even offered to rescue them during the last days of Arrow Cross rule, but did so for money. The Struckys hid people or for a large financial gain "overlooked" that their documents were forged. The Strucky-Szamocseta family's wealth rapidly increased in 1944: they paid back the mortgage on their Göd house at the bank of the Danube, 23 km north to Budapest.

4 Piroska Dely in Budapest

> An Arrow Cross Party woman who served in the Svábhegy section of Gestapo and arrived with SS and Arrow Cross lads. [...] They killed upon her command. She had no mercy over a 14 year old child, and had people forcibly taken away in three turns. [...] She plundered [...] She faked pregnancy to dodge death penalty. [...] She was not a woman but a bloodthirsty beast in human skin, a soulless slattern, a callous criminal, and a devout servant of German and Arrow Cross killers.[58]

This was the vivid description by the Csengery 64 survivor Andor Lichter of the woman he identified as Piroska Dely. However, Andor Lichter did not personally witness Piroska Dely robbing and killing in Csengery Street. Lichter was in forced labor service and returned home a day after the massacre. It was through his wife that he learned about the events of October 15, 1944. Lichter's mother, father and only son were all killed in this massacre, and his wife was soon after deported to Bergen-Belsen and murdered there. Piroska Dely had certainly nothing to do with this latter event, still, Lichter held her responsible for the death of his wife too. Lichter followed Dely's trial with special attention. Actual eyewitnesses talked in a more nuanced manner about Dely: "she seemed to have executive power," said one of them.[59] For this "semblance" of executive power that lasted less than a day, Piroska Dely paid a great price: with her life.

Lichter gave a statement to the police and later served as a witness during the trial. His narration of the event exemplifies how "Arrow Cross women" were – and are – imagined even today. In the historiography there are three emblematic female figures related to Arrow Cross terror: Piroska Dely, Etel Pap, and Mrs. Salzer, née Lujza Háy, an active participant of the Városház Street Arrow Cross house massacre. Piroska Dely was charged with illegal wealth acquisition and war crimes and executed.[60] During the trial she had already become the embodiment of "the typical Arrow Cross woman" though, as I will discuss, she had nothing to do with the Arrow Cross Party. While she became a prominent symbol of the "Arrow Cross Beast," on the other hand her real motives for committing

---

[58] Excerpts from Andor Lichter's letter to Zoltán Tildy President of the Republic, February 1, 1946. (MOL) XIXE-1-l-Tank-2000-1946 (6401).
[59] Simon Zweig's testimony, February 12, 1945. (BFL 2442/1947. 11.)
[60] During the trials of German women perpetrators, the expression "woman beast" was used in a similar context; see Insa Eschebach, "Gespaltene Frauenbilder. Geschlechtsdramaturgie im juristischen Diskurs ostdeutscher Gerichte," in *"Bestien" und "Befehlsempfänger"*, ed., Edgar Wolfrum and Ulrike Weckel (Göttingen: Vandenhoeck & Ruprecht, 2003), 112.

the crime together with other female perpetrarors had been forgotten. How did that happen? Who was she?

4.1 Her biography

The first official sources about Piroska Dely (sometimes: Delly, Deli, Delli) are her indictment and the records of her police hearing. There are no other sources about her previous life other than police and court materials, which largely determine the value of these sources though it provides only a partial picture of her biography.

Piroska Dely was born in Jászkisér in the poor central part of the country, east of Budapest in 1913 or 1916. Her father died during the First World War, her brother in the Second World War on the battlefield. She inherited a piece of land that she sold to her younger sister, Terézia Dely, and moved to the capital to try her luck.[61] She was married to, then legally divorced from, Sándor Temesváry (elsewhere: Temesvári), but in spite of this, all throughout the court process she was addressed by and mentioned only using her maiden name, which was quite unusual at the time. Only years later, during the re-consolidation of state socialist gender politics was she mentioned again in official documents with her married name as Mrs. Temesváry. Piroska Dely was a mother of two and a Roman Catholic by denomination. She had no criminal record. We have no information about her children, and her husband was impossible to find, though he was sought for years. The legal document proving their lawful divorce also went missing. To top it all, in one of her testimonies Dely identified herself as a widow.

She provided contradictory data concerning her employment history too. In one testimony she said that in 1936 she worked as a nurse in the Sopron Military Hospital, moved to Budapest in 1939, where at first she worked in a sanatorium but later became a military nurse again. In another testimony she claimed that she was an accountant in the Braun Liqueur Factory till 1941, although she did not have the required degree.[62] She also stated that she had worked in 1943 as a war nurse on the Russian frontline, where she claimed to have gotten a heart condition.[63] This statement could not be verified, because the databases on Hun-

---

61 BFL 2442/1947. 41.
62 BFL 2442/1947. 46.
63 BFL 2442/1947. 47.

garian military personnel including civilians in service was destroyed at the end of the war.⁶⁴ According to this testimony after her return from the frontline she remained a nurse, and in 1944 she worked in the Svábhegy Sanatorium in Buda.⁶⁵ However, according to yet another testimony, she was a factory worker in the Burányi and Mátrai Company till December 22, 1944.

It is certainly true that for Piroska Dely work was not a source of self-fulfillment or joy. Her employment history shows a single mother's struggle for a livelihood. It is also true that the quality of her livelihood was enhanced when the state and its institutions had collapsed and it became legal to rob from a group within Hungarian society, the Jews.

4.2 Her trial

Piroska Dely's case was one of the very first cases of the Budapest People's Tribunal. Her trial started on March 13, 1945, and the people's tribunals were put in effect only a month beforehand. The first people's tribunal verdict was brought on February 4, 1945 in the trial of two former military forced-labor guards who were sentenced for the death of 124 forced laborers.⁶⁶ Still, until September 16, 1945 when Law No. VII/1945 was signed into act, the people's tribunals were regulated by decree only.⁶⁷

4.2.1 The People's Tribunals

May's argument applies to post-Holocaust Hungary: "Trials are not the only possible remedies for group-based harm. Other reconciliatory strategies will provide what victims are owed, and also sometimes better exemplify the principle of equity that is crucial, especially for crimes that involve large segments of the population as both victims and perpetrators."⁶⁸ I use the case of the war crimes

---

64 Personal statement by Péter Szabó. On the German military service, see Karen Hagemann, "Mobilizing Women for War: The History, Historiography, and Memory of German Women's War Service in the Two World Wars," *Journal of Military History* 5.3 (2011): 1055–1093.
65 BFL 2442/1947. 44.
66 Karsai Elek, ed. *"Fegyvertelen álltak az aknamezőkön..." I – II. Dokumentumok a munkaszolgálat történetéhez Magyarországon* (Budapest: Hungarian Izraeliták Országos Képviselete, 1962).
67 Major Ákos, *Népbíráskodás. Forradalomtörvényesség* (Budapest: Minerva, 1988), 123.
68 Larry May, *Crimes Against Humanity. A Normative Account* (Cambridge: Cambridge University Press, 2005), 22.

committed at Csengery Street 64 to trace different possible interpretations of post-Holocaust transitional justice. An important point is that this case led to the erection of the first privately funded Holocaust memorial in Budapest.

As part of the armistices, Hungary made a commitment to retribution.[69] From 1945 on, expert supervisory committees performed the inspections necessary for the restoring of the legal order. Altogether there were 25 People's Tribunals organized in Hungary.[70] A law on People's Tribunals was necessary because in large, precedent-setting cases this was the only way to attribute liability to those who gave the orders; also, this was the sole legal framework within which the argument that "we only followed orders" was invalid. In other words, without a specific law the political and military elite of the Horthy system responsible for the war could not have been sentenced without much difficulty.[71] On the other hand the legal absurdity that, until Law No. 7/1946 was signed into act such a severe question was regulated by decrees, had to be discontinued under the pressure of the armistice agreement that was in the process of being made.

Those who drafted the People's Tribunal's law in Debrecen for the Provisional Hungarian Government performed a nearly impossible stunt when they tried to fuse the existing Hungarian penal code and the decrees on the People's Tribunals together into a law that would define and penalize previously non-existent criminal offences such as war crimes and crimes against humanity. The legislators made a wise choice when they integrated the new criminal stance into the existing legal framework (although possibly because of international pressure they had no other choice). Until the act on People's Tribunals was signed into law, the tribunals operated according to previously effective decrees and reclaimed remnants of earlier legislation, i.e. Law No. 3/1921 ("on crimes and misdemeanors that aim at the perturbation or shattering of the state and social order"), originally implemented against the Communists of the short lived People's Republic in 1919, was now implemented against the members of the Arrow

---

69 On the People's Tribunals, see Ildikó Barna and Andrea Pető, *Political Justice in Post War Budapest* (Budapest: CEU Press, 2015). and Nánási László, *A magyarországi népbíróság joganyaga 1945-1950. Pártatlan igazságszolgáltatás vagy megtorlás?* [Legal material of Hungarian people's court 1945-1950] (Kecskemét: Bács Kiskun Megyei Önkormányzat Levéltára. 2011), 6–56.
70 On the process, see Tibor Zinner, "Háborús bűnösök perei" [Trials of the war criminals] *Történelmi Szemle* 1 (1985): 118–140.
71 The Provisional National Government's 81/1945. ME. decree on people's tribunals. "War criminal" is defined by 13§, while the definition of "crime against people" signifies state office bearers (MPs, high ranking public sector employee).

Cross Party and other war criminals.[72] The next phase was the post-war Sovietization of the Hungarian legal system, the first step of which was the transformation of the penal code.[73]

The reason why the Hungarian people's tribunal system was different from that of some other countries' under Soviet occupation was because of Hungarian exiles living in the Soviet Union: they, though ranking rather low in the Soviet hierarchy, had a decisive effect on the shaping of Hungarian judicial processes. The legislators and the advisors, as well as the jurists running the system – attorneys, prosecutors and judges – were the people meant to represent the continuity of institutional practices and its principles. However, when the fresh cadres arrived from Moscow together with the Red Army, the old guard needed to adapt to new values, practices and expectations. During the Hungarian lustration process, the Soviet lay people's tribunal system was used as a model.[74]

The social and political climate, as well as the legislation was very different in 1945 than it was in 1946 or 1947, and that left its mark on the Dely trials too. The 1945 People's Tribunal law was necessarily a hastily composed piece of legislation, but later the operation of the People's Tribunals was increasingly regulated and tightened. The process began with Law No. 7/1946 on democratic state order, which extended the protection of criminal law onto the republic and introduced the rather wide category of "anti-democratic statement." This law had a profound effect on the legal situation: the People's Tribunal became a stage for large-scale political games. Tellingly, the last verdict brought by the Budapest People's Tribunal was in the Rajk trial in 1949.[75] After the 1956 revolution, Law-Decree No. 34/1957 on NOT (*Népbíróságok Országos Tanácsa* – National Council of People's Tribunals) had reestablished the organization – with entirely different purposes.[76]

The Communist Party controlled the Hungarian police, or in particularly important cases the Department of State Protection (from October 1946 ÁVO, *Állam-*

---

[72] On the Sovietization of Bulgarian legal system, see Nikola Dolapchiev "Law and Human Rights in Bulgaria," *International Affairs* 29.1 (1953): 59–68, especially 59–61.
[73] Pető Andrea, "A magyar büntetőjog szovjetizálása: egyéni közvetítők és intézmények (1945–1961)," *Aetas* 33.2 (2018): 69–82.
[74] About Czechoslovakia, see Szarka László, ed., *Jogfosztó jogszabályok Csehszlovákiában, 1944–1949.* [Regulation of deprivations of rights in Czechoslovakia] (Komárom: Kecskés László Társ, 2005), 111–112.
[75] See more in Pető Andrea, *Rajk Júlia* (Budapest: Balassi, 2001), and Pető Andrea, *Geschlecht, Politik und Stalinismus in Ungarn. Eine Biographie von Júlia Rajk* (Herne: Gabriele Schäfer Verlag, 2007).
[76] I am grateful for Kinga Pétervári's help with collecting the decrees and laws on People's Tribunals.

védelmi Osztály – State Protection Authority) ran the investigations before the case was handed over to the people's prosecutor's office (*népügyészség*). Then, when the prosecutor's investigation was concluded, the files were transferred to the People's Tribunal. The tribunals were led by professional judges, but their members had no legal degrees, as they were party delegates from the Hungarian National Independence Front's five parties.[77] As the People's Tribunals were overwhelmed, their functioning was largely dependent on the precision of the prosecutors.[78] However, it was not uncommon that the prosecutor received the files on the very day of the trial while the defendant, given that they had a lawyer, could prepare for weeks ahead.[79] On the executive section of the judicial process very little data remained.

The operation of the People's Tribunals was also divided along party lines. For instance, when it came to femaleperpetrators, the representatives of the Independent Smallholders' Party – a right-wing umbrella party – argued for less severe sentences because of women's "gullibility" and "lesser intellectual capacity." Due to the majority vote system, their stance was not validated.

The NOT operated as the appellate court. It acted in five-member committees, the members of which were all professional judges delegated by the five parties. The NOT as the second instance court could not start a new process, instead its task was to examine whether People's Tribunal processes abided by the law. The NOT's investigations often ended with release because they found that procedural mistakes were made in the first instance.

The verdict of a People's Tribunal's trial could depend on many factors, among them timing. During the first wave of trials, in the spring of 1945 there were still fights in the western part of the country, therefore rigorous court work was unfeasible (the Dely trial was symptomatic in that regard). Then from the second part of 1945, after the survivors had returned, the People's Tribunals became overwhelmed with work. The justice system was not ready to process the huge number of cases, and as a result the accused often received lighter sentences.

After 1945 the language of the law became the discourse of consolidation. The operation of the People's Tribunals was meant to alleviate social pain;

---

[77] Civil Democratic Party, Hungarian Communist Party, Independent Smallholders' Party, National Peasant Party, Social Democratic Party.
[78] MOL I-F-24. On November 18, 1946, two-third of the cases the NOT received were incomplete. In turn, the Ministry of Justice paradoxically urged a withdrawal of second instance appeals because they "either offered atonement for the people or represented the state of affairs as established by judicial praxis."
[79] Interview with Gy. K., People's Tribunal judge, March 22, 2005.

they represented the institutionalized form of a much needed process of mourning. The lawyers had a huge influence on the court process, but they also played a central role in negotiating what counted as a crime. Legal professionals mediate between state and individuals; they serve as a transmission belt of norms and values as well as of disciplining power. This was especially true after 1945, when legal discourse was the discourse of normalization: the People's Tribunals were expected to mark the end of an era and the start of a "new" one.

The reinstatement of gender hierarchy was crucial to this process, and trial records show that lawyers used the courts' gender bias to their defendants' advantage. Whereas in the case of men, indictments were fitted to individuals and paid lawyers offered the possibility of an escape from the rigors of the justice system, in the case of female perpetrators, the "femaleness" of the accused party, as a defense category, held out the prospect of a more lenient sentence. Piroska Dely did not have a private defense lawyer and that left its mark on her process. She did not conform to the gendered expectations of the court either as she was a divorced, single employed women with two children who were not living with her.

In the Budapest City Archives (BFL) and the Historical Archive of the State Security Services (ÁBTL), I examined the files of woman perpetrators and collected the names of their assigned and appointed lawyers. I wanted to know more about those men, all 62 of them, who defended femaleperpetrators, so I also examined their private files at the Budapest Bar Association (BÜKI – *Budapesti Ügyvédi Kamara*).[80] I found that in terms of their social and family background the group was very balanced: 48 percent came from lower classes and 52 percent from a middle-class background. The first-generation lawyers were featured in very high numbers among the lawyers, which suggests that they were more willing to take risky, controversial, very political but lucrative People's Tribunal cases. More than a third (24) of these lawyers were former members of the MÜNE (*Magyar Ügyvédek Nemzeti Egyesülete* – National Association of Hungarian Lawyers) the corporate organization of Christian legal professionals, but only one left the anti-Semitic association "cursing the Germans and the Arrow Cross,"[81] for the rest of them leaving apparently seemed "too risky."[82] During

---

[80] Unfortunately, there is no such source concerning the people's judges. Lóránt Tilkovszky quotes a February 16, 1946 report of the Social Democratic Party, according to which 80 percent of the party's people's judges were of Jewish origin and 90 percent of them were driven by revenge or worked as judges as a side job besides trading. See Tilkovszky Lóránt, "Vád, védelem, valóság. Basch Ferenc a népbíróság előtt," *Századok* 6 (1996):1405.
[81] BÜKI 4770
[82] BÜKI 7573

the post-war attestation processes, 71 percent of former MÜNE members were cleared, 21 percent were reprimanded, three percent were excluded from the Bar Association and five percent were suspended. This shows that within the elite of the legal profession MÜNE membership was not necessarily punished during the first wave of lustrations. The continuity within the legal profession greatly contributed to the controversies of the people's tribunals' trials.[83]

4.2.2 Between sloppiness and rigor: The People's Tribunals' activity

Besides the difficulties caused by the sheer number of cases, the literature on People's Tribunals also regularly discusses the role and effect of the Soviet pattern. The Soviet justice system was rigorous in dealing with collaborators and they held trials in large quantities. As the Stalinist legal system reached back to the tradition of the 1917 military tribunals, Hungarian courts reached back to the extraordinary legal practices established after the 1919 Hungarian Soviet Republic.

The analysis of trial records shows that the Stalin era's justice system could neither clearly define nor appropriately punish the war crimes committed by Germans, but it stepped up very effectively against its own citizens. The massive amount of trials in the Soviet system were rife with inconsistent verdicts, which is hardly a surprise given that the trials were held in bulk and many of the judges were party delegates who had not even finished high school. Furthermore, in the legal system in the USSR appeal was disallowed. Although the Hungarian People's Tribunal's structure and processes were shaped after these Soviet patterns, the praxis of appeal was integral to Hungarian justice system, and the judges were also professionals who had passed their bar exam. The Soviet tribunals examined whether the defendant was guilty of the accusations *and* whether they exhibited any sort of behavior opposing the Soviet system. The Hungarian system followed suit with Law No. 7/1946 on democratic state order and the protection of the democratic republic. At the Soviet tribunals, the testimonies were the most important parts of the trial. As the tribunals were operating under heavy ideological control, the evidence used during building the case was mostly based on the testimony often obtained under physical and psychological pressure. Although the trials were not open to the public, the testimonies

---

[83] For more on this, see Andrea Pető, "'I switched sides'. Lawyers Creating the Memory of Shoah in Budapest," in *Confronting the Past. European Experiences*, ed., Davor Paukovic, Vjeran Pavlakovic and Viseslav Raos. (Zagreb: Political Science Research Centre, Series of Political Science Research Forum, 10, 2012): 223–235.

assumed the ritualistic and highly symbolic character of a confession.[84] Research also shows that there were great regional differences within the Soviet Union, even though the limited accessibility of archives makes it hard to come to definite conclusions.[85]

From the summer of 1945, the Hungarian Ministry of Justice started receiving letters of complaint from practicing people's prosecutors. They criticized the legal system but mainly complained about the slow, unfair, lax and improvised verdicts of the People's Tribunals. An offence that was worth six months prison time at one tribunal received six years at another; innocents were being imprisoned while Arrow Cross members walked away, etc.[86] The most common complaint was, however, that the courts were overburdened. This problem could have been resolved by singling out "smaller cases." Although this was a practice abroad, in Hungary it was not introduced, that is why, as a people's prosecutor ironically remarked, "the Hungarian people's punitive fist, the people's tribunal spends hours each day mulling over whether Mrs. Smith told to Mrs. White that the Germans would win the war and that the Jews were bad people."[87] The Dely case also contained minor, yet important details the careful consideration of which exceeded the capacity and skills of the people's tribunal.

The history of People's Tribunals in Hungary recently received unexpected political and professional interest due to blankspots in the literature. The systematic and methodical mapping of the Hungarian post-war justice system's operation has not been conducted yet, therefore the substantial regional differences have remained undetected. Available studies either focus on the court case of one remarkable personality or a single municipality based on material of that people's court. The scarcity of comparative and comprehensive works on the topic contributed to the political instrumentalization of the unquestionable flaws of the People's Tribunal process as a part of the revisionist historical turn effected by the Hungarian government's switch to illiberal memory politics. As a result, since 2010 new historical research has aimed to undermine the legitimacy of post-Second World War retribution process by focusing exclusively on

---

[84] Alexander Victor Prusin, "Fascist Criminals to the Gallows. The Holocaust and the Soviet War Crimes Trials December 1945–February 1946," *Holocaust and Genocide Studies* 17.1 (2003): 1–30.
[85] On the Soviet style justice system in Ukraine, see Tanja Penter, "Local Collaborators on Trial," *Cahier du Monde Russe* 49.2–3 (2008.): 341–364.
[86] MOL XIX-E-1-L X. 2. box Bö 117/1945. Miklós Kátai, people's persecutor, July 31, 1945.
[87] MOL XIX-E-1-L X. 2. box Bö 117/1945. 10.

the Sovietization of the legal system and the impact of the Communist Party.[88] In the framework of "mnemonic security,"[89] revisionist political forces challenge the anti-fascist agenda and promote the myth of Hungarian "double victimhood" (i.e. victim of both Nazi and Soviet occupation) while ignoring Hungarian collaboration with both countries. In that framework, the People's Tribunal are presented as tools of the Communist takeover without acknowledging that real crimes had been committed. Exactly because of the legal paradigm change that the establishment of the illiberal state in Hungary has brought with it, the analysis of historical precedents, like the case of Dely, is ever more imperative.[90]

4.2.3 Piroska Dely in front of the People's Tribunal

Dely's case became one of the early high-profile cases of the Budapest People's Tribunal. Yet, it did not start as a court case that would enter history textbooks discussing post-war political justice. Dely's case started as an ordinary crime process. If there were no survivors, then the people's prosecutor's office had to take its own initiative. In practice though in most of the cases the victims or their surviving relatives filed a report with the police.[91] Returning survivors, like survivors in Csengery, wanted to know what happened to their loved ones, or wanted to reclaim their belongings because they found someone else in their apartment, someone else wearing their clothes.[92] These issues made up the bulk of the People's Tribunals' "small cases," which had so far largely been ignored by historiography, as it focused on high profile trials.[93] One of

---

[88] About the illiberal turn in memory politics, see Andrea Pető, "Roots of Illiberal Memory Politics: Remembering Women in the 1956 Hungarian Revolution," *Baltic Worlds* 10.4 (2017): 42–58.
[89] Maria Mälksoo, "Memory must be Defended: Beyond the Politics of Mnemonical Security," *Security Dialogue* 46.3 (2015): 221–237.
[90] Andrea Pető, "Hungary's Illiberal Polypore State," *European Politics and Society Newsletter* 21.4 (2017): 18–21.
[91] In addition, the people's tribunals or denouncements were occasionally used for resolving family feuds and personal conflicts. See Karol Sauerland, *Dreissig Silberlinge. Denunziation in Gegenwart und Geschichte* (Berlin: Volk und Welt Verlag, 2000). I am grateful to András Karácsony for this source.
[92] For more on this, see Andrea Pető, "Privatised Memory? The Story of Erecting of the First 'Private' Holocaust Memorial in Budapest," in *Memory and Narrating Mass Repression*, ed., Nanci Adler, Mary Chamberlaine and Leyla Neyzi, 157–175 (New Brunswick, N.J: Transaction, 2009).
[93] For instance, see Mária Kralik's case (BFL 270/1945) who reported on Jewish people. One victim, Jolán Katz returned and denounced Králik, who was sentenced to forced labor and served her sentence till the 1955 amnesty.

the eyewitnesses of the Hársfa Street robbery, one of the four robberies Dely and her accomplices committed on the October 15, 1944, recognized Piroska Dely as she walked by on the street, followed her home then filed a handwritten denunciation letter to the police.[94] There were still ongoing fights in the west of the country when in March 1945 Dely was already charged for the robbery in Hársfa Street.

The perpetrators expected that the deported victims would never return. During the Csengery 64 massacre they tried to eliminate all eyewitnesses. Those whom they could not kill (because there were too many of them) and those whom they had no reason to kill (because they readily handed over their assets) were organized in three groups and forcibly taken to a nearby police station. The perpetrators – among them Dely – did not expect that the police would allow them home the following day, nor that several tenants would later return from deportation too. Andor Lichter, who lost his mother, father and only son in the massacre, was among the returned ones. Lichter was a successful businessman in his late forties with considerable expertise in international correspondence. He was not personally present on the night of October 15, 1944, because as a forced labor serviceman he simulated dysentery (with the widely used method of beetroot) and he was hospitalized.

Upon his return to Budapest, Lichter took on the mission to bring punishment to the culprits.[95] He became an ardent reader of the People's Tribunals' press releases, which played a crucial role in shaping the public discourse about crime and punishment.[96] Lichter also regularly visited the People's Tribunals' trials. Perhaps he tried to alleviate his guilty conscience for not being present on that fatal night with his family. As a survivor said: "My mother and uncle Andi [Lichter] went to the tribunals almost every day, because they needed this kind of retaliation I think."[97] This was a pre-Nürnberg trial when the language and the practice of justice was being created.[98] Lichter was present at Piroska

---

94 Elsewhere survivors also bumped into perpetrators on the street then turned to the police. See the analysis of four such cases, in Natalia Aleksiun, "Intimate violence: Jewish testimonies on victims and perpetrators in Eastern Galicia," *Holocaust Studies* (2016.), DOI: 10.1080/17504902.2016.1209833.
95 Interview, March 3, 2005.
96 On May 17, 1947 János Szűcs, the chief people's prosecutor visited the Association of Hungarian Journalists (*Magyar Újságírók Szövetsége*), and said, that "[t]he deterrent effect is the main reason for the death penalty. However, if the press hides the news that a murderer or a thief was executed, the effect will be almost indiscernible." (MOL XIX-A-L.)
97 Interview, March 3, 2005.
98 For more on this, see Natalia Aleksiun, "Organizing for Justice: Jewish Leadership in Poland and the Trial of the Nazi War Criminals at Nuremberg," in *Beyond Camps and Forced Labour*.

Dely's first trial too, and he recognized the similarities between the Hársfa Street robbery and the Csengery 64 massacre.

Andor Lichter turned to the police and claimed that the perpetrator of Hársfa Street and Csengery Street was the same person;[99] moreover, he stated that he saw Dely in an Arrow Cross uniform.[100] During this first police hearing on March 5, 1945 Lichter told the story in the first person singular, i.e. he talked as if he was also present in Csengery 64 during that fatal night. Lichter was a respectable man and later the house overseer, that is the elected representative of the house who supervised the janitor, Strucky. The survivor eyewitnesses entrusted Lichter with their story of that night, so Lichter might have felt as if he had been personally present at the events.

With this the Dely case began. After the first police hearing, Lichter mobilized the massacre's other survivors. However, their testimonies were in many ways contradictory. The tenants had very different perspectives on the events, and since they were in different parts of the house, they could claim to have witnessed different things. There were apparent factual variations (who was where, who saw or said what) among the police hearings and among the court testimonies too. The polyphony of the testimonies tested the patience of the overburdened staff of the police and the court.

Dely was charged with threatening to torture, forcible removal ("elhurcoltatás" the Hungarian legal term for deportation), and execution. The investigation identified four crime scenes: one in Hársfa Street, one in Nagyatádi Street (today: Kertész Street), and two in Csengery Street. According to the charges Dely controlled, monitored and deported the Jewish tenants on German commands. In the Hársfa Street case (at the trial at which Lichter was present), she was accused of locking the gate and handing the key to the Arrow Cross. In the Nagyatádi (today: Kertész) Street case, Dely first admitted having taken some assets (a coat and a ring) but later claimed to have tried to return the ring but according to Dely the owner allegedly refused to take it back. Concerning the rest of her items she claimed to have bought them at the Teleki Square flea market. Regarding the Hársfa Street case where she was accused of threatening with torture, she said that she just "coincidentally passed by" and somehow ended up being part of the events. Later, as more and more eyewitnesses identified her, she changed her testimony and claimed that an SS soldier had "dragged her" to the crime

---

Current International Research on Survivors of Nazi Persecution, ed., Johannes-Dieter Steinert and Inge Weber-Newth, 184–194 (Osnabrzuck, Germany: Secolo, 2006).
99 ÁBTL V 48889, 17654/1949. 127.
100 ÁBTL V 48889, 17654/1949. 20.

scene.¹⁰¹ This was probably the version that Lichter himself also heard at the trial:

> An SS soldier dragged me into Hársfa Street 57. It was not an SS soldier, actually, but an acquaintance of mine, I don't even know his name, more accurately, he was not even an acquaintance, but a tall man in black uniform with an Arrow Cross armband, who took me there. Because I complained to this stranger about my workplace problems... or rather I asked him whether he could find a better position for me, and I also complained that I have no winter coat. He said that I should go with them to escort the Jews, and I will get a coat. I admit being present in Hársfa Street 57, I participated in the rounding up of women, we took them to the Nagykörút [Grand Boulevard]. More accurately, now I remember, we did not take them to the boulevard, because the Germans sent them back in the house due lack of space. I deny that I had mistreated women. It is a fact that I got a coat, the one that I'm wearing now. I also received a golden ring. Both were handed over by the already mentioned Arrow Cross man. I also received a blue blouse and a blue polka dot dress. This is the coat. All the rest of the confiscated items were my long time belongings [...]¹⁰²

The Csengery Street case was entirely different though. It was not about small-scale theft anymore: in Csengery 64, 18 people were shot dead.

4.2.4 Was she present at all?

Based on the testimonies it is not possible to determine how many men in what kind of uniform (green or black shirt?), with what armband (green with an arrow cross or black with a death skull?), speaking what language entered Csengery 64 on that warm October evening in 1944. Some saw Arrow Cross uniforms, other saw SS soldiers, and there are some who saw ethnic Germans from Hungary (in which case it would be hard to explain why Dely would have acted as a "translator" as was stated during a trial). The relationship between the armed men and Piroska Dely was also not clarified. According to the testimonies some eyewitnesses saw no woman among the intruders. Fifty years later, the stories told by the survivors during the oral history interviews are still contradictory:

---

101 ÁBTL V 48889, 17654/1949. 73.
102 BFL 2442/1947. 42. (February 13) "She bought the fur coat, the golden ring, the blouse and the polka dot dress on the Teleki Square flea market for 350 *pengős* [...] she didn't say so because she wasn't asked." BFL 2442/1947. 54.

4.2 Her trial

We saw the end of a car in front of the gate. Maybe she sat by the driver so we could not see her getting out of the car. It was beyond dispute that she was there. I don't remember the uniforms, only the German army boots.[103]

I think there were more Germans. The Arrow Cross men came back the next day but Piroska Dely wasn't with them anymore. Because when they were to… We were taken away I already told that, my mother, my grandmother, and then this officer brought us back to 64. And then my mother went to the Struckys. Because we did not know what happened because the house was empty by then. […] I saw an armband, for sure. […] I don't think that they wore the Arrow Cross outfit that one sees in documentaries. […] Most of them wore those tall riding boots, the breeches boots. […] Semi-long coats and green shirts. That's what they usually wore. A dark green shirt. […] And the armband.[104]

I don't remember seeing a woman among them, among the Arrow Cross men. […] I remember seeing a German-Arrow Cross mix of men jumping off the truck and entering the house. […] I remember the armband.[105]

I can't swear that the Germans were from the SS. But they had German uniforms. Unquestionably.[106]

When we peeked out from behind the shades after that we had heard the shots then we saw the truck and the German and Arrow Cross men jumping out of its back. And that's when I saw an armbanded Arrow Cross man jumping off the truck. […] I have no idea [about their number]. It was a closed truck. […] It had a canvas top and they jumped out from underneath. I saw approximately three people jump out but I cannot tell how many of them were Germans and how many were Arrow Cross, because my father sent us away from the window to the bathroom, because the bathroom was the only place where no bullet could enter from the courtyard or from the street front.[107]

I remember men, four or five of them. In black uniforms with armband.[108]

The interviews bear witness to the uncertainty of remembrance but also point at an actual source of uncertainty: in the dark it was hard to discern how many people came, who they were and where they came from. When I went around Csengery 64 I checked the vantage points of the eyewitnesses to see what they could potentially have seen during that night. Based on that I can claim with certainty that the testimonies do not reconstruct the story in full. Still, most of the interviewees assuredly stated that Piroska Dely was present.[109] The reason why

---

103 Interview with Magda Kun, January 9, 2007.
104 Interview, March 3, 2005.
105 Interview, April 1, 2005.
106 Interview, April 1, 2005.
107 Interview, April 1, 2005.
108 Edit Rosenberg, Interview, August 13, 2007.
109 According to Mrs. (Miklós) Faragó, 10 to 15 SS-soldiers were present and Dely got out of a car. (BFL 19273/1949. 225, December 26, 1946. Testimony.)

the survivors were so certain of this is to be examined later in connection with Andor Lichter's activity.

4.2.5 Changing explanations

Piroska Dely's court testimony was a "testimony-performance" and her trial was a political drama.[110] Perpetrators often use the technique of "doubling," i.e. they posit themselves as model citizens in order to compensate for being guilty.[111] Dely did not use this method, although she could have used the opportunity to "re-invent" her past in her testimonies. She could also have talked about her past in a manner conforming to gendered expectations and invoke her poor family, that she was a single mother of two, and might have mentioned that she was widowed. She did not do that either. Instead she kept on saying that through her deeds she "wanted to avoid a greater evil" which, given the consequences of those deeds, could only fail to convince.[112]

The first fact that she mentioned in her police testimony was her workplace, the Svábhegy Sanatorium in Buda. An important detail, because after the German occupation on March 19, 1944, the sanatorium was transformed into a German military hospital and the Gestapo moved into the nearby well-defendable hotels. Supposedly it was here, in the sanatorium that she became intimate with Otto Willinger (elsewhere: Wildinger), a German general. As there was no such high-ranking German officer her statement can be interpreted in multiple ways. Perhaps she meant Otto Willigman (1898–1945), the General of the Army Group South who disappeared in 1945 on the Eastern front, or Otto Winkelmann (1894–1977), General of the Waffen-SS and Higher SS and Police Leader in Hungary, briefly city commander of Budapest. Perhaps the minute taker at the people's tribunal misspelled the German name and it went on record inaccurately. Piroska Dely spent quite some time in military surroundings, therefore we can exclude the possibility that she had mixed up a sergeant with a general (uniforms play a huge role in this story, as this was the time of men in uniform). It is also possible that Dely made up this love affair in order to hint at her high-level connections – not a wise strategy in an era when abroad women's col-

---

110 Leigh A. Payne, *Unsettling Accounts. Neither Truth nor Reconciliation in Confessions of State Violence* (Durham, NC/London: Duke University Press, 2008), 15.
111 Ibid., 17.
112 On the typology of testimonies, see Ibid., 19–21.

laboration was punished with other forms of humiliation like head shaving.¹¹³ However, perhaps Piroska Dely needed an imagined high-ranking German officer in her story as the tempter who led her astray. This was not a bad defense strategy: the structural analysis of the People's Tribunals' trials showed that a much-repeated and rather successful defense argument was that the accused had been acting under the influence or pressure of others.¹¹⁴ In the case of accused women, this argument worked particularly well – especially when they had to answer for their crimes to male judges. In Dely's words:

> I was the girlfriend of Otto Wildinger German general, who painted a very advantageous picture about my future as well as about my children's future, and kept on saying that the Germans would win the war and he completely misled me and it was under his effect that I took that filthy and sinful role to assist the SS.¹¹⁵

In her later testimonies further versions of the story were presented. In one of them Dely was asked by (in yet another version she was commanded by) her German lover to translate for the SS soldiers which is how she got to the Hársfa and then to the Csengery Street at the head of armed troops.

The janitor Struckys' nephew, Nándor Szamocseta also served on the Svábhegy with the German occupying forces. Perhaps he came up with the idea of the robbery and knew Dely personally, although he denied that throughout. If this had been the case Dely would not have hesitated to share it with the tribunal. I will come back to this supposed connection and another tie to Strucky's lodger, Széplaki in a separate section.

In yet another version of Dely's testimony a "finance guard" called "Pista," whose family name she did not know, gave her an Arrow Cross armband and badge, and "pushed" her into the Hársfa Street house where under German orders she swept up the money the Jewish tenants had thrown on the ground. What made them act so irrationally, i.e. who threatened them and with what, was not part of Dely's narrative, she only mentioned that she warned someone – supposedly out of the goodness of her heart – that the person should not hold money in their hands. Allegedly in her willingness to help, she also took away two Jewish children from their mother and sent them back to the janitor:

---

113 Besides France it was also used in Northern Italy as a punishment for collaborating women. See Mirco Dondi, *La lunga liberazione. Giustizia e violenza nel dopo Guerra italiano* (Rome: Riuniti, 2004). 125–130.
114 Barna Ildikó and Pető Andrea, *Political Justice in Budapest after World War II* (Budapest: CEU Press, 2015).
115 BFL 2442/1947. 40.

> I passed Hársfa Street 57 and I saw that the Arrow Cross was taking away Jewish children and women. I saw that some women took their children with them. I took two children from a woman and I took these kids back to the janitor, and I asked the janitor to take care of them, because if those women were to be taken to forced labor service then the children would get in danger. The women were against this, they wanted the children back, but I still took the children because that was the right thing to do, because I saw that the Germans, the SS and the Arrow Cross were cruel to children too.[116]

This was not the only occasion that Dely tried to posit herself as a rescuer in order to save herself:

> I told a woman in the courtyard to not have cash in her hands because that will bring trouble on her. When the Arrow Cross men heard that I warned the Jews one of them grabbed my coat and threw me on the street… Pista wanted to give me a golden ring he found there… But I refused to accept it I didn't want to take such a thing. Then they said that they don't need a woman like me.[117]

Mrs. Veréb, the wife of the Csengery 45 janitor claimed in her testimony that "a seven men SS patrol led by a woman in a black dress" stopped in front of their gate.[118] During the trial Mrs. Veréb identified Piroska Dely as the woman in black dress. It is important that in Csengery 45 people were not shot dead in their apartments. According to Mrs. Veréb's testimony, Piroska Dely had commanding power over the armed men: twice she ordered them to shoot. This was when Ernő Gruber was killed while trying to escape. After that seven tenants were forcibly taken away. Those who were hiding in the cellar survived and were not taken away, at least not yet. Mrs. Veréb did not mention theft at the court, which is why Dely got a lighter sentence for the crimes she committed at Csengery 45. This was a very early People's Tribunal trial, and the police was not exactly exhibiting mastery in investigation.

Several eyewitnesses mentioned a certain Etel Simon as the person who supposedly led the Arrow Cross to Csengery 64. During her court hearing Piroska Dely denied having used the pseudonym Etel Simon, and she insisted that she was never called Sister Etel either[119] moreover, she claimed she never wore an Arrow Cross armband,[120] she never hurt anyone and played no role in the deportation of the tenants.[121]

---

116 BFL 2442/1947. 41.
117 BFL 2442/1947. 41.
118 BFL 19273/1949. 197. January 25, 1946. Testimony. Steiner mentioned 3 to 4 "German SS soldiers."
119 February 26, 1945. Police hearing.
120 BFL 19273/1949. 45. Mrs. Miksa Tenczer's testimony, January 25, 1946.

4.2 Her trial

Although the victims were usually precise in remembering the names the perpetrators used for each other, in principle it is plausible that there was an Arrow Cross woman called Etel Simon who escaped conviction. At the beginning of the hearings the figure of Sister Etel Simon was often mixed up with Piroska Dely but later entirely disappeared. Therefore most probably we will never find out whether Dely used a pseudonym, or if there was an actual Etel Simon who participated in the robberies but escaped justice, or perhaps Etel Pap, notorious for the Nagyatádi (Kertész) Street case, made some incursions into Csengery Street.[122]

Before examining Dely's role in the events we shall trace how she explained her presence in Csengery Street. When the "I coincidentally passed by" version of her narrative was not tenable any more Dely started to come up with newer and newer stories. First, she claimed that her dire existential situation was the culprit:

> An Arrow Cross man showed up at my workplace. He wore a black uniform with an armband. I asked him to put me in a better position, to which he said he could not help for now but told me to go with him to help round up and guard Jewish women. He also promised that he would buy me a winter coat. This is how I got to Hársfa Street 57. When we entered, the Arrow Cross and German soldiers organized the Jewish women into a line. A uniformed man asked me to lock the gate and let no one in. I locked the gate and handed the key to the janitor. [...] They were not taken away because an SS soldier came and said that there is no space for them... He sent me away. I got a fur coat, the one that I'm wearing now, and a golden ring. I never met this Arrow Cross man nor any other ever again.[123]

What makes her reasoning hard to credit here is that during the trials Piroska Dely, despite her rather adventurous employment history, depicted herself as a woman with a steady income and a good job on the Svábhegy.

In her later testimonies, the "I followed an order" explanation came to the fore. Dely repeated several times in her testimony that she "got orders from the German headquarters,"[124] because she was familiar with the neighborhood and spoke "some" German. When asked about the identity of her commissioners she gave various responses. First, she claimed that she was sent from the Svábhegy to translate for the patrol crews. Another time she said that she was in the Andrássy Avenue Arrow Cross Headquarter, the House of Faith, which was right

---

121 BFL 19273/1949. 45. Mrs. Miksa Tenczer's testimony, January 25, 1946.
122 BFL 2442/1947. 39. Etel Pap was sentenced by the people's tribunal for participation in tortures in Nagyatádi Street. Pelle János, "A nyilas terror Budán," *Valóság* 10 (2015): 65–87.
123 BFL 2442/1947. 104.
124 BFL 19273/1949. 63.

down the street from Csengery Steet 64, where someone – an unknown person for an unknown reason – told her to lead a penal squad because she knows the area."[S]he performed these deeds because the captain at the German headquarters ordered her to lead the SS soldiers to the houses and to translate for them."[125]

The story has a further variant in which Dely has no ties to any official organization or institution. Once she said that on October 15, 1944 she had dinner with Arrow Cross and/or SS soldiers in a restaurant and during the dinner they discussed a potential robbery (given the then current political situation, the choice of topic is not surprising). Dely knew the neighborhood and urged the Arrow Cross men and/or Germans to take their chance and sack the vulnerable tenants. Probably Dely was particularly keen on robbing the Steiner jeweler family in Csengery 64 whom she had possibly known from before as they had a signboard on the wall. It is certain that she knew where to go. It is also possible that she got a lead from the janitor's relative, Nándor Szamocseta. Lichter considered that most likely there was a connection between Dely and Szamocseta even though he had no evidence for that. Both of them plundered, both were motivated by greed, but possibly they acted independently from each other. A tragedy like the one that Lichter went through is extremely hard to process, therefore it is understandable that he was in desperate search for logical explanations.

The thus far quoted witnesses did not see Piroska Dely on Csengery Street, but some claimed that they did. In a March 17, 1945 letter Pál Laub described what he saw on Csengery Street on October 15 around noon:

> [It was] a middle-aged woman in a black coat... four-five men with yellow stars were in a conversation in front of Csengery 45. The woman attacked them with unrepeatable offences and accused them that they halt traffic on the sidewalk; they idly hang out while her husband is on the battlefield. Then she walked away in the direction of the Andrássy Avenue 60 Arrow Cross house all the while cussing and cursing the Jews. [...] I went downstairs to warn the men to get lost because she could bring the Arrow Cross men. She had a high-stepped gait. She wore a short skirt. She had good legs.[126]

There is one detail that makes it dubious that the woman Laub saw was indeed Piroska Dely: especially in combination with a short skirt and the coat, which had to be a rather unusual outfit on such a warm, sunny afternoon. The black coat that many eyewitnesses recognized came into Dely's possession only later that day in the Hársfa Street robberies. There is a chance that another, unknown

---

125 BFL 2442/1947. 104.
126 BFL 2442/1947. 177.

female passerby reported that the excited tenants of the Csengery Street house took the yellow star off the entrance door and as a consequence the penal squad turned up that night.

However, if the massacre was a plotted penal action then further questions arise. Did Dely really arrive in Csengery with the list of tenants prepared in advance, as Mrs. Propper maintained?[127] The intruders might have had a copy of the tenant registry from the janitor and used that to organize the transport groups of tenants. If they arrived with a list that would be a sign of a premeditated action and it would also signal that Strucky collaborated all along. This, like many others, remained an unresolved question, because the court did not examine whether the massacre constituted malice aforethought. It is certainly a pity because such an investigation could have contributed to our knowledge about the aims and motives of the perpetrators of this unusual crime.

The trial turned Piroska Dely into a notorious "Arrow Cross woman." In 1948, two years after her execution on 23 March, 1946, testimonies still mentioned her as the organizer of a grand scale women's conspiracy.[128] In an April 2, 1948 denouncement letter, Margit Szabó listed women who to her knowledge collaborated with the Arrow Cross in the Zichy Street area. According to this testimony Piroska Dely (there: Delli) was but one among the many "Arrow Cross commissioned translator women" such as Ibolya Kovács, Mrs. Száll, Mrs. Csizik, Mrs. Kállászár, Paula Gubicsek (whose brother stole deported people's belongings), Mária Hergarocs, Mrs. Kiss (whose husband, Géza Kiss was the 8th district Arrow Cross section foreman), Szilvia Sipics (one of the leaders of the Death Skull Legion, a "Hungarist" far-right paramilitary organization whose members wore an armband with a death skull), and Miss Erzsi, Miss Viki and Miss Lilli, who were possibly waitresses at the King Confectionery on Andrássy Avenue and made and distributed anti-Soviet propaganda posters. In 1948, Piroska Dely, long dead by then, still re-appeared on Szabó's list, probably because her name was familiar from People's Tribunals' press releases. Margit Szabó's letter also suggests that of the many variants of Dely's story the "translator" version was the most widespread at the time, although Piroska Dely denied speaking German.

---

127 BFL 19273/1949. 51., January 25, 1946. Testimony.
128 ÁBTL V 48889. 20–29. Margit Szabó's denouncement: April 2, 1948. 31–46.

4.2.6 The power objects: The Arrow Cross armband and the weapon

It was a key question of the trial whether Piroska Dely's ties to the Arrow Cross should be proven or be treated as a fact. The testimonies repeatedly claimed that she wore Arrow Cross markers from the nonexistent "Arrow Cross hairband" to the actual Arrow Cross armband.[129] The Arrow Cross power symbols were mentioned to prove that Dely was an "Arrow Cross woman" although she was not a "woman of the Arrow Cross" as she held no party membership. The witnesses and particularly Lichter knew that the overwhelmed justice system would soon divert its attention from the case if there was no convincing political aspect to it. The testimonies had obviously become increasingly canonical with time, i.e. they were more and more alike, while a witness's narrative usually acquired a standard form already by the second telling. These were the steps through which the unified narrative of the events, presented in the verdict, had been developed.[130]

Piroska Dely was sentenced to death as a member of the Arrow Cross Party for 19 counts of murder. The verdict assumed that she was a party member and that she was present at the crime scene. However, Dely denied having a firearm and denied the murders too: "I had no weapon, I don't know how to handle one, but I admit that I helped the executing soldiers all throughout the events."[131] Yet, the court testimonies uniformly depicted her as an armed "amazon." Strucky, the Csengery 64 janitor, was the sole exception: he did not mention a weapon in his testimony, though he was the one who let Piroska Dely into the house and therefore the one who could really examine the woman as she entered.[132] And was there really a revolver in Dely's hand when she entered Csengery 45? András Veréb, the only person who might have seen that stated otherwise:

> This woman in black uniform with an armband had limitless power, she ruled over life and death. There literally everything happened the way she wanted it to happen. She was not armed, but the German SS soldiers obeyed her commands: they killed and they took the tenants away.[133]

---

129 ÁBTL V 48889, 17654/1949. 10.
130 On police records as sources, see Andrea Pető and Klaartje Schrijvers, "The Theatre of Historical Sources. Some Methodological Problems in Analyzing post-WWII Extreme Right Movements in Belgium and in Hungary," in *Professions and Social Identity. New European Historical Research on Work, Gender and Society*, ed., Berteke Waaldijk, 39–63 (Pisa: Edizioni Plus – University of Pisa Press, 2006).
131 ÁBTL V 48889., March 8, 1945 testimony.
132 BFL 2442/1947. 104.
133 Mrs. (Ervin) Gábor's testimony, BFL 2442/1947. 32.

In a similar vein a Csengery 64 survivor claimed that: "The Arrow Cross woman decided what happened there... Those whom she wanted dead, died, and those whom she wanted ... were taken away, and if she wanted so, they were saved."[134] As evidenced by the memories of the survivors from sixty years later, the situation was more complex than that: "I think she had a gun because she pointed it at my mother. I don't know... That's what my mother told. Now you cannot make someone stand by the wall with a slingshot." When I asked if it was possible that an SS soldier or an Arrow Cross man handled the gun, he said: "Certainly someone was there with [her]. Because she alone could not drive away so many people. Armed men accompanied the groups. We were also accompanied by gunmen but Piroska Dely was not with us."[135]

According to the witnesses, Piroska Dely was a member of the Arrow Cross Party. She denied that all along and no evidence proves that she had ties to the party, though such documents tend to be hard to find. Dely stated that "I was rude to Jewish women, but I had no connection to Arrow Cross women."[136] With this statement Dely challenged the widespread discourse of the time that Arrow Cross members exclusively harmed Jews. In my interpretation, Piroska Dely was, to use Christopher Browning's expression, an "ordinary perpetrator"[137] who took advantage of the Hungarian state's October 15, 1944 collapse, and when the opportunity presented itself, she went for her prey. She was an easy target for the Communist police and become a symbol of something she was not, and in this way those women who participated in looting and killing were invisibilized.

4.2.7 The power of "executive power"[138]

If Piroska Dely did not shoot, and she had no weapon either, then who committed the murders? If it all happened on her command, then as a civilian woman how and whom could she give orders to? What did "executive power"– a term that was crucial in her verdict – mean in that context?[139] These are burning ques-

---

134 BFL 2442/1947. 36. Mrs. (Alajos) Steiner's testimony, March 26, 1945.
135 Interview, April 1, 2005.
136 BFL 2442/1947. 15., February 13, 1945 police hearing.
137 Christopher R. Browning, *Ordinary Men. Reserve Police Battalion 101 and the Final Solution in Poland* (New York: HarperCollins, 1992).
138 BFL 17654/1949. 11.
139 Mrs. Strucky, the janitor's wife, who was locked in her ground floor apartment during the massacre, at the first police hearing said that "[t]he named woman organized and directed the

tions especially that the four armed men who participated in the crime were never found, partly because Piroska Dely only mentioned their given names. It is also unclear how many people entered Csengery 64 on the evening of October 15. And who were these men? Arrow Cross people or SS soldiers? Were they uniformed or only wore armbands? If they were in uniforms, were those black or green? How did they arrive? Were they on foot? Or did they come in a truck? Or by car? Did Piroska Dely arrive with them or join them at the crime scene? None of these questions can be reassuringly answered because of the contradictory nature of the testimonies.

Dely once stated that her accomplices talked about a certain Alexander Werner who was shot dead in Nagyatádi (Kertész) Street. If this was true, then perhaps the Csengery event was part of a German revenge mission that aimed to destroy alleged resistance to the Arrow Cross takeover. Such "assassinations" and the myth of "Jewish resistance" appeared in other testimonies too. According to these variants, the janitor family only protected the soldiers from potential but unspecified assassinations:

> I don't know what kind of soldiers were those who walked the streets, I didn't tell the soldiers to take away the Jews, I only told them to search the house, because there was a reason to worry that from the house on the opposite side of the street someone would shoot over.[140]

Dely stated that she was accompanied by two Germans, Stefan and Josef, who later left with the retreating German troops and she never heard from them again. Another man, a certain Józsi (most probably not the same as Josef), she got to know on that day in an Erzsébet Boulevard buffet. "I never met him before or after,"[141] stated Dely. These vague statements with which she tried to shift responsibility to male partners in the crime did not help the identification of the perpetrators and didn't lessen her responsibility either.

In the indictment, Dely appeared as a "nurse employed at the German headquarters"[142] who led four SS soldiers to Csengery 45.[143] Dely herself talked about two soldiers in her testimony, and later the verdict mentioned seven men in unspecified uniforms. According to the indictment, she had a pistol and she wore

---

events in the house, she kept on giving orders and they had to do as she commanded." BFL 17654/1949. 23., March 19, 1945.

140 BFL 1322692/1949. 24., Mrs. Borbély, December 15, 1945. The house on the opposite side of the street was a yellow star house.
141 March 13, 1945 testimony. BFL 2442/1947.
142 BFL 2442/1947. 101.
143 BFL 2442/1947. 98.

an armband. There was a shot in the gateway. Dely ordered the janitor's wife to be shot but she dodged the bullet. In Csengery 64 she also led the SS soldiers with a pistol in her hand (there the number of soldiers was unspecified). The noise of gunshots brought the tenants out from their apartments. Dely again ordered fire in Steiner's apartment, then she had 70 people forcibly taken away and left 18 behind dead. Lichter's father died from a heart attack due the effect of the events. However, whether it was legally possible for a civilian woman to give orders to uniformed men remains a question.

The tenants of Csengery Street were driven away in three transports, most probably much more than seventy of them. The men were taken to Nagyatádi (Kertész) Street, women with their children into the Szeged Street church, and the third transport consisting of elderly and children went to Nagyatádi (Kertész) Street again. This I reconstructed through my interviews with the survivors as there was no relevant data among the court records, because those who survived the massacre remained under the radar of the court. For the People's Tribunal the perpetrators' attempt to eliminate witnesses was an insignificant detail, the 18 or 19 murders sufficed for the most severe sentence. Whether Dely acted as an armed "escort" besides the Csengery tenants on their way to the gathering points – and as the perpetrators convinced, their later deportation – was not a question of importance.

4.2.8 The endgame

According to the People's Tribunal's papers it was during a February 28, 1945 hearing that Piroska Dely mentioned that she was pregnant.[144] She remembered the exact date of her last period (December 18, 1944) and the date she last had sexual intercourse (December 23). That as a divorced woman she had sexual affairs further strengthened the image of the "lewd Arrow Cross woman." However, the fact that she was pregnant and that she had two children (whose whereabouts were unknown) could possibly have led to her acquittal. Perhaps that was the reason why the police did not make much of an effort to locate the children, because they would have weakened the prosecutor's position during the trial. Piroska Dely's death sentence was suspended till the birth of her child.[145] On May 8, 1945, a gynecological exam confirmed that she was in the sixth month of pregnancy. However, when she did not deliver after nine months

---

[144] BFL 2442/1947. 50.
[145] BFL 2442/1947. 92.

– she received official inquiries in October and December – the Hungarian justice system ordered her reexamination. During her January 9, 1946 reexamination the gynecologist diagnosed ovarian cancer *(cysta ovarii)*, which the prison physician mistakenly identified as pregnancy.[146] The President of the Republic, Zoltán Tildy (1889-1961) ordered her execution on January 30. The course of the pregnancy was closely followed by Andor Lichter too. In a February 1, 1946 letter he "reminded" Zoltán Tildy of the fact that Dely was an Arrow Cross member, and he called Dely a "servant of the Gestapo" for the first time who killed at least 18 people: "she was not a woman but a bloodthirsty beast in human skin."[147] Piroska Dely was executed on March 23, 1946.

---

[146] BFL 2442/1947. 125.
[147] MOL XIX-E-1-l-Tank-2000-1946. 28.

5 Death and the Maiden

"I think that one was not shot because there was no blood."[148]

According to the indictment Piroska Dely was "the abettor and aider of people's unlawful execution and torture"[149] in atrocities committed on October 15, 1944 in Budapest Csengery Street 45 and 64, Hársfa Street 57 and Nagyatádi (Kertész) Street 1. Abettor and aider: these are serious accusations. Will we ever know what Piroska Dely's exact role was in the murders? Did the people's tribunal make an honest attempt to find out what happened during the massacre? For the court it was of key importance that a witness heard Dely order fire in German: "Schiessen!" But was it really possible to hear that through two closed doors and among all the mayhem and noise? Why was such an order necessary? And how could a nurse (or a translator for that matter) give orders to armed soldiers? And how did this statement about the fire order make it into a later testimony when it was missing from earlier ones?

The indictment also stated that in Csengery Street 64, "19 persons were executed on the spot."[150] Indeed, 19 names were preserved on the marble commemoration plaque in the inner courtyard of the building but among them there are victims who were not executed at Csengery 64 and there were victims at Csengery 64 whose names did not make it on the plaque. Why these names were put on the plaque and why others are missing is also hard to reconstruct. Most probably Lichter wanted to give extra gravity to the events that he wished to commemorate. We will come back to the memory plaque's story in a separate chapter.

Besides biological and personal aspects, death has a cultural aspect too. A dead human body acquires different meanings at different times and places, and this also holds true for the corpses of the 19 people recorded on the plaque.[151] They were regarded differently by the janitors, by their former neighbors and family members, and again differently by the police investigators. After the massacre Mária Verebes, the loyal Christian maid of the Lichters looked for the family, and Strucky told her: "[T]here are no more Lichters... I know that they [the police] started an investigation on the massacre but I don't know anything

---

148 BFL 2442/1947. 33. Mrs. (Andor) Steiner's testimony, March 24, 1945.
149 BFL 2442/1947. 96.
150 BFL 2442/1947. 98.
151 David Simpson, "Naming the Dead," *London Review of Books* 23/22 (2001): 3.

Figure 5: The commemorative plaque (Photo by Erika Gabányi).

about their findings."¹⁵² The fact that police investigators came to the crime scene on October 16 and took minutes (even though those were later lost), i.e. the fact that during the short orderly period after the Arrow Cross coup this event drew the attention of the police, suggests that the massacre was not a plotted political penal action to break Jewish resistance but a straightforward common offence of armed robbery. This could also explain why Piroska Dely's group returned to the location of the events.¹⁵³

The Csengery 64 massacre did not dehumanize its victims as mass killings do, because it was a set of "intimate murders" many of which happened in the victims' own apartments. The perpetrators consumed no alcohol unlike the German soldiers on the Eastern Front who killed Jews one by one, or the Arrow Cross men who a few days later in Budapest killed as part of an orgy. The Csengery 64 killings were not meant to bring cohesion to a team of perpe-

---

152 BFL 19273/1949. 79.
153 BFL 19273/1949. 1. Lichter's denouncement letter.

trators either – although perhaps they brought cohesion to a group of men instead of whom Piroska Dely was punished.

The question of exactly how many people were killed in Csengery Street remains unresolved because it is unknown where the corpses were taken. I examined every potential trace but found no lead. The perpetrators certainly aimed to ensure that no one would identify their victims.[154] After the Hungarian publication of my book, a survivor contacted me and informed me that her uncle was among the victims. Ernő Singer was buried in the Kozma Street Jewish Cemetery's 5th parcel's C_7_9 grave. The inscription, "Died as a martyr on October 15, 1944," is written on the tombstone.[155] Most probably the Csengery 64 victims were placed, together with many other unidentified corpses, into a mass grave, which later became the Kerepesi Cemetery's Parcel of Martyrs.

5.1 Those who speak for the dead

The fact that an armed group would break into apartments and murder civilians was unprecedented in Budapest before October 15, 1944. The massacre of Csengery Street 64 was the first occasion that the tenants of the building encountered scenes of violent death; therefore, the researcher should handle their testimonies with increased caution. In the following section, I will analyze the testimonies of witnesses to present the different versions and show how they changed throughout the years.

The court testimony of József Strucky, the Csengery 64 janitor who assisted during the first Dely-razzia deserves close attention. During his own trial, Strucky stated that the SS and/or Arrow Cross locked him and his wife into their apartment to be let out only after the massacre when he was ordered to turn off the lights as it was blackout time. Next Strucky described what he saw as he went from apartment to apartment that night. His statements should be treated with skepticism because, as I will analyze later, his primary aim was to cover up his own actions. Consequently, the testimony is full of contradictions, which is not a surprise: recalling complex events which happened quickly and months previously is not easy, especially if some parts of the story are to be kept secret. For instance, in an apartment that Strucky, according to his first tes-

---

154 On the fate of corpses during the Ustasha massacres, see Alexander Korb, "The disposal of corpses in an ethnicized civil war: Croatia, 1941–45," *Human remains and mass violence*, (March 31, 2017): 106–128.
155 Erika Gabányi's email, June 19, 2019.

timony, found empty in the evening by the morning another dead body had materialized.

Another group of eyewitnesses consists of the women of the jeweler Steiner family. They were locked in their apartment's room while the men were slaughtered in the bathroom. Although they were deported in November 1944, they returned and testified in front of the People's Tribunal.

Thirdly, some tenants were hiding in the cellar or elsewhere in the building. They saw nothing, but heard gunshots and yelling and screaming. The grandson of the tenant of the fourth floor apartment 1 wrote me after the book was published in Hungarian: when his grandmother, Livia Schillinger, heard that "shouting and shooting Arrow Cross members are coming to search for hiding Jews," she opened all the doors of her apartment to trick them into thinking that no one was hiding there. Thanks to her smart strategy she remained undetected.[156]

Lastly, Piroska Dely was a witness herself and all throughout her trial she steadfastly denied having a weapon or having issued a firing order. She never once mentioned the victims because from her defense narrative's point of view they were nonexistent. Had she acknowledged knowing them she could have been accused of premeditated murders.

As stated, there are discrepancies between the names of the deceased and the names on the commemorative plaque; partly because the bodies were not all found at the same time, and partly because several bodies were found in apartments other than their own. Ernő Singer's body, for instance, was in the Steiner's apartment for still unknown reasons. "My mother never talked about that day" – wrote Singer's niece to me upon reading my research.[157] Since there was no comprehensive list of the tenants of the house, nor of the victims of the massacre, the plaque contains the names of those victims who had surviving relatives in the house.[158] Lichter added his father's name too, although Izrael Lichter died from the after effects of the severe shock he had endured.

---

156 János Polgár's Facebook message, June 20, 2019.
157 Erika Gabányi's email, June 19, 2019.
158 Lujza Erdélyi MD's sister, Mrs. Mezey, was also taken from Csengery Street as part of the Nagyatádi (Kertész) Street transport. Mrs. Mezey never returned. Erdélyi MD wrote a letter to the National Council (Nemzeti Bizottság) in which she told her own version of the story that the deportations happened because of the building's "Arrow Cross symphatizer" janitor. Mrs. Mezey's name is not included in any of the lists, only this letter revealed that she lived in Csengery Street 64. BFL XVII-2.19. IV. 6. letter, 167. February 26, 1945.

5.1.1 Why were they killed? The "Jewish resistance" version

The reason behind this disproportionately large armed action will never be truly uncovered. One explanation holds that it was the reaction of the newly in power Arrow Cross to the news of Jewish resistance. This explanation relies on two sources. On the one hand it was fueled by Dely's testimony:

> [T]he German Headquarters controlled the Svábhegy Sanatorium [...] A German captain ordered me to go to Csengery 64 with 5-6 soldiers. He told me to lead them because I know Budapest, while these Germans don't and I also speak some German... They were to search for ammunition and firearms in the house at question and the order was that if someone exhibits resistance the person should be taken in. I was not given a weapon. [...] They rang the bell then went inside and fired alarm shots. There were shots from the 2nd or 3rd floor and one of the lieutenants got wounded on his hand. I stayed with him but the other soldiers went upstairs and I don't know what happened there... I heard shots from upstairs. ... The soldiers told me that they shot out the locks of doors. They did not shoot at the people rounded up on the courtyard. ... [T]he next morning I was ordered again to guide German soldiers... [T]hey caught three persons idling on the courtyard at Nagyatádi... on October 15 we also went to a house on Csengery Street, I don't remember the number... [I] waited in the gateway while they took action. [T]hey took [them] to Nagyatádi, one person tried to escape, he was shot.[159]
>
> In a house the soldiers gathered a whole basketful of firearms. I heard gunshots in both houses when the soldiers were upstairs but I don't know if they wounded or killed anyone. I witnessed no murder, I was never cruel, I helped them whenever I could, separated the children and the elderly... Once, while the soldiers were distracted, I sent a woman and her small child home to protect them. The deportation of the Jews was not my doing.[160]

These descriptions suggest well-organized military actions – on both sides. But there were no two sides, and there was no "basketful of firearms." The only form of resistance Csengery 64 tenants exhibited was that they removed the yellow Star of David from the gate after the Horthy proclamation.[161]

The other sources of the "Jewish resistance" narrative are testimonies about men in the house deciding to keep guard at the gateway after the news about Szálasi's coup.[162] As the story goes, a certain Széplaki, to be introduced later, reported the "Jewish conspiracy" to the Arrow Cross. Andor Lichter considered that for the perpetrators the narrative about the "Jewish resistance" served as an alibi, as he was certain that the main reason behind the events was sheer

---

159   April 25, 1945 trial, BFL 2442/1947. 63.
160   BFL 2442/1947. 65.
161   BFL 19273/1949. 37. Mrs. Miksa Eisenstadter's testimony.
162   János Kun, interview, March 3, 2005.

blood thirstiness. The interviews I conducted with the survivors clarified the picture: the Jewish tenants of the house had no other weapons other than a stick and brass knuckle dusters.

> Dely Piroska and her Svábhegy SS group came because of an accusation that the tenants of Csengery 64 secretly armed themselves. Of course they found no weapons, the accusation was a complete lie. [...] The SS soldiers were Schwab people who spoke good Hungarian, their junior army officer was a Schwab named Lenhart or Lenhard, and the commander was an SS officer who snatched the assets and documents of the deported ones.[163]

During the Strucky family's trial the survivors all claimed that the Struckys were the minds behind the crime. In her testimony Mrs. Sárdi stated:

> Our cellar was right underneath György Szamocseta's tailor shop and through the vents we could hear the conversations in Szamocseta's shop. The shop seemed to have been the headquarters where people came all day long and discussed whatever happened in the building. Of course in these conversations those horrid events were mentioned with the greatest expression of joy.[164]

The narrative of "Jewish resistance" was certainly not favored by the justice system established under the Hungarian people's democracy in 1947. The concept of resistance has been discussed widely even today, but right after the war resistance was equated with armed resistance.[165] As in Hungary, Jewish resistance was mostly organized by the Zionist movements with their international connections and strong ideological commitment, therefore they were targeted by the Communist police.[166] The policies of the Communist Party-state towards Jewish institutions were basically no different from the policies directed towards other religious denominations. The pogroms of 1946, banning of Jewish religious institutions, anti-Zionist campaigns and revival of Communist anti-Semitism all contribute to the forgetting of this aspect of the events. Zionism was increasingly perceived as an ideological foe, so another framework was needed to explain the unusual event.[167]

---

163 BFL 19273/1949. 230. Lichter's testimony.
164 BFL 19273/1949.43. Mrs. Sárdi's testimony, January 28, 1946.
165 Yehuda Bauer, *Flight and Rescue* (New York: Random House, 1970).
166 Asher Cohen, *The Halutz Resistance in Hungary 1942–1944* (Boulder, Colorado: East European Monographs, 1986).
167 For more, see Attila Novák, "Resistance or Saving One's Skin? Notes to the Problem of 1944's Hungarian Zionist Resistance." *State and Equality*, ed., Attila Károly Molnár and Milán Pap, 93–117 (Budapest: Dialog Campus, 2018), and Robert Rozett, *Jewish and Hungarian Armed Resistance in Hungary.* (Jerusalem, 1988), reprint from Yad Vashem Studies Vol. XIX.

5.1.2 Why were they killed? The Széplaki version

The survivors of the Csengery massacre were not the only ones who closely followed the people's tribunal's trials. An old farmer from Szekszárd, a small city 150 km south to Budapest, György Széplaki (Szedlacsek) Sr, the father of György Széplaki Jr, a Soviet prisoner of war at the time, wanted to clear his son of allegations that he had played a role in the Csengery events. Namely, some survivors explained the appearance of armed men by introducing a new aspect:

> [T]he tenants gathered in front of the apartment of Strucky janitor who had the only radio in the house. I stood in the doorway and heard that inside their apartment [Mrs. Strucky] said: "My weakling husband cannot take care of anything. If the Arrow Cross comes I will be whacked together with them." [Then an] unknown man's voice interjected: "Wait, I will take care of that." I stepped away from the door not to be noticed that I had been eavesdropping. A fair-haired, about 172 cm tall, approximately 25 years old man came out of the apartment. I didn't know his name but I was told later that he was called some Széplaki. He left then came back 2-3 minutes later and then it all started.[168]

György Széplaki (Szedlacsek) Jr was born in 1925 (the arrest warrant stated 1920) in Szekszárd. His father, György Szedlacsek Sr was a wealthy farmer. Széplaki Jr was schooled at the Kalocsa Jesuits. In 1943, the Szedlacsek family took on the more Hungarian sounding name Széplaki. During the 1943/44 academic year, Széplaki Jr was a student of the Archduke Joseph University of Technology and Economy's Faculty of Veterinary Medicine. His last known Budapest address was District 6 Csengery Street 64.

After several survivors had unanimously confirmed that Széplaki Jr had called the Arrow Cross, the People's Tribunal issued an arrest warrant against him. Although the tribunal did not follow this thread, Széplaki Sr readily invested time and energy into providing an alibi for his son. In the meantime, an article portrayed Széplaki Jr as responsible for calling the armed men with the catchy title: "Exposing the mind behind the first Arrow Cross mass murder." The article presented the Széplaki version (using his former name Szedlacsek), and questioned the police's inability to solve the case.[169]

Thus Széplaki Sr had several reasons to be eager to prove that after visiting his landlady, Mrs. Strucky, Széplaki Jr went straight to his own third floor apartment and not the House of Faith, and that it was a mere coincidence that the

---

168 BFL 19273/1949. 215. Mrs. Rosenberg's testimony.
169 László Zsolnai, "Leleplezzük az első nyilas tömeggyilkosság értelmi szerzőjét," *A Reggel*, (July 9, 1945). 4.

Arrow Cross arrived right after and locked Mrs. Strucky and Széplaki into their apartments to "keep them safe."[170]

Széplaki Sr's report suggests an active relationship between Széplaki Jr and the Struckys, which the janitors kept carefully hidden from the court, as it could have exposed them as potential abettors. Instead Mrs. Strucky repeatedly emphasized that Széplaki Jr and their daughter, Éva, "talked about school things";[171] because the only undeniable tie between the Struckys and Széplaki was that he was Éva Strucky's boyfriend. Perhaps he walked to Andrássy 60 and reported on the Jewish tenants to impress his lady and show her that he was different from her father.[172] Was it because of him that the armed men entered Csengery 64 or that Piroska Dely wanted the wealth of the Steiners; there is no way to know.

Interestingly, Széplaki Jr is absent from all accessible lists of Hungarians in Soviet captivity.[173] According to Andor Lichter's denunciation letter against the Struckys, Széplaki Jr had deserted the country to the west.[174] For a fact Széplaki Jr managed to remain under the radar of the police and consequently avoided the People's Tribunal.

5.2 Murders at night

Based on the information in the testimonies, the possible sequence of events is the following. On October 15, 1944 at 9:30pm Piroska Dely and several armed civilians and/or men in uniform arrived at Csengery 45 and started to plunder it. Then by mistake they went to Csengery 62 where they moved on to 64 and rattled the gate. Hearing the noise at the entrance many of the tenants rushed to the air raid shelter cellar. Piroska Dely and the armed group broke into the building, went from apartment to apartment and shot 18 people dead. Next, they rounded up the tenants in the courtyard. As the courtyard was small, it was quickly filled up and when the previous group filled the premises armed guards herded them to a nearby police station. Dely and the armed men returned to the house one more time that night, then early the following morning and in the evening too. In the meantime, the remaining tenants were hiding in the cellar and at

---

[170] BFL 19273/1949. 136.
[171] BFL 19273/1949. 243.
[172] BFL 19273/1949. 212. Mrs. Rosenberg's testimony, January 29, 1946.
[173] MOL XIX-j-1-q. The Hungarian Ministry of Foreign Affairs' Lists of Prisoners of War. I am grateful for Piroska Kocsis and Éva Varga's assistance.
[174] BFL 19273/1949, 5. September 3, 1946.

the janitor's apartment. On October 17 at dawn two German soldiers and Hungarian police officers also robbed the house, but this action later remained under the radar of the police and the attorney's office. The tenants who were driven away by the intruders returned on October 18 and 19. Between November 5 and November 20 all tenants were deported except for those few who were hidden by the Struckys for monetary compensation.

5.2.1 The Strucky version

According to József Strucky's testimony,[175] on October 15, 1944 at 9:45pm someone rattled the gate, then Piroska Dely broke in together with several SS and Arrow Cross soldiers. When they found out that he was the Christian janitor they locked him and his wife into their apartment. From inside he heard shooting and screaming. In the meantime, 30 tenants were herded into their apartment (the people who later remained) while others found shelter in the cellar. Before leaving the house, the armed men ordered Strucky to turn off the lights on the upper floors. There was a blackout in the city and the lights could draw the attention of official bodies. They also told him to keep quiet about what had happened, and "Dely warned me not to be shocked by the sight in the apartments," added Strucky.

The janitor went upstairs together with the local administrator of the house (*házgondnoknő*) to perform the order. Both were suddenly granted official power in the moment of a power vacuum. In his first testimony, the janitor said that on the first floor the doors were locked, but later he said that they found five corpses in a first floor apartment. In apartment 2 on the second floor they found the body of István Faragó, the owner of the apartment, in apartment 3 they found five dead bodies, among them the two Grünberger girls. From here on the local administrator of the house did not accompany Strucky – she either did not want to see what the intruders had done, or she did not want to witness what Strucky was doing.

Then the janitor went and turned off the lights in the empty third and fourth floor apartments. In apartment 4 on the fourth floor he found six further corpses (although if he found the Steiners on the first floor, as he claimed, then on the fourth floor there could be only three bodies). While he walked around on the upper floors the tenants were rounded up in the courtyard and approximately seventy of them were taken away. This certainly took a while, which suggests

---

[175] BFL 2442/1947. 72.

that Strucky spent quite some time in the apartments, so he could have had enough time to steal the assets that Dely and her accomplices left untouched.

On October 16, Mrs. Grünberger climbed out of the lightwell of her apartment where she had been hiding since the night before. She asked Strucky to search the pockets of her dead relatives, Vilmos, Margit, and Ilona Grünberger and gather their personal belongings. The janitor responded that he had already examined the bodies and "found nothing valuable on them" and he returned an empty wallet.[176] Mrs. Grünberger's testimony indicates that the janitor took advantage of the situation: while the Jewish tenants were afraid to leave their hideouts he freely rummaged through their apartments. Strucky denied that and blamed the armed intruders for the missing items.

The janitor claimed that the intruders were continuously shooting while rounding up the tenants.[177] That would have explained why he had not resisted. While the armed intruders were roaming in the house, he also started to collect some valuables hoping that their owners would either fall victim to the shooting or would not return from the deportation so he would escape punishment. Later he refined his statement to try to shift any responsibility for the events and said, that "the soldiers shot out the locks if the doors were not opened for them."[178]

On the morning of October 16, Strucky visited the apartments once more and found two further bodies in the second floor 1, and three more in the third floor 1. Later that day he found the lodger Faragó in second floor 2, and the third Grünberger girl in second floor 1. In other words, according to his testimony the number of victims changed during the night. Other witnesses unanimously stated that between the night and the morning there were no more shots, therefore there could be no more victims either. Possibly Strucky did not notice all the casualties at once, although it is hard to imagine that he turned off the lights without seeing the dead bodies on the floors. During Dely's April 25, 1945 trial, Strucky did not mention the numeric discrepancies, instead he turned the massacre into a continuous storyline probably to cover up for the time he spent upstairs.

After the apartments were emptied the tenants were forcibly taken away in three turns. In the meantime, there were further gunshots. When Mrs. Gábor, who was among the first tenants to be taken away, turned back from the corner of Csengery and Andrássy Avenue and returned to the house – we will come back later to how she explained she was saved – she still heard gunshots.[179] Mrs. Gábor's testimony suggests that someone was still shooting on the upper

---

[176] BFL 19273/1949. 41. Mrs. Grünberger's testimony.
[177] BFL 2442/1947. 29–30.
[178] BFL 19273/1949. 29.
[179] BFL 2442/1947. 25.

floors when Strucky was already upstairs turning off the lights – Strucky failed to mention this in his testimony, as it would have implicated him as complicit with the perpetrators. Mrs. Gábor's testimony also hints at the possibility that the intruding armed men were not a unified group that followed commands, but the intruders individually decided whom to kill in which apartment.

5.2.2 The Steiner version

Mrs. Andor Steiner, a survivor of the Csengery street massacre described the events with vivid details. Her testimony is particularly relevant as she had firsthand knowledge of the events.[180]

> The men were body searched then taken in the anteroom and we women stayed locked in the room. From the anteroom they were taken to the bathroom, first Róbert Tenczer, then my husband, then my brother-in-law. [...] Mr Singer was pushed into the toilet where he got a heart attack and died.[181] I think that one was not shot because there was no blood. They brought two unknown men into the apartment. I found them dead. My husband and my brother in law were still alive. I brought my brother in law in the room [...] then my husband called for me, I led him into the room and I wanted to comfort him because his hand was wounded. Then they came back and I pleaded them to leave my husband alone because we are poor working people. First they listened but then they shot my husband three times in the back. They shot me too. I fell into the wardrobe and played dead. The Arrow Cross and the Germans came into the apartment once more to check if everyone died. One of them said this woman is still alive but they left nevertheless. I climbed under the bed that's how I survived. Dely and her company returned few more times.[182]

Mrs. Lajos Steiner, who was in the same apartment, said the following:

> [There were] three SS soldiers and a woman in a black coat held together by a belt and she had an Arrow Cross armband. [They said] bring out the gold and the jewelry. As we had no such possessions we could not give them anything. Then they took the men out and locked the women in the room. Before this happened we tearfully pleaded the Arrow Cross woman who had limitless executive power to save our men, because we are poor working people, to which the Arrow Cross woman [...] categorically told my sister in law that she should be glad that she had not been killed [...] From inside the room we heard gunshots and whimpering. [...] We managed to open the door and we found Róbert Tenczer in the bathroom with mutilated head and my husband, Steiner, shot ... He was still alive but he died that

---

180 BFL 2442/1947. 33–34.
181 According to this story, Ernő Singer was not shot either, which further complicates the analysis of the plaque's contents.
182 BFL 2442/1947. 33.

night… My brother in law died of lung shots. […] A person called Singer who was in my apartment at the time also died there.[183]

During subsequent police hearings, the description of the events became increasingly detailed; for instance, the German fire order ("Schiessen!") was included. The later testimonies sometimes contain elements that were taken from other survivors' witness accounts, i.e. they became enriched with details that the survivors simply could not see or hear. This was Mrs. (Andor) Steiner's second testimony:

> Around 9:30pm several SS soldiers entered in our apartment. They were led by Piroska Dely who had a revolver in her hand. She held us gunpoint and yelled not to move. Then she told the men to leave the room and herded them into the bathroom… I stayed in the room with my female relatives because they locked us in. Anxiously we waited. I heard several shots from up close. When we got into the bathroom the sight was horrid. First I noticed my brother in law, Lajos Steiner severely wounded on his head. I led him into the room and tended to his wound. Then my husband left the bathroom, his hand was shot and I aided him too. Then I went to my little nephew, Róbert Tenczer, but I could not help him, he also got a headshot and his brain was out, it was spilled out next to him. After these horrific events the murderer Piroska Dely left our apartment with her accomplices in murder. As I was nursing my husband and my brother in law with the severe headshot Piroska Dely and the SS soldiers and the Arrow Cross men came back to check on us. Then me and my husband pleaded Piroska Dely to leave us alone because we are working people. She did not care the least instead she ordered fire in German, scheiesen [sic!]. Then the German SS soldiers shot my husband three times and he immediately died. I went on pleading but then I was shot in the back too, it was the German SS soldier, but the order came from Dely. I state it as a fact, and I swear that it was Piroska Dely who gave the fire order that is the order to kill. When I got wounded, I fell into the wardrobe and I stayed there for a while. From there I climbed under the bed and laid there till next morning often unconsciously, then I got to my senses and I looked around in the apartment and I know it for a fact that there were six deceased people in the apartment, all of them were my relatives, all of them killed by Piroska Dely and her murderers.[184]

Mrs. Lajos Steiner's second testimony:

> They looked around in the room, there were chairs on the top of the wardrobes, the five families lived crammed together, and they complimented on the furniture. Then they took my husband, his brother and nephew and took them into the anteroom, and they locked the door on us, and we eavesdropped wondering what would happen. […] In German she said Sieseh [sic!][…] They led them one after another into the toilet […] His jaw was mutilated by the bullet, he died immediately, then my brother in law came next, he got a shot in his

---

183 BFL 2442/79.
184 BFL 19273/1949. 191. Mrs. (Andor) Steiner's testimony.

hand, he survived, then my husband came next, he got a shot into his head but he also survived. Then everything went quiet. We opened the door and we saw that sorrowful sight. Me and my mother in law helped my husband into the room, he walked on his own, we put compresses on him, he could have been saved, but then Dely and the soldiers came back and took us out on the courtyard. They took me to the Gestapo, my mother in law and my child were placed into the apartment by the janitor's. Whatever happened next I don't know because I was taken away, but my mother in law pleaded Strucky janitor that night to let her upstairs into the apartment to tend to her son who was still alive. [Strucky] didn't let her upstairs, you should be glad that you are alive, that's what he yelled at her, and that she should be no bother, because he would not let her upstairs. My sister in law was hiding in Andor Steiner's apartment, she was shot too, and she said that those sadists came back several times, and she [Dely] ordered my husband and his brother to be shot dead. Unfortunately by the time I got home they were not in the house anymore, they all died.[185]

Almost half of the Csengery 64 casualties were from the Steiner family. The surviving Steiner women had to battle their own conscience as well as the slovenliness of Hungarian political justice system. They molded the later, more graphic narrative of the events to the expectations of the latter. Their descriptions indicate a well-organized, predmeditated robbery. The fact that men were separated from women suggests a pre-determined choreography.

5.3 What happened to the dead?

The answer – just like the answer to many other questions in this book – is that we do not know. Strucky knew who took the bodies and where, but he remained silent. The corpses were certainly still in the apartments on the afternoon of October 16.[186] However, by the time the family members returned the dead were gone, only a bloody woolen blanket was there as a reminder – a blanket that the janitor's wife washed because she did not want it to be wasted. Many survivors remembered the bloody blanket drying on the carpet-beater. It came up during the Strucky trial too:

> By the time we arrived home the bodies were removed from the apartments but there was a huge dry blood stain in our anteroom that my father and Laci tried to clean up for days. One of the victims held [...] a woolen blanket in his hands when he was killed and his blood spilled onto the blanket. Mrs. Strucky, the janitor's wife took the blanket and soaked it in water in the courtyard then dried it, it hung there on the carpet-beater [...] for a week.[187]

---

[185] January 24, 1946. Testimony. (BFL 19273/1949. 187–189.)
[186] BFL 19273/1949. 8.
[187] Miklós Bodor's letter.

According to some testimonies the body of Izrael Lichter, Andor Lichter's father, who had a heart attack, was left in an armchair on the courtyard for several days after the events. The elderly man was buried right there in the courtyard underneath the yellow cobblestones. An eyewitness remembered how hard it was to dig the frozen earth because "it was a cold winter."[188] These words could denote an early October frost, or they can be interpreted symbolically, i.e. that it was difficult to bury the old man, but maybe the burial was actually postponed till the winter. Izrael Lichter was buried in the yard possibly because the rest of the corpses were removed earlier, potentially to a mass grave. Lujza Erdélyi MD visited the Institute of Pathology (*Bonctani Intézet*) several times in search of her sister, but the institute was so overloaded with corpses that they could not provide her assistance with identifying the dead.

Erdélyi MD went to the Institute of Pathology because at first the deed was classified as murder.[189] According to Strucky, the detectives who came to the house by mistake brought the files of another case and then they left, never to return. Still, the fact of their visit in and by itself suggests that the massacre was an individual action which was duly reported to the police as crimes are usually reported in peace time.[190]

Andor Lichter remembered the events quite differently:

> My wife told me that sometimes after October 19 three detectives came to the house. They talked to Strucky for a long while then they questioned the tenants who survived the night of October 15, among them my wife. They told her that they came from the Svábhegy Political Police to investigate the October 15 events, because what happened was not in line with the Arrow Cross government's intentions, and the culprits will be found and punished. My wife gave them a detailed account of the happenings. She also told them that seven men were forcibly taken away among them our son, and she tearfully pleaded them to find him. The detectives took minutes and promised to look for our son and that they would return to the house. They never did of course. Before they left they talked once more to Strucky so Strucky should know a lot about this case. I asked him after the liberation what did he talk about with the detectives but he gave me a meaningless answer.[191]

The differences between the two testimonies show how Strucky tried to monopolize the memory of the event. Appearently he was convinced at the time of the murder that no one would remain alive to tell another version. He was wrong.

---

[188] Interview with Edit Rosenberg.
[189] BFL XVII-2.19. IV. 6. 167.
[190] BFL 19273/1949. 70. Strucky's testimony.
[191] BFL 19273/1949. 230. Lichter's testimony.

6 The Perpetrators

> [T]hey did not enter each apartment. [...] Someone certainly told Piroska Dely where to go. I am suspicious of the janitor and his relative Szamocseta.[192]

During Piroska Dely's first trial not much attention was paid to the janitor family. While interrogated the Struckys emphasized their benevolence and willingness to help and tried to clear up every possible trace leading to them.[193] However, they could not mislead Andor Lichter. Allegedly, Lichter warned them that if his son had not returned within a year he would denounce them because it was "a common belief among the house's tenants [...] that Piroska Dely and the 19 murders happened because of this family."[194] The "continuous amnesty orders"[195] also urged the survivors to act, i.e. as time passed the forcefulness of political justice lessened and the verdicts of war criminals became lighter and lighter. Finally, Lichter waited no longer and at the end of 1946 denounced the whole Strucky-Szamocseta family.

The Strucky-Szamocseta family was connected by the Kalliszta sisters: one of them married József Strucky, the other György Szamocseta. They lived as neighbors in Csengery Street, György Szamocseta's tailor shop was in 64. Their children, Nándor Szamocseta and Éva Strucky grew up together. Nándor Szamocseta became the main accused of the case.[196]

But why was this family put on trial? Most of the janitors easily found their place in the new regime.[197] Why not this family? The answer is because of the existence of proactive survivors who did not wait till the legal system took its course, but actively moved the process forward. The question is also valid as there had already been a People's Tribunal trial on the Csengery 64 case, which, as even Lichter acknowledged, "could not prove that Nándor Szamocseta caused the tragedy." Still, Lichter added:

---

[192] BFL 19273/1949. 187–189. Mrs. (Lajos) Steiner's testimony.
[193] Alan Rosen, "Autobiography from the Other Side. The Reading of Nazi Memoirs and Confessional Ambiguity," *Biography. An Interdisciplinary Quarterly* 24.3 (2001): 553–570.
[194] BFL 19273/1949. 8.
[195] BFL 19273/1949. 3.
[196] BFL 19273/1949. 1–6. This also contained Strucky's cousine István Kiss, who later ceased to be mentioned during the court process.
[197] Ádám Pál István, *Budapest Building Managers and the Holocaust in Hungary* (London: Palgrave, 2017).

> [Nándor Szamocseta's] conduct and the whole family's anti-Semitic and extremist attitude and greediness seem to prove my hypothesis. [...] although it was not possible to identify who denounced the house, I had to come to the conclusion that it was certainly a common agreement of the actors.[198]

In January 1947 Nándor Szamocseta, György Szamocseta, Mrs. György Szamocseta née Mária Kalliszta, József Strucky and Mrs. József Strucky née Emília Kalliszta were provisionally arrested.

6.1 The janitors' greed

The indictment against the arrested family members was war crimes and crimes against the people. For the June 23, 1947 public trial Mrs. Temesvári (i.e. Piroska Dely) was ordered as witness. According to the court records she failed to show up, which was hardly a surprise given that she had by then been dead a long time. Therefore, sections of the Dely case's court records and parts of Dely's testimony got attached to the Szamocseta–Strucky case file, which turned Dely's statements into "truth" since their cross-examination was impossible.

Shortly before her execution Dely was questioned two more times. The terminally ill woman accused Strucky of "having to return to" Csengery 64. She said that Strucky did not want to give up all the Jewish tenants at first. Of course Strucky denied the accusation during their cross-examination.[199] In her January 31, 1946 testimony "Dely delivered that she saw the accused person [Strucky] talk to the leader of the Arrow Cross and the SS and that conversation had an effect [on the massacre]. They came to the house and took away many people."[200] Strucky denied this accusation too. In other words, in 1947 the People's Tribunal had to decide whom to believe: an executed "Arrow Cross woman" or what by that time Strucky had became: an "Arrow Cross janitor."

Strucky was also accused of not preventing Miksa Eisenstadter's deportation. Had he said that he had stomach issues, so ran the accusation, Eisenstadter would have been saved.[201] It is certainly true that the soldiers asked a question

---

[198] BFL 19273/1949. 9. Lichter's testimony.
[199] BFL 19273/1949. 206.
[200] BFL 19273/1949. 10.
[201] "Mrs. Eisenstadter pleaded the leader of the Arrow Cross men, who was rather benevolent I should say, because he accepted various excuses and left some people in the house, to leave her husband who had a surgery recently. The Arrow Cross man looked at Strucky, who shrugged to signal his indifference. [...] The tiniest benevolence from Strucky's side could have prevented Eisenstadter's deportation, because [...] that Arrow Cross man was unusually agreeable." BFL

and the janitor at that moment gave the morally wrong answer, still, the accusation wrongly assumed the janitor's power to be high. Had Strucky said the truth, namely that Eisenstadter had stomach issues, that would not have saved his life, because the point of the deportation was to eliminate witnesses. He was also accused of not letting the house's Jewish tenants leave their apartments and of plundering their assets. These were proven without much further ado.[202]

"[T]hey made [the Jews' lives] harder whenever it was possible. [T]hey asked a high price for every service and demonstrated their power at every occasion," was the summary of the accusations against the Strucky's.[203] Certainly there are times when even corruption can offer a sense of security: the vulnerable tenants knew that if they paid the Strucky's, they would receive services. But as the times were getting increasingly insecure, the janitor made more and more ad hoc decisions. The house's tenants could not forget when Strucky had "rung the bells and told the tenants that they were his captives, and no one can leave their apartments any more."[204] This was certainly an autonomous action on his part and his way of demonstrating his power.

The charge against Mrs. Strucky née Emília Kalliszta was that Széplaki, who lived as a lodger on the third floor, was in her kitchen right before he called the Arrow Cross. According to the indictment Széplaki listened to her moaning about her husband and how he could not take care of anything, to which Széplaki replied: "I will take care of them [the Jews]!" With that Széplaki left and according to the first testimonies he phoned whereas in later testimonies he walked over and personally called the Arrow Cross. Furthermore, on October 15, 1944 Mrs. Rózsa and Mrs. Stongl heard Mrs. Strucky stated that if the Russians came she would "stand up against them with a machine gun." The woman was also accused of stealing textiles (gowns, crocheted tablecloths, bedding) from the ten-

---

19273/1949. 49. It is no wonder that the strongest accusations against the Struckys were coming from the widow, Mrs. Eisenstadter, who claimed to have seen them on Arrow Cross Party rallies and that Arrow Cross men helped them to transport the belongings of the deceased Stern family. (BFL 19273/1949. 36–38.)

202 A vészkorszakról lásd Lévai Jenő: *A pesti gettó csodálatos megmenekülésének hiteles története*. Budapest, Officina, 1946., Lévai Jenő: *Fekete könyv a magyar zsidóság szenvedéseiről*. Budapest, Officina, 1946., Lévai Jenő, *Zsidósors Magyarországon. Az üldözés kora* (Budapest: Magyar Téka, 1948), and Ferenc Laczó, "The foundational dilemmas of Jenő Lévai: on the birth of Hungarian Holocaust historiography in the 1940s," *Holocaust Studies* 21.1–2 (2015): 93–119.

203 BFL 19273/1949. 44. Grünberger's testimony. On the legal background, see Mátraházi Ferenc, ed., *Szemelvények a magyarországi zsidóság életét korlátozó törvényekből és rendeletekből*. (H. n., K. n., 2004), and Székely Gábor and Vértes Róbert, eds., *Magyarországi zsidótörvények és rendeletek, 1938–1945* (Budapest: Polgár Kiadó, 1997).

204 BFL 19273/1949. 11.

ants, which after liberation she gave back upon their request. Lastly, multiple testimonies emphasized that Mrs. Strucky washed, dried and used the bloody, bullet-torn woolen blanket (elsewhere a Persian rug) of the Stern family.

Their daughter, Éva Strucky, Széplaki's girlfriend was not arrested, because she had no enemies in the house other than Lichter, who considered that "Éva Strucky worked at the House Office responsible for the redistribution of Jewish property and she placed her acquaintances and relatives into forsaken Jewish apartments. [...] [S]he did not talk to the Jewish tenants of the house because in my opinion she was a huge anti-Semite."[205] Had this been true she would certainly have gotten an apartment for Nándor Szamocseta too. Instead Szamocseta used a forged Gestapo permit, or as he put it:

> I knew that the apartment was empty and since I had no apartment I announced on the Svábhegy that there was an empty apartment and asked them to get it for me. German soldiers went to the apartment and confiscated it for the German police and took the keys. I got the keys on the Svábhegy and a permit with which I could prove to the Hungarian housing administration that the police does not need it. With this permit I went to the housing administration and the apartment was mine.[206]

Importantly, the testimonies suggested that the Struckys were not all equally wicked, but that the wife was the family's "evil spirit." A detail from Mrs. Bydeskuti's testimony:

> I lived with forged documents in the house and I was not deported. I was checked in front of the janitor's apartment and let on my way. I heard when Mrs. Strucky asked her husband who was checked and who remained. The janitor listed me and three other persons. Then Mrs. Strucky reprimanded him for leaving one alive, for not giving all of us up, they should all perish, she said. Then Strucky started yelling at her, to shut her big mouth up, because "you can be in their place one day." The next morning József Strucky let me out of the house again [...] he knew that I had forged documents. I gave him 250 pengős as I remember.[207]

Mrs. Bydeskuti's testimony would come to Strucky's rescue, but the family was accused even by their own relative, Nándor Szamocseta: "Mrs. Strucky, my mother's sister is a greedy woman who would do anything for money. Strucky was an Arrow Cross Party member already in 1938."[208] This time the court had no reason

---

205 BFL 19273/1949. 30.
206 BFL 19273/1949. 234., BFL 19273/1949., Szamocseta's testimony, January 2, 1947.
207 BFL 19273/1949. 64.
208 BFL 19273/1949. 236.

to doubt Nándor Szamocseta's sincerity, as these statements did not protect his own interests, thus his testimony probably aggravated the Struckys' sentence.

Andor Lichter claimed that the tailor, György Szamocseta, was an Arrow Cross badge wearing party member who hid stolen goods. Also, the tailor drove Mrs. Krámer and her little daughter away who were hiding at their place and threatened to call the Arrow Cross on them. Lichter also added some crucial information for the police that since his internment György Szamocseta had been in contact with suspicious people. Pál Kádár, himself a people's prosecutor, whose father lived in Csengery 64, stated that he saw György Szamocseta in his tailor shop with an Arrow Cross badge reading the extreme right daily, *Magyarság*. The People's Tribunal's priority was to confirm whether the tailor had collaborated with the Arrow Cross. György Szamocseta denied wearing the party badge but did not deny reading the paper.[209] Kádár in his testimony used the phrase "I heard" several times, but since he talked as an employee of the people's tribunal his words had considerable weight for the court.[210]

Interestingly Mrs. Szamocseta was also considered the family's "evil spirit." "Mrs. Szamocseta acted like a crazy Cesar" – wrote Lichter.[211] Another testimony held that when "the house's women were to be taken by the Arrow Cross to the Teréz Boulevard Arrow Cross house to clean and we were lined up on the courtyard Mrs. Szamocseta showed up and gleefully watched our plight."[212] In addition, Mrs. Szamocseta as the house's air-raid shelter commander separated the Jewish tenants in the air-raid shelter.[213]

6.2 The collaborating projectionist, translator, courier, driver, SS-soldier, and father

The main culprit of the trial, Nándor Szamocseta had an adventurous life. As a youth he spent time at the Aszód Reformatory, then between 1938 and 1944 he had 13 jobs and performed five illegal border crossings. Since those employed in the defense industry could avoid active military service, he tried to get in a defense plant or to work for the occupying German forces.[214] On October 22, 1944 he left his German employers and moved to Szentes. He constructed func-

---

[209] BFL 19273/1949. 261.
[210] BFL 19273/1949. 260.
[211] BFL 19273/1949. 266., Lichter's testimony.
[212] Mrs. Gábor's testimony.
[213] BFL 19273/1949. 34.
[214] BFL 19273/1949. 234., Szamocseta's testimony, January 2, 1947.

tional vehicles from run down old trucks and transported vendors and goods to Budapest markets. How this young man avoided the military draft is unknown but almost certainly the solution exceeded the limits of legality. At the time of his arrest he worked for the SZEB (*Szövetséges Ellenőrző Bizottság* – Allied Commission) in the same job as earlier in the Gestapo.

According to the indictment, Nándor Szamocseta "was an agitator who went to Germany, [then] served at the Svábhegy Gestapo, and furnished an apartment in Csengery 55 with Jewish belongings. He participated in the arrest of Katalin Karády[215], held an orgy at his parent's apartment with Arrow Cross men Bandi, Pista, Tomi, who "assumedly participated in crimes," and asked money from Piroska Dely "for his intermediary services." Lichter, the source of accusations obviously did not care that the personal, direct relationship between Dely and Szamocseta failed to be proven during Dely's trial. He held on to the fact that Szamocseta, just like Dely, "worked at the Svábhegy as a translator in the service of the Gestapo."[216] Probably on his lawyer's advice, Szamocseta later supplemented his first testimony: he never volunteered at the Gestapo, instead two cars stopped at his house and he was taken to the Svábhegy as a captive. When the Germans found out that he spoke Polish they used him as a translator.[217] Next to this statement there is a January 8, 1947 comment: "I don't think that's true and it's unlikely that the Gestapo used such a primitive man with such low level of language proficiency as a translator."[218]

The connection with Piroska Dely – that Szamocseta denied all along – could not be proven during this trial either. "I don't know how Piroska Dely [and her people] entered the house. I only learned from the newspapers that the woman who showed up with the SS soldiers and the Arrow Cross was called Piroska Dely,"[219] said Szamocseta. It is a fact that during the Dely trials he and his family did not live in the Csengery Street anymore, so they certainly did not participate in the everyday corridor conversations about the Dely case.

Based on the testimonies it was proven that Nándor Szamocseta took advantage of his power in the sudden power vacuum of the Arrow Cross takeover. A witness remembered:

---

215 Katalin Karády (1910-1990) was the shining femme fatal actress of the interwar period, who achieved iconic status. That her name popped up out of the blue during the trial shows that they wanted to present Nándor Szamocseta as a serious case.
216 BFL 19273/1949. 225. Mrs. (Miklós) Faragó.
217 BFL 19273/1949.
218 BFL 19273/1949. 7.
219 BFL 19273/1949. 236. Mária Szabó, who closely followed everything that happened in Csengery 64, said: "The first time I heard Dely's name was after liberation." BFL 19273/1949. 13.

I saw Nándor Szamocseta talk to an unknown man through one of the windows of the ground floor Szamocseta apartment. I wanted to know what they were talking about so I bowed to tie my shoelaces, and when Nándor Szamocseta said that "they had to be taken care of radically otherwise it would never end," and the unknown man repeated it affirmatively then I had the impression that they were talking about the Jews.[220]

Another Csengery tenant, Mrs. Bauer, who also overheard the conversation, shared this impression. The circumstances under which she heard it were not part of her testimony.

What made the whole house believe that Nándor Szamocseta had power? Allegedly, to increase her own authority Mrs. Strucky enthusiastically bragged about his nephew's important position among the Gestapo. The tenants of the house certainly hid their opinions about the modestly educated young man's comet-like career because when they needed help from "official" Hungary they had no one else to turn to.

Nándor Szamocseta denied requesting money for his services; moreover, he stated that he helped "out of sheer benevolence." Basically, he denied everything: he never asked for and never received money and if he did, he returned it:

[I] was a poor man and I needed money several times and I borrowed some from the Jews and told them that in turn I would take care of their affairs. If I couldn't help, then I returned the money immediately after liberation. Because I was poor, I usually spent the borrowed money right after I borrowed it. I helped the persecuted people whenever possible.[221]

He allegedly returned Mrs. Aupek's money[222] from a loan that he took from his aunt, Mrs. Strucky. Where Mrs. Strucky got the money from, when before the war they were living rather modestly, was not revealed.

Besides the rumors about his "good job" the other source of Nándor Szamocseta's notoriety was that he regularly showed up in the house in a uniform. What kind of uniform was that? Testimonies held that it was a dark grey, metal buttoned, "uniform-like" short jacket.[223] One of the witnesses described it as follows:

I heard that the Strucky and the Szamocseta families used to go to the Andrássy Avenue Műcsarnok Coffee House after the Germans came [and occupied Budapest] but before

---

220 BFL 19273/1949. 219. Mrs. Aupek.
221 BFL 19273/1949. 68.
222 Moved in after June 1944.
223 BFL 19273/1949. 19. Mrs. Gábor's testimony.

the Jews were moved in [to yellow star houses]. I saw Szamocseta Nándor several times in some kind of uniform made of dark grey cloth with gilded buttons.[224]

Mrs. Szamocseta stated that her son used to wear a grey civilian outfit with three gilded buttons because he worked at the Kálmán Tisza Square (later: *Köztársaság tér*, i.e. Republic Square, today: John Paul II Square) *Volksbund* house as a junior officer. Therefore, argued Mrs. Szamocseta, he did not and could not collect protection money from the Jewish tenants.[225] However, Szamocseta stated that his son was the *Volksbund* house's projectionist but then he would not have had a uniform.[226] Mrs. Schwartz considered that "the Szamocseta boy" wore an SS uniform,[227] Ilona Bodor saw a German armband on him,[228] and Mária Szabó saw him with a revolver.[229] Nándor Szamocseta himself said that he was a courier and not an SS soldier.[230] In any case his by now unidentifiable uniform made the impression that he had good connections and he could protect the house's tenants from harassment. The following scene accurately depicts Nándor Szamocseta's "influence":

> I went over only on the afternoon of [October] 16. I found two deaf-dumb Arrow Cross soldiers there who complained that they were very hungry. I told them to go and eat but they said they were ordered to stay. I told them that nothing bad would happen. They eventually left. I called the tenants and told them to go in the air-raid shelter and that they should not worry because I would be home all day and should anything happen my aunt would send for me. I went home and then around 6 or 7 my aunt came over. She said that some Hungarian soldiers and an SS came, and they seek for the Jews. I went over and asked the Hungarians' leader, a sergeant for the house search warrant. He asked who I was and on what right I asked for the search warrant. I told I was a Gestapo translator and I was mandated to keep everyone in the house because they would be questioned. He told me that they would search through the house and the apartments and had they found Jews I would get in trouble too. We went upstairs on the fourth floor and they started to examine the Uprimny's apartment, but the point of their search was to steal whatever they could. Then we went to the Roth apartment where they went on plundering. When they had their fill, they stopped. After they had left, I told the people in the shelter that they should not worry, there had been a house search but it was over, they could go back to their apartments, everything

---

224 BFL 19273/1949. 227. Mrs. Singer's testimony.
225 BFL 19273/1949. 75.
226 BFL 19273/1949. 247. György Szamocseta, January 31, 1946.
227 BFL 19273/1949. 76. I am grateful to Krisztián Ungváry for his help identifying the uniforms in the testimonies. Unfortunately, because of the contradictory nature of the testimonies, we could not come to conclusions.
228 BFL 19273/1949. 221., December 27, 1946 police hearing.
229 BFL 19273/1949. 13. Mária Szabó's testimony.
230 BFL 19273/1949. 79.

would be alright. Bindeskutiné [Bydeskutiné] put some money in my hand. I did not ask for it she gave it on her own saying that she knew that my wife was ill, and the money was for hospital expenses. I gave half of it, about 3-400 pengős to Strucky [...].[231]

This was probably just the beginning of Nándor Szamocseta's lucrative rescue business.[232] Later he acknowledged that he accepted money from a tenant for whom he promised to find one of his relatives although he had no intention of doing so.[233]

6.3 The verdict[234]

This people's tribunal's process was not exempt from procedural mistakes either: the first public trial had to be repeated a month later. The August 21, 1947 testimonies perceptively shifted towards a more simplified and ritualized version of the story. The Szamocsetas' lawyer tried to classify the case as a straightforward common offence in order to exonerate his clients from the charge of crimes against the people, but he failed. Andor Lichter and the other survivors deployed a very deliberate strategy: they concertedly claimed that it was not a simple robbery but robbery of persecuted people, as it could not have happened had it not been October 15, 1944. The final word came from the NOT (National Council of People's Tribunals – *Népbíróságok Országos Tanácsa*) on November 15, 1948.[235] The Szamocsetas' deeds were qualified as "robbery from persecuted persons." József Strucky was sentenced for failing to save Eisenstadter who was just recovering after an operation, i.e. he was considered personally responsible for a person's death – as if his word against the armed men could weigh much. The second appeal trial increased their sentences, that is, though it was not customary, the NOT added to the punishment issued by the Budapest People's Tribunal.

---

231 BFL 19273/1949. 68. Nándor Szamocseta
232 For more on rescue for money in Poland, see Joanna Tokarska-Bakir, "The Unrighteous Righteous and the Righteous Unrighteous," *Dapim: Studies on the Holocaust* 1.24 (2010): 11-63, DOI: 10.1080/23256249.2010.10744397; Jan Grabowski, *Rescue for Money. Paid Helpers in Poland. 1939–1945* (Jerusalem: Yad Vashem, 2008); Agnieszka Wierzcholska, "Helping, Denouncing, and Profiteering: a Process-Oriented Approach to Jewish–Gentile Relations in Occupied Poland from a Microhistorical Perspective," *Holocaust Studies* 23. 1–2 (2017): 34–58, DOI: 10.1080/17504902.2016.1209842.
233 BFL 19273/1949. 68.
234 BFL 19273/1949. 97., BFL 19273/1949. 89–95.
235 BFL 19273/1949. 96–99.

Nándor Szamocseta was sentenced to ten years of forced labor service,[236] József Strucky got three years and his wife received a four year prison sentence. Mr. and Mrs. Szamocseta were each handed a year's prison sentence.

During the People's Tribunal process, complicated stories got simplified, details got lost – or sometimes added –, and nuances disappeared. The investigation material was full of assumptions: "Although it was not established with certainty who denounced the house it is unquestionable that it was a concerted effort of the actors."[237]

The indictment also included the detail that after the robbery Nándor Szamocseta collected a thousand *pengős* and some other assets from Mrs. Aupek, Dr. Pál Kádár and Endre Uprimny, in exchange for their "protection." Furthermore:

> Although he is a Hungarian citizen he joined the German security forces [...] used fascist power tools for his own benefit to blackmail and swindle, i.e. he committed crimes against property [...] His defense, that he acted in the interest of the persecuted and without personal financial gain because the collected sums went to the Gestapo officers, [the court] could not accept because the accused person never actually helped. [...] He used the gullibility of frightened people to gain financial advances.[238]

The defense achieved the People's Tribunal's confirmation that Nándor Szamocseta was not present at the massacre and had no ties to it. The People's Tribunal also took into consideration his "occasional willingness to help," but that he did so for money that he collected "from persecuted people" aggravated his sentence.[239] The tribunal was not concerned with the "voluntarily given document," the *Persilschein* that was attached to the Szamocseta-files (see appendix 2 and 4). When the appeal was rejected the sentence became a binding decision. Szamocseta was eventually released in 1957.

József Strucky was held responsible for not saving the sick Eisenstadter. According to the verdict:

> [When the men were taken away], he acted as if he did not know that named person was ill as a result of which named person was forcibly taken away. [...] [I]n general he was not hostile towards the Jewish tenants of the house. However, after the tenants were taken away, he appropriated their remaining assets.

---

[236] BFL 19273/1949., on March 16, 1956. Per Mrs. Strucky's request his release was not approved.
[237] BFL 19273/1949. 9.
[238] BFL 19273/1949. 90.
[239] BFL 19273/1949. 90.

The people's tribunal took in consideration Strucky's "lower level of education" and the effect that "propaganda" and "his violent and racist wife" had on him, also that he helped persecuted people multiple times. Although Mrs. Krámer stated that "József Strucky did everything for money, his benevolence always had a price," the Struckys hid her in their apartment for eight days, and their daughter got her a transit letter because there was "some human sentiment in her."[240] Éva Strucky tried to help other tenants too, for instance she tried to convince Edit Rosenberg's mother to convert to Catholicism and she volunteered to be her godmother.[241]

Mrs. Strucky's verdict went as follows:

> [S]he told people in her apartment that her husband was a weakling as he did nothing against the house's Jewish tenants who gathered under their window to listen to the radio. To that an Arrow Cross person named György Széplaki who was at her apartment told that he would take care of that and with that he left the apartment. A short while later the Arrow Cross arrived at the house and the massacre begun. She took the blanket off the deceased Sterns and washed it and used it as her own. She behaved in the worst way towards the house's Jewish tenants, she cursed Jewry and glorified Arrow Cross rule. After the deportations she moved into an empty Jewish apartment and appropriated whatever she found there. When Mrs. Strucky moved into Mrs. Krámer's apartment she did not let Mrs. Krámer back. [...] Mrs. Strucky took all her belongings and used her food supplies as her own.[242]

The verdict established that "the court could not reassuringly appraise the facts concerning the conversation in the janitor's apartment with the Arrow Cross tenant present."[243] After his disappearance, Széplaki was labeled as an Arrow Cross member and he became the person who could be conveniently blamed for the massacre. The verdict on Mrs. Strucky also took in consideration her "lower intelligence level" but established that "she urged her husband to an unlawful demeanor."[244]

Concerning Szamocseta György and his wife the verdict established the following:

---

240 BFL 19273/1949. 266. Mrs. Krámer corrected: "She got back her belongings from the Struckys. She also acknowledged that the Struckys wanted to move her to Felsőgöd to protect her from deportation, but they ran out of time." BFL 19273/1949. 76.
241 Interview with Edit Rosenberg, August 13, 2007.
242 BFL 19273/1949. 34.
243 BFL 19273/1949. 34.
244 BFL 19273/1949. 82.

> Together and with joint intention they moved into an apartment forsaken by deported Jewish persons and they took their belongings in their possession, used them as their own, [...] and mainly owned them in such a way that after liberation the returning persecuted persons could only get back a small share of their assets.²⁴⁵

The verdict emphasized that Mrs. Szamocseta was the house's air-raid shelter commander who "with her actions aided military formations," furthermore that, concerning the Jews in the cellar, Szamocseta said that "the most practical would be to open the water and gas taps and make them drown."²⁴⁶ (There were no gas pipes in the house.)²⁴⁷ The Szamocsetas were held culpable of the same charges as the Struckys.

The Szamocsetas divorced in 1950. The police and court processes put their already conflicted relationship under severe pressure, which the marriage could not endure. ²⁴⁸

6.4 The truth of the perpetrators' memories

From the Szamocseta–Strucky families' perspective the events ran a very different course than the one reconstructed by the People's Tribunal or through my conversations with the survivors.²⁴⁹

Victims usually search for a definite truth, but perpetrators also do, except thus far their attempts had received less publicity.²⁵⁰ Their search for the truth

---

245 BFL 19273/1949. 82.
246 BFL 19273/1949. 82.
247 BFL 19273/1949. 56. "We were away for four days and when we returned the other Jews told us that they overheard the conversation of Mrs. Strucky, Mrs. Szamocseta and the Arrow Cross men who looked for Jews [...] [T]hey said that certainly there are more Jews in the house, they must be in the cellar [...] the gas should be opened, they should be smoked out like rats." BFL 19273/1949. 57.
248 The Szamocsetas are not unique. For instance, Lower focused on the husband-wife dynamics in the case of a couple who shot hiding Jewish people on their estate in Ukraine. The couple thought they could trust each other, or rather the wife thought that the husband would save her with his testimony, but the tribunal trials necessitated a different, more individualistic strategy. Wendy Lower, "Male and Female Holocaust Perpetrators and the East German Approach to Justice 1949–1963," *Holocaust and Genocide Studies* 24.1 (2010): 56–84, 68.
249 See Margit Reiter, *Die Generation danach. Der Nationalsozialismus im Famielengedächtnis* (Innsbruck/Vienna/Bozen: Studienverlag, 2006), and Dan Bar-on, *Legacy of Silence. Encounters with Children of the Third Reich* (Cambridge, Mass.: Harvard University Press, 1989).
250 Sibylle Schmidt, "Perpetrators' Knowledge: What and How Can we Lear from Perpetrator Testimony?" *Journal of Perpetrator Research* 1.1 (2017): 85–104.

commonly aim to separate participation, responsibility and crime. Both parties want to actively shape memory, and this leads to memory wars,[251] a sign of which are the increasingly common media appearances of Nazi perpetrators' children. For instance, in a German talk show, Amon Göth, widely known from *Schindler's List*, was depicted as a lovable father. In Hungary a feature film was made about the family of László Endre, state secretary of the Ministry of Interior Affairs and main coordinator of the deportations, although it certainly reached smaller audiences.[252]

In Austria, the perpetrators' children sought psychological explanations for their parents' deeds. Their arguments were in harmony with the canonic postwar framework of explanations: their parents were "misled," "too young," "idealistic," "only behind a desk," "following orders," etc. Hungary followed a different route. The Hungarian framework of remembrance was built on the fallacies of the Communist system and in particular the People's Tribunal processes. This framework, which during the past decade increasingly determined Hungarian memory politics, allows for and sometimes downright supports the avoidance of responsibility for the past. Since 2010, government funded research has increasingly aimed to revise the anti-fascist historical canon through the reevaluation of well-known men's (politicians, high ranking officers and writers) biographies.

From the point of view of "truth-content," the memories of perpetrators' children are even more problematic than the memories of victims. In this regard Hungary again follows a different route than Austria. While in Austria the perpetrators' children had nowhere to turn to if they wished to reconstruct their parents' lives, in Hungary often even the victims had nowhere to turn to, as the Dely case exemplifies. Many of the survivors could not find the place of their story within the official Holocaust canon either. For instance, the victims on the memory plaque arranged by Lichter were not registered by the Chevra Kadisha.[253] In Hungary there is no institutional framework supporting inquiries about atypical events like the Csengery Street massacre. I will come back to these issues in the chapter on the massacre's remembrance.

The contradiction between emotional needs and desires, on the one hand, and available information, on the other, creates a very strong, potentially life-de-

---

251 Saul Friedländer, "History, Memory and the Historian. Dilemmas and Responsibilities," *New German Critique* 80 (Spring/Summer, 2000): 9.
252 *Leszármazottak* [Ascendants, 2005], directed by Ágota Varga. On the memories of survivors: *Beágyazott emlékeink* [Our embedded memories, 2017], directed by Kata Oláh.
253 Zsuzsa Toronyi's information taken from the Hungarian Jewish Archives.

fining tie to the parent. The children of war survivors have great responsibility in the shaping of memory dynamics. It is unclear whether perpetrators' remembrance can be legitimately discussed within the framework of "recovered memory."[254] Memories cannot be interpreted in a "true-false" framework, because the narrator always believes that their memories are "true." Rather, remembrance is a process, within which an interview (for instance the one I conducted with the Szamocsetas) can bring memories into motion, i.e. "recover" them. The "recovery" process should happen in the appropriate historical framework and without the glorification of victimhood. Truth has a healing effect, and it may have a public effect too as it can shift communal values.[255] However, as a necessary prerequisite those who remember should get rid off the self-fetish of memory, i.e. that their story is "truth itself," and they should do so without questioning the authenticity of the experience of remembrance. Lastly, the process of forgetting should not be demonized, because it is impossible to live without forgetting.

6.5 The Szamocseta story – As told by them

The monologue below was composed from my interview with Nándor Szamocseta's son.[256] The interview served as the space of memory.[257] The method of publication follows Margit Reiter's work in which she examines how the remembrance of the Nazi era affected the children and grandchildren of famous and ordinary perpetrators.[258] I edited the interview when it veered from the topic but did not change the sentences or the wording. Here I will publish the text in its entirety, and later I will devote a whole chapter to memory formation.[259]

---

[254] Marita Sturken, "The Remembering of Forgetting. Recovered Memory and the Question of Experience" *Social Text* 57 (1998): 103–125.
[255] Gabriele Rosenthal, ed., *The Holocaust in Three Generations. Families of Victims and Perpetrators of the Nazi Regime* (London: Cassell, 1998).
[256] On the portrait method, see Raphael S. Ezekiel, *The Racist Mind. Portraits of American Neo Nazis and Klansmen* (New York: Viking, 1995).
[257] Pierre Nora, "Between Memory and History: Les Lieux de Mémoire," *Representations* 26 (1989): 7–24.
[258] Margit Reiter, *Die Generation danach. Der Nationalsozialismus im Famielengedächtnis* (Innsbruck/Vienna/Bozen: Studienverlag, 2006).
[259] I could also analyze the narrative using Harald Welzer or Margit Reiter's method, who in turn built on Gabriele Rosenthal's method. See Gabriele Rosenthal, *"Wenn alles in Scherben fällt..." Von Leben und Sinnwelt der Kriegsgeneration* (Opladen, Leske + Budrich, 1987), Gabriele Rosenthal, "German War Memories. Narrability and the Biographical and Social Functions of Remembering," *Oral History* 19.2 (1991): 34–41, Gabriele Rosenthal, "Reconstruction of Life Stories.

Rosenthal noted that non-persecuted Germans were rather talkative about their memories of the Second World War.[260] The Hungarian case is different in this regard too. As a result of the changing political frameworks the topic became silenced, while the remembrance of the Communist era allowed for the relativization of Second World War events. Moreover, the perpetrators entered a "conspiracy of silence" which did not allow them to ask questions about their past.[261]

Dan Diner and Joel Golb differentiated various forms of guilt depending on whether it was caused by political, moral or metaphysical transgressions. Political guilt is felt by the member of a community for having committed something against the community. However, none of the Csengery Street perpetrators, neither Piroska Dely nor the janitor family belonged to any community (e.g. a political party), therefore they could feel no political guilt. The experience of moral guilt was disabled by the problematic operation of the people's tribunals, and metaphysical guilt was not possible in the ostracizing political culture of the Horthy era and the Anti-Jewish Laws. [262] The Csengery Street massacre is a classic example of sin without guilt. [263]

The interview below in and of itself is not suitable for the examination of the memory structures of various generations but it allows tendencies to be pointed at.[264] The perpetrators are also given a voice within this book; their perspective

---

Principles of Selection in Generating Stories for Narrative Biographical Interviews," *The Narrative Study of Lives* 1.1 (1993): 59–91, Gabriele Rosenthal, *Erlebte und erzählte Lebensgeschichte. Gestalt und Struktur biographischer Selbstbeschreibungen* (Frankfurt am Main: Campus, 1995), Gabriele Rosenthal, "The Healing Effects of Storytelling. On the Conditions of Curative Storytelling in the Context of Research and Counseling," *Qualitative Inquiry* 9.6 (2003): 915–933, Gabriele Rosenthal, ed. *Interpretative Sozialforschung. Eine Einführung* (Weinheim–München: Juventa, 2005), Gabriele Rosenthal, ed., *"Als der Krieg kam, hatte ich mit Hitler nichts mehr zu tun". Zur Gegenwärtigkeit des "Dritten Reiches" in erzählten Lebensgeschichten.* (Opladen: Leske + Budrich, 1990), Gabriele Rosenthal, ed., *Der Holocaust im Leben von drei Generationen. Familien von Überlebenden der Shoah und von Nazi-Tätern* (Gießen: Psychosozial Verlag, 1997), Gabriele Rosenthal, and Dan Bar-on, "A Biographical Case Study of a Victimizer's Daughter," *Journal of Narrative and Life History* 2.2 (1992): 105–127.

260 Gabriele Rosenthal, "German War Memories: Narratability and the Biographical and Social Functions of Remembering," *Oral History* 19.2 (1991): 189.
261 Margit Reiter, *Die Generation danach. Der Nationalsozialismus im Famielengedächtnis* (Innsbruck/Vienna/Bozen: Studienverlag, 2006), 68.
262 Dan Diner and Joel Golb, "Source on Guilt Discourse and Other Narratives: Epistemological Observations regarding the Holocaust," *History and Memory* 9.1–2 (1997): 303.
263 Ibid., 314.
264 The Hungarian processes followed the German pattern, see Michael L. Hughes, "'Through No Fault of Our Own.' West Germans Remember Their War Losses," *German History* 2 (2000): 193–213.

and memories are also represented. Complexity is part and parcel of memory and that is how in the interview the Szamocseta–Strucky family can show up not only as the victim of Communism but also as a group of anti-fascist rescuers who helped the Jews whenever needed.[265]

The story that Szamocseta's son told is a fantasy narrative in which the past is an important element of identity creation: the perpetrator father becomes the victim because that makes his son's life more bearable. The interview demonstrates two tendencies. The first is unconditional devotion towards the father and the grandfather, which is in part based on their retouched biography.[266] This devotion could be explained with deep psychological dynamics, which in the Austrian cases often lead to the rejection of the father figure.[267] Here, unlike Austrian (and German) cases, there was no distancing from the father's politics, instead the father appears as a victim and not as a perpetrator.[268] The other remarkable tendency is the view of the complete ineffectiveness of post-war punishment as, unlike in Austria or in West Germany, the whole post-war legal process is considered to be fraudulent as it happened under the auspices of the Hungarian Communist Party. Firstly, Szamocseta kept quiet about the ten years he spent in forced labor even in front of his most immediate relatives; secondly, he depicted himself as the victim of a Communist "political trial" – and this is what was preserved in family history.[269] Suffering during Communism be-

---

[265] In Austria, the children of perpetrators also often remembered family stories about their parents' wartime resistance. See Margit Reiter, *Die Generation danach. Der Nationalsozialismus im Famielengedächtnis* (Innsbruck/Vienna/Bozen: Studienverlag, 2006), especially 49–51.

[266] For a parallel in fascist Italy, see Luisa Passerini, *Torino operaia e fascismo.* Roma, Laterza, 1984. or in Austria, Margit Reiter, ibid.

[267] Ibid., 183.

[268] For more from this developing literature, see Donald Bloxham, *Genocide on Trial. War Crimes Trials and the Formation of Holocaust History and Memory* (Oxford: Oxford University Press, 2001), Lawrence Douglas, *The Memory Judgement. Making Law and History in the Trials of the Holocaust* (New Haven – London: Yale University Press, 2001), Norbert Frei, Dirk van Laak, and Michael Stolleis, ed., *Geschichte vor Gericht. Historiker, Richter und die Suche nach Gerechtigkeit* (München: Beck, 2000), Claudia Kuretsidis-Haider, and Winfried R. Garscha, ed., *Keine "Abrechnung". NS-Verbrechen, Justiz und Gesellschaft in Europa nach 1945* (Leipzig: AVA / Wien DÖW, 1998), Thomas Albrich, Winfried R. Garscha, and Martin Polaschek, ed., *Holocaust und Kriegsverbrechen vor Gericht. Der Fall Österreich* (Innsbruck/Vienna/Bozen: Studienverlag, 2006), Carlos Santiago Nino, *Radical Evil on Trial* (New Haven – London: Yale University Press, 1996).

[269] See Ruth Wodak, *"Wir sind alle unschuldige Täter". Diskurshistorische Studien zum Nachkriegsantisemitismus* (Frankfurt am Main: Suhrkamp, 1990).

comes the "cover-story"[270] which makes it possible to avoid facing responsibility for Second World War crimes. The story of the interviewee, the son of Nándor Szamocseta, is not a passive product of collective remembrance but itself a producer and transmitter of memory. (For the transcript see appendix 9)

Since the Strucky–Szamocseta families were motivated primarily by financial gain, in the next chapter I will examine how wealth disappeared and reappeared within Csengery 64.

---

[270] Gabriele Rosenthal, "German War Memories. Narrability and the Biographical and Social Functions of Remembering," *Oral History* 19.2 (1991): 199.

7 The Greed

> After liberation we had no one but the three of us: my aunt, Laci and I. When we went back Mrs. Strucky received my aunt in my aunt's silk gown and served her tea in my grandmother's Rosenthal tea set.[271]

The Dely trial's focus was on the unprecedented and brutal murders at Csengery 64, but the court process failed to clarify who fired and how many people died. In the Szamocseta trial the focus was on financial loss[272] and restitution, and the Strucky–Szamocseta families were indeed sentenced for the confiscation of assets, but because of an administrative mistake the verdict was never executed. Analysing the dispossession of Jews in Hungary is absent from the international literature, therefore this case study is even more valuable as it shows the process by which the state and individuals enriched themselves by creating legal and psychological circumstances whereby the owners gave over their property to them.[273] This process is labelled by Frank Bajohr as the "race for personal enrichment" (*Bereicherungswettlauf*).[274] Thus the war profiteer family could keep all the wealth they plundered: everything they stole from those who never returned and additionally those items the loss of which they blamed on the Arrow Cross or the Russians. The stolen goods were quickly liquidated so when the Struckys moved out from Csengery 64 the eager tenants could not recognize anything other than a perhaps familiar looking carpet among the Struckys' packed-up items.

There were no particularly wealthy people in Csengery 64, as most of the tenants belonged to the lower middle class. During the hearings they regretted the loss of chrome watches, crocheted tablecloths, embroidered duvet covers and undergarments.[275] The fact that the first things the janitors grabbed from

---

271 Miklós Bodor's personal letter.
272 On the systematic dispossession of Hungarian Jewry, see Kádár Gábor and Vági Zoltán, *Aranyvonat. Fejezetek a zsidóvagyon történetéből* (Budapest: Osiris Kiadó, 2001), Kádár Gábor and Vági Zoltán, *Hullarablás. A magyar zsidók gazdasági megsemmisítése* (Budapest: Jaffa Kiadó, 2005), Rigó Róbert, "A zsidóvagyon sorsa Kecskeméten," *Forrás* 40.9 (2008): 42–80, Bibó István, *Zsidókérdés Magyarországon 1944 után* (Budapest: Katalizátor Iroda, 1994), 18.
273 Christoph Kreutzmüller and Jonathan R. Zatlin, ed., *Dispossession: Plundering German Jewry, 1933-1953* (Ann Arbor: University of Michigan Press, 2020).
274 The original German phrase, found in Frank Bajohr, "Arisierung" in *Hamburg. Die Verdrängung der jüdischen Unternehmer 1933–45* (Hamburg: Hans Christians Verlag, 1997). Quoted in introduction to Christoph Kreutzmüller and Jonathan R Zatlin, ed., *Dispossession: Plundering German Jewry*, 1933-1953 (Ann Arbor: University of Michigan Press, 2020), 9.
275 BFL 19273/1949. 20.

the abandoned apartments were undergarments shows the intimacy of these murders. The items were usually returned later to their owners. But generally, it was very hard to trace the route of particular items. In the steel safe deposit box of the allegedly wealthy Steiners there were supposedly only 800 *pengős*, which may explain the sudden aggression of the armed men.[276] In the Grünfeld's Wertheim safe the intruders found 3200 *pengős* and 13 bottles of spirits (*pálinka*) and the Grünfelds were not shot.[277] In her testimony, Mrs. Steiner mentioned that the armed men stole her 'Floris' chocolate and her sister in law's gown.[278] Gowns often played a central role in the testimonies, perhaps because the post-war stories were primarily women's stories (way fewer men returned from deportation) and personal items like gowns have an identity-making effect with their intimacy. The engine of the events, Andor Lichter, missed his typewriter the most, but later he found it in the Struckys' apartment alongside several other typewriters.

Unquestionably their apartments were the returned tenants' most valuable assets: in war-ruined Budapest, inhabitable apartments represented great value. As already discussed, the Csengery 64 tenants often changed between June and November 1944 when the deportations started. After the deportations a total of 34 of the building's apartments were assigned to new tenants because those were "forsaken by the persecuted."[279] The new tenants paid a considerable rent for these apartments and for months on end János Pál, the new janitor, collected that rent and gave it to the Strucky family instead of the Jewish owner of the house.[280]

7.1 The birth of wealth

At the beginning, the Struckys perhaps felt that it was not worth staying in a yellow star house as the sole Christian family. Soon though as the ghettoization began they had more and more opportunities for profiteering. The families who had to move into the yellow star houses were crammed together and they stored their assets in the apartments and in lockable cellars. Some tenants gave part of their belongings to the janitor for safekeeping. These transactions were all trust-based as the tenants could not ask for a receipt. Some tenants

---

276 BFL 2442/1947. 35.
277 BFL 19273/1949. 48.
278 BFL 2442/1947. 35.
279 BFL 19273/1949. 61.
280 BFL 19273/1949. 21. Mrs. Pál's testimony, January 6, 1946.

gave them their apartment keys. The janitors took advantage of the trust they accumulated before the Jewish Acts were put in effect.

The most feasible explanation for the fact that many Christian janitor families, who could have moved elsewhere, chose to stay in the yellow star houses, is that they recognized that their position could help them become lucrative money-makers. Did they know that the Jewish tenants would be deported? They most probably didn't, but they used the law to their advantage when the systematic dispossession of the tenants had begun. One tenant remembers:

> [T]he Jellinek family moved to the ghetto. Soon after they left their apartment I was coming upstairs to my own apartment and on the way, I glanced into theirs because the door was wide open. In the anteroom I saw Nándor Szamocseta on the top of a chair as he handed things from the top of a wardrobe to his parents who were both there with him.[281]

The janitors requested money for all their otherwise free services. Thus, the yellow star houses turned into "private prisons" where the tenants lived according to rules set by the janitors. The aim of these rules was constant monitoring and ceaseless theft. For instance, one had to pay 200 *pengős* (which was then a very lavish monthly salary) to be let out of the house, but Strucky often took the money and still did not open the gate.[282]

Confinement increased vulnerability and the Strucky–Szamocseta families were prepared to reap harvest of the situation's psychological effects, which is what happened on October 15, 1944. Although Horthy's proclamation seemed to have signaled the end of their little private business, the later news about the Szálasi coup promised further increase of wealth and a quick end to the mortgage on their Göd house. Whether it was Mrs. Strucky's lodger Széplaki who reported on the Jewish tenants is unknown, but it is certain that as soon as the first group of tenants was taken to the police station the Struckys took the opportunity.

First, they looted the dead and their apartments – they were aware that this was something they could easily blame on the leaving Arrow Cross and SS soldiers. When the hiding tenants emerged, they locked them in the air raid shelter in order to be able to search and rob the apartments undisturbed. In the meantime, in the air raid shelter the still deeply shocked Jewish tenants gathered money to be able to buy Nándor Szamocseta's benevolence – as suggested by Nándor Szamocseta himself. The fact that the Arrow Cross or SS troops returned to the house provided a great cover story for the janitors as they could claim that

---
281 BFL 19273/1949. 227. Mrs. Singer's testimony.
282 BFL 19273/1949. 59.

the armed men robbed the apartments too. This was one of the reasons why the tenants did not openly confront them challenging their version of the events.

The Sterns' woolen blanket became the symbol of the Csengery 64 robbery. Mr and Mrs. Stern were either holding it when they were shot, or their dead bodies were covered with it. According to a witness it was not a blanket but a Persian rug that soaked up their blood. This would explain why Mrs. Strucky kept it. Strucky picked it up, Mrs. Strucky washed it and it was dried hanging on the courtyard's carpet-beater for several days. The blanket or rug that was still in their possession during the Dely trial ("because no one wanted it") symbolized the bloody redistribution of wealth that took place in Csengery 64.

When the house's tenants were herded away, the Struckys settled into the new situation. However, to their great surprise on October 18 and 19 the tenants came back. After that the tenants were consciously preparing for their future deportation and entrusted more and more of their assets to the only family they could turn to for assistance, the janitors. The deportations started on November 5 and went on until November 20. In the chaos of the deportations the janitors offered a helping hand as trustworthy "friends." Around this time, they had already collaborated with János Pál and his wife, the future janitors of Csengery 64.

> [W]hen we only had minutes to leave the house the present time janitor, János Pál and his wife intruded into my apartment, they opened my wardrobes and he started to rummage in them and then he took clothing items that he liked, underwear and shirts etc. and left with them but beforehand told his wife that she could take whatever she felt like. When I returned to my request Mrs. Pál gave back part of my belongings and also said that she is ready to testify that Mrs. Strucky took my white angora yarn with the knitting needles. After the battle I saw my white angora yarn on Éva Strucky, knitted. This was suspicious because Strucky did not work in 1944 only Éva Strucky worked in the House Office, where she issued apartments to the incomers of the Szálasi-era, including their relatives, unlawfully, so it was not likely that they would have had the means to buy something like that not to mention that back then it was not possible to buy angora yarn as the stores were closed. When the Germans were finally ousted from the country in the spring of 1945 then Mrs. Strucky all at once remembered to bring back my crocheted tablecloth and my sister in law's two embroidered duvet covers; Mrs. Szamocseta returned my sister in law's gown, my brother's Royal typewriter, and they said that these items were in their apartment for safekeeping. Beforehand they did not remember that although the house overseer [Lichter] warned them several times. They always said that the Russians robbed the house.[283]

---

[283] BFL 19273/1949. 25. Mrs. Gábor's testimony.

When everyone else was deported from the house the larger items such as the furniture and greater objects could be safely sold off. But first the Struckys moved upstairs into the nicest apartment of the building, the Krámer's, and to their own place they installed newcomers in the house, the new janitors, Pál János and his wife, who were completely at their mercy and followed each of their commands. According to the testimonies "the assets of the murdered Stern family were taken away by Arrow Cross trucks,"[284] and "they went upstairs in the forsaken apartments and gathered the more valuable items."[285]

Éva, their daughter, was employed at the House Office responsible for the redistribution of Jewish property, the "emptied" apartments. She collaborated in assigning these apartments in the house to trustworthy people who accepted the Strucky family's unquestionable rule in the building. Still, not every new tenant robbed the apartment they inhabited. Sándor Bán, a policeman, lived in Lichter's apartment for a short while. Strucky gave him the keys to the apartment together with an inventory list of all equipment. Lichter got everything back: "Bán returned all my belongings on the inventory list."[286] The inventory meant responsibility, but it was seldom that such a list was put together. Most of the tenants who returned after the liberation found empty wardrobes, cellars and pantries.[287]

Nándor Szamocseta also acquired an allegedly empty apartment in the neighborhood that he filled with furniture and other items. Most probably some of the robbed goods were taken to the Strucky's Göd house. As stated, Nándor Szamocseta started working as a driver, and the trucks that he fixed up could provide a great help moving the stolen furniture of Csengery 64. Stolen goods had a well-developed black market by then: the larger and easily recognizable furniture and carpets were immediately taken to the countryside. In the mayhem of war, the chances of being caught were minimal, plus it was easy to attribute the robberies to the Arrow Cross or later to the Russians when the returned Jews looked for their assets. Mrs. Strucky confirmed:

> After liberation Russian soldiers installed phone cables in the house and while they worked the gate was wide open. In the meantime, anyone could enter the house and we could not

---

[284] BFL 19273/1949. 47. Mrs. Grünberg's testimony.
[285] BFL 19273/1949. 57.
[286] BFL 19273/1949. 200. Lichter's testimony.
[287] For more, see Borbála Klacsmann, "Abandoned, confiscated, and stolen property: Jewish–Gentile relations in Hungary as reflected in restitution letters," *Holocaust Studies* 23 (2017): 133–148.

prevent robberies. When the Krámers were deported Mrs. Krámer asked me to safeguard their furniture, therefore we moved into their apartment.[288]

On the other hand, according to Mrs. Krámer's version, the Struckys not only appropriated their belongings including their food supplies but they moved into their apartment and did not want to let the Krámers back. When the family returned Mrs. Strucky shouted at them: "My sweet lord what shall I do with you now?" However, at least the apartment's equipment was preserved.[289]

When the returned tenants wanted to know the whereabouts of their items, the Struckys pointed at the new janitors, the Páls, and the Páls pointed at the Struckys:

> When I returned into my apartment after liberation, I saw that much of my belongings disappeared. When I inquired the janitors told it was the Struckys and the Struckys told it was the janitors. So I never found my assets.[290]
>
> [A]fter liberation I found at the new janitor's wife, Mrs. Pál, or rather I saw her wearing my daughter's blouse and shoes that she returned upon my request. She said that she got them from the Russians.[291]

The intimacy of the robberies affected the two janitors differently. Strucky, who always liked to drink, reached for the bottle increasingly often and one night he yelled drunk at his wife: "You stole everything from the Jews!"[292] At the same time his wife increasingly enjoyed her power and kept on complaining about her husband's meekness.

7.2 The loss of wealth

Andor Lichter's return to Budapest after the liberation marked a turning point in the wrangle over the stolen assets. It certainly did not contribute to the establishment of a good relationship that Mrs. Strucky received Lichter in the gown of his wife who was killed in Bergen-Belsen.[293] As soon as he arrived Lichter became the house overseer, the elected representative of the house who supervised the

---

288 BFL 19273/1949. 73–74. Mrs. Strucky's testimony.
289 Interview with Magda Kun, October 7, 2005.
290 BFL 19273/1949. 62. Mrs. Propper's testimony.
291 BFL 19273/1949. 226. Mrs. Faragó's testimony.
292 BFL 19273/1949. 29. Mrs. Krámer's and Mrs. Sárdi's testimonies (BFL 19273/1949. 263.): Strucky "was often drunk."
293 Magda Kun's personal statement.

janitor, thus he had the authority to demand the return of his stolen assets, among them his typewriter. By April some of his items, e.g. the typewriter was returned.

After liberation it became part of the returned people's everyday routine that they looked for their belongings that were either stolen or that they themselves had handed over for safekeeping before the deportations. In parallel they tried to convince the new tenants of their apartments to move out. A survivor remembered:

> We went back to our old apartment in the Csengery. In the meantime, things happened. It was a separated section of the apartment. Someone moved into the other half, used it but then left. A woman with a small child. She had a hard time leaving… It was not about big things: what she returned me was something from my father. That hurt me.[294]

Another stated:

> After liberation Mrs. Szamocseta handed over a typewriter and told me that she was unsure whether it was mine, and later my sister in law also got back a few clothing items again from the Szamocsetas. Later we also got back some bedding and undergarments from the Struckys. All of them said that the apartments were robbed by the Arrow Cross and then by the Russians, still, we found our own underwear in their apartments.[295]

After many failed attempts to reclaim their belongings the house overseer and the angry tenants held a house search at the Struckys'. This most probably contributed to the Struckys' quick move from Csengery Street to their house in Göd, which by that time was free from its mortgage. In Mrs. Strucky's words: "[W]hen after liberation the returned persecuted tenants held a house search in our apartment they found nothing. Whatever we had for safekeeping I gave back to their rightful owners right after their return." [296]

The assets were of very different value. Some lost carpets and furniture, others lost clothing items such as silk neckties, and there was someone who looked for a barrel of lard (which could be a lifesaver then). [297] For instance, from the

---

[294] Interview with Edit Rosenberg, August 13, 2007.
[295] BFL 19273/1949. 30., Mrs. Gábor's testimony
[296] BFL 19273/1949. 72. Ilona Bodor also stated that what she gave to Strucky she received back, but the contents of her wardrobes that she entrusted to Mrs. Strucky were completely gone. (BFL 19273/1949. 222.)
[297] Mrs. Schwartz: "While I was deported my apartment and several other apartments in the house were robbed. Once I took a barrel of lard to Mrs. Strucky but I never got it back. When I was deported, I messaged Mrs. Strucky to send that lard after me but she said that the Arrow Cross took it." 19273/1949. 78.

Krámer apartment the four families' whole food supply disappeared on October 16, 1944. Later, when the Krámers were hiding in the Szamocseta's apartment, they had to pay for their own food.[298] The objects were strictly kept count of as Mrs. Rosenberg on May 10, 1947 still stated that some of her items were at the Struckys. [299]

The Szamocseta trial was a late trial in the history of the People's Tribunals. By then it was more comfortable to frame the trial as an account of what happened in the Csengery Street primarily for financial accountability. The emotions disappeared form the recorded texts, the witnesses cold headedly listed their financial losses and the endured injustices. Because of the earlier Dely trial, by this time the stories became narratable and they took on a standardized form. Nevertheless, the returned tenants were deeply hurt, and they harbored a lot of bitter hatred too. From the interviews it is clear that the survivors were not satisfied with the operation of the People's Tribunals, the process of compensation and, first of all, with the fact that the janitor family could get away with all those goods they robbed from the tenants. This dissatisfaction was discussed at home and among relatives. What could remedy those feelings – and whether the People's Tribunal, which at the time had no alternative, was suitable for that – remains a question.

---

298 BFL 19273/1949. 29.
299 BFL 19273/1949. 215.

8 Revenge and Forgiveness

My foster father [Lichter] was the one who pushed this thing forward.[300]
In the morning they went to see an execution. I don't know what their afternoon was like.[301]

8.1 The frameworks of justice

Post-Second World War justice represented the institutionalized remembrance of the past. W. James Booth differentiated three methods of "justice as it deals with the past: trial and punishment (criminal charges); illumination and acknowledgement (truth commissions); and forgetting for a sake of a future in common (amnesty)."[302] All three were present in the Hungarian case; at the same time most denouncements were fueled by revenge. [303] There is a general silence from survivors about feelings of satisfaction and happiness experienced when witnessing trials and executions are strictly tabooed topics. The post-Second World War trials were expected to negotiate and harmonize emotions to form "emotional communities"[304] besides marking out what is good, bad or acceptable. The court was a highly ritualized space where the audience was expected to be silent, therefore we can access the emotions constructed during the trials only through the testimonies. Emotions usually escape the attention of historians, as they do not leave any written trace behind. The VHA video testimony collection is unique as it explicitly asks questions about feelings.[305]

---

[300] Interview with Magda Kun, March 3, 2005.
[301] Interview, April 1, 2005. Until March 1946 women could not watch the executions, but then this discriminative measure was found unconstitutional. (MOL XIX-E-1-L X. 2. box Bö 1466/1945. 5.)
[302] W. James Booth, "The Unforgotten. Memories of Justice," *The American Political Science Review* 4 (2001): 777–791, 778.
[303] Andrea Pető, "Digitalized Memories of the Holocaust in Hungary in the Visual History Archive," in *Holocaust in Hungary 70 years after*, ed., Randolph Braham and András Kovács (CEU Press, Budapest, 2016), 253–261.
[304] Barbara Rosenwein, "Worrying about Emotions in History," *American Historical Review* 107.3 (2002): 842.
[305] More on this see Andrea Pető, "Historicizing Hate: Testimonies and Photos about the Holocaust Trauma during the Hungarian post-WWII Trials," in *Tapestry of Memory. Evidence and Testimony in Life Story Narratives*, ed., Nanci Adler and Selma Leydesdorff (New York/London: Transaction Publishers, 2013), 3–19.

But who could take revenge and for what? Special importance was given to the process because of the victims who could not stand up for themselves: the denouncers fought for their own dignity. However, punishment should be just.

Hungary established two institutions for the examination of wartime events, the people's tribunals following the Soviet example and the bottom up initiative of the Committee for the Investigation of Nazi and Arrow Cross Atrocities, founded on March 7, 1945 after the lead of Béla Varga. Until September 17, 1945 the Committee collected 12,000 questionnaires in which Budapest inhabitants listed house by house what happened during the Arrow Cross rule. The Committee's goals were defined as follows:

> [In order to] not let the past fall into the waters of forgetfulness. [...] [T]o find out what happened for the sake of the future of Hungarian nation. The people's tribunals execute dozens of mass murderers, the political police investigates case x, but terminates investigation in case y because the perpetrators are unknown. This is not enough. We also need to know and share with the international community the psychological reasons and the evidences, which prove that the mass murderers were criminals under other circumstances too. [...] [T]o prove that they were foreign to Hungarian people, sometimes even their names were foreign like Mesztl who took on the Hungarian name Murai [...].[306]

The declared aim of the committee's work was to contribute to social science research, but in particular cases it could also provide a basis for criminal procedures.[307] In the meantime, the Hungarian Communist Party (MKP – *Magyar Kommunista Párt*) tried to sabotage the committee's operation. For the MKP such a wide-based democratic project seemed uncontrollable. Therefore, soon enough the People's Tribunals, which were supervised by the Ministry of Justice, which in turn was controlled by the Communist Party, remained the only institutional channels of punishment.

Besides Andor Lichter there was another engine behind the Csengery 64 justice process: Pál Kádár people's prosecutor, later people's judge.[308] Although during the shooting Kádár played dead, he was put into the first transport from where he escaped with forged papers. For the purposes of the Committee for the Investigation of Nazi and Arrow Cross Atrocities, Kádár summarized what happened in the Csengery Street. In his view there were 21 "improvised" killings by "8-10 SS soldiers, 3 Arrow Cross men and an Arrow Cross woman."[309]

---

[306] BFL XVII-2.18. 13–14.
[307] BFL XVII-2.19. 38. March 9, 1945.
[308] BFL XVII-2.19. 164. Application for the people's prosecutor's office. (MOL XIX-E-1-L X. 1. Ta 1777/1945.)
[309] BFL XVII-2.19. 164. on February 23, 1945

Nothing proves that Lichter and Kádár collaborated, but the fact that a people's prosecutor was a witness during the Csengery 64 trials gave the case extra gravity. Pál Kádár always talked straightforwardly and genuinely by which he greatly aided the justice process. When he applied for the position of people's judge (with recommendations from Zoltán Tildy, the first, and Árpád Szakasits, the second President of Hungary after 1945), his argument was: "The Arrow Cross and the fascists partly killed partly deported my family and they deported me too. For these personal reasons my deepest commitment and desire is to chase fascists and reactionaries within the framework of legality but with all strictness of law."[310]

8.2 Moral witness or political witness?

Whom did Andor Lichter represent? Did he have a choice? Avishai Margalit holds that someone is a moral witness if they act upon clear moral aims,[311] while they take personal risk.[312] Lichter took a risk indeed, and not a negligible one. That is one of the reasons, when he believed that Communist Hungary had collapsed, on 23 October, 1956 that he made sure his meticulously collected files would be burned.[313]

Annette Wieviorka describes the complex process through which survivors become witnesses: the process of remembrance is taken to a new space and this new space provides legitimacy to their memories.[314] Could Lichter come to terms with himself had he not acted the way he did? Moral witnesses should establish a moral community of their present and future selves; but as a prerequisite they should validate a moral standpoint. The authority of a moral witness is rooted in a deep commitment that allows for no compromise: "[A] strong congruence between his emotions and his avowals, and with his not making concessions to himself."[315]

---

310 MOL Ta 1777/1945.
311 Avishai Margalit, *The Ethics of Memory* (Cambridge, Mass.: Harvard University Press, 2001), 151.
312 Ibid., 157.
313 Interview, April 1, 2005.
314 Annette Wieviorka, "From Survivor to Witness. Voices from the Shoah," in *War and Remembrance in the Twentieth Century*, ed., Jay Winter and Emmanuel Sivan (Cambridge: Cambridge University Press, 1999).
315 Avishai Margalit, *The Ethics of Memory* (Cambridge, Mass.: Harvard University Press, 2001), 170.

Margalit compares the concept of moral witness to the concept of political witness. The political witness says what happened, but the moral witness says what it was like to face the devil.[316] For that Lichter did not have to be personally present in Csengery Street on October 15, 1944. "The moral witness plays a special role in uncovering the evil he or she encounters.[317] Piroska Dely was "devil-like" exactly because she was so ordinary.

But what about the fact that Lichter lied to those institutions, which were officially after the "truth"?[318] To answer that question we should separate the truth of memory and the memory of truth:

> Truth-memory is [...] an act of fidelity [...] to members of one's community who have been lost. Memory-truth is not a gesture of fidelity to just anyone it is faithfulness in the context of a community, whether a marriage, a religion, or a nation. The truth of remembrance differs from the truth of law and history in that its core is fidelity to the victim. [...] Remembrance serves to reintegrate the victims into their community and to restore that community after the rupture induced by the crime. Faithfulness and the (re)integration of the community are two sides of the same phenomenon.[319]

Leigh A. Payne – borrowing from Elizabeth Jelin – uses the term *memory entrepreneur*.[320] A memory entrepreneur is a person who "turns" past events into political deeds. Andor Lichter was a memory entrepreneur as well as a memory militant: he put principles of his memory politics into practice. Lichter's memories conformed to the 'memory of truth' but not to 'the truth of memory.' The way he fought for the truth of law did not restore the community, although that was what he wished for. As he individually waged this fight against forgetting, his impact on the process was therefore provisional and lacked long term perspective.

---

316 Ibid., 168.
317 Ibid., 165.
318 For more, see Daniel L. Schacter, ed., *Memory Distortion. How Minds, Brains and Societies Reconstruct the Past* (Cambridge, Mass.: Harvard University Press, 1994).
319 W. James Booth, "The Unforgotten. Memories of Justice," *The American Political Science Review* 4 (2001):787.
320 Leigh A. Payne, *Unsettling Accounts. Neither Truth nor Reconciliation in Confessions of State Violence* (Durham, NC/London: Duke University Press, 2008), 37.

8.3 The affect of testimony

What if Lichter had died on October 15, 1944 in the Újpest Hospital, if he really had dysentery? How much would we know about the Csengery Street massacre today? How would we think about invisible perpetrators? Would we consider Piroska Dely a "beast in human skin"? How would we remember the first massacre committed by the Arrow Cross? The answers are twofold: on the one hand, Lichter's denouncements should be interpreted within the matrix of forgiving and forgetting in post-war Hungary.[321] Secondly, it should be analyzed whether Lichter was truly a moral witness since he was not part of the events, he did not see the massacre, but still, he testified as an eyewitness.[322]

Dori Laub separates three levels of witnessing. The first level is being witness to oneself in the experience, the second level is being witness to someone else's testimony, and the third level is being witness to someone else's witnessing.[323] Laub considers that the third level to be missing from the Holocaust experience.[324] However, in the Csengery case the opposite is true. The remembrance of the experience was created through the act of witnessing.

But we would misrepresent the events if we posited Lichter as the sole engine of them. Lichter as a lettered, respectable man certainly played a huge role during the trials but the rest of the tenants also participated in the process. Edit Rosenberg, from Csengery Street, could not imagine the belligerent and passionate statements her mother made in front of the people's tribunal until I showed her the court records. She remembered her mother as "bunny-like."[325] This shows that although the People's Tribunal played a key role in the shaping of post-war memory their later experiences modified their remembrance of events. In the long run in socialist Hungary it was more beneficial to adopt a "bunny-like" attitude than to be a fierce warrior.

---

321 Martha Minow, *Between Vengeance and Forgiveness. Facing History after Genocide and Mass Violence* (Boston: Beacon Press, 1998).
322 See his detailed, descriptive testimony made on December 26, 1946. (BFL 19273/1949. 231– 233.) The basis of the testimony was that he questioned his wife thoroughly. In his testimony he tried to accuse Mrs. Strucky's cousin, István Kiss and his wife too because they regularly visited the Struckys and participated in the transport of stolen goods. During his testimony he exhibited exceptional preparedness concerning the structure and functioning of the Arrow Cross.
323 Dori Laub, "An Event Without a Witness. Truth, Testimony and Survival," in *Testimony. Crises of Witnessing on Literature, Psychoanalysis and History*, ed., Soshana Felman and Dori Laub (New York: Routledge, 1992), 75.
324 Ibid., 80.
325 Interview with Edit Rosenberg.

Hannah Arendt in *Eichmann in Jerusalem* says: "*One man* will *always* be left to *tell the story.*"³²⁶ This is certainly true, however in the case of Csengery Street the one man who told the story was not an eyewitness. Lichter was a sharp man though. He strategically placed Mária Verebes, the Lichter family's loyal maid, at the Szamocseta's home when the Jews were not allowed to employ Christian maids anymore: "[I told her to] Please keep your eyes open and tell me everything that happens around the Struckys and the Szamocsetas, because I expected that they would pay for their crimes."³²⁷ Verebes's information and her testimonies were indeed very useful during the court process.

"Forgiving means overcoming anger and vengefulness,"³²⁸ says Avishai Margalit. Lichter was far from that. But what could the opposite strategy be? Forgetting? "Forgetfulness may in the last analysis be the most effective method of overcoming anger and vengefulness, but since it is an omission rather than a decision, it is not forgiveness."³²⁹ Margalit argues that it is not forgetting that should be the base of forgiveness but the ignorance of sin.³³⁰ However, the ignorance of sin cannot be an accidental mental act, it should be an active process, which brings with it mental change. This is why it cannot be connected to forgetting, because forgetting is involuntary while forgiveness is deliberate.³³¹ Forgiveness is a process and a result at the same time.³³²

For the returned Jews it was key to assuaging the damage.³³³ In a European comparison – as Pierre Lagrou demonstrates – Hungary did not differ from other countries where the Germans exterminated local Jewry in collaboration with representatives of local institutions.³³⁴ After the war, national organizations buried

---

326 Hannah Arendt, Eichmann in Jerusalem. *A Report on the Banality of Evil* (London/New York: Penguin Books/Viking Press, 1994). 232–233.
327 Andor Lichter's testimony, December 27, 1946. BFL 19273/1949. 229–230.
328 Avishai Margalit: *The Ethics of Memory* (Cambridge, Mass.: Harvard University Press, 2002). 192.
329 Ibid., 193.
330 Ibid., 197.
331 Ibid., 203.
332 Ibid., 205.
333 On the post-1945 social history of Hungarian Jewry, see Karády Viktor, *Szociológiai kísérlet a magyar zsidóság 1945–1956 közötti helyzetének elemzésére, Zsidóság az 1945 utáni Magyarországon.* in ed., Karády Viktor, Kende Péter, Kovács András, et al, 37–180 (Párizs, Magyar Füzetek, 1985), Karády Viktor, *Túlélők és újrakezdők* (Budapest: Múlt és Jövő, 2002).
334 Pierre Lagrou, "Return to a Vanished World. European Societies and the Remnants of their Jewish Communities," in *The Jews Are Coming Back. The Return of the Jews to Their Countries of Origin after WWII*, ed., David Bankier, 1–25 (Jerusalem: Yad Vashem, 2005). Between 1946 and 1960 in Poland, 16,819 Nazi war criminals and Polish collaborators were sentenced. There

the dead, aided the survivors, but not because they were Jewish, but because this way they could claim to be anti-fascists. Anti-fascism provided an appropriate and comfortable enough framework of memory within which the war became discussable. For the surviving Jews it was an especially suitable framework of assimilation.[335]

The post-war reconstruction of the country entailed the redefinition of the concept of citizenship. The question was who should benefit from the newly launched welfare services. In Eastern Europe the Communists were against the return of Jewish wealth – this is why the heirs of the Csengery Street apartment building lost their right to their inheritance. The argument was that the return of Jewish wealth could spark anti-Semitism. However, anti-Semitism did not need a spark for it to flare up. The concept of "Jewish revenge" was already present at the time of the people's tribunals' trials – and even before.[336]

A former investigator of the Ministry of Internal Affairs told me in an interview what had been on his mind when he was liberated as an 18 year old boy in an Austrian labor camp:

> "I had two great resolutions. I was not religious. I took two vows. I went through such horrid events that I would never leave my mother again. Two: I will devote my life to what happened to us, the Jewry."[337]

It was hard to move beyond the "us and them" framework. During the trial Lichter described the Szamocseta–Strucky family as "the maffia of Aryan Hungarians"[338] In her testimony Mrs. Szamocseta said the following: "I did not know that internment camps existed, I learned about them only when Christians got interned."[339] These statements clearly mark the clear dividing line between the

---

were 1,214 death penalty verdicts. See Leszek Kubicki, *Zbrodnie wojenne w swietle prawa polskiego* (Warszawa: PWN, 1963), 40–41, 180–183. I am grateful for Krzysztof Persak's help.

335 On the role of Hungarian Jewish organizations, see Kinga Frojimovics, "Different Interprerations of Reconstructions. The AJDC and the WJC in Hungary after the Holocaust," in *The Jews Are Coming Back. The Return of the Jews to Their Countries of Origin after WWII*, ed., David Bankier, 277–293 (Jerusalem: Yad Vashem, 2005).

336 Karsai László, "'Shylock is Whetting his Blade.' Fear of the Jews' Revenge in Hungary during World War II," in *The Jews Are Coming Back. The Return of the Jews to Their Countries of Origin after WWII*, ed., David Bankier, 293–312 (Jerusalem: Yad Vashem, 2005). On revenge, see Andrea Pető, "Digitalized Memories of the Holocaust in Hungary in the Visual History Archive," in *Holocaust in Hungary 70 years after*, ed., Randolph Braham and András Kovács 253–261 (Budapest: CEU Press, 2016).

337 Interview with Iván Svéd, August 6, 2007.
338 BFL 19273/1949. 265. Lichter's court testimony.
339 BFL 19273/1949. 261.

two worlds: when Jews were taken away this process remained allegedly unnoticed by the gentiles. This exclusion of course had an impact on Jewish-Hungarian relations. As the psychologist István Kulcsár (1901-1986) characterized the post-war mood of Hungarian Jewry: "Untreated memories, unacknowledged losses, infertile ressentiment, collective residual neurosis, further self-deception, intellectual civil war, see, this is the psychic cross-cut of the remaining Jewry at the fall of 1946."[340]

For his part, Lichter did everything to "treat" memories and for that he used the only forum of judicial remedy: the People's Tribunal.

---

340 Kulcsár István, "A maradék zsidóság lelki keresztmetszete 1946-ban," *Thalassa* 1–2 (1994): 336.

9 The Survivors and the Surviving Memories

> Unfortunately, I'm turning into a professional testifier.[341]
> Who cares for high politics, it's all in the history books, but why did they do that to us?[342]

"History is the way in which a culture accounts for its past" – wrote Johan Huizinga in 1929.[343] This accounting is present through historiography, but also through museums, commemorations, court trials, state issued public apologies, historical fiction, photographs and family stories. Though historians play an important role in memory culture they do not play a decisive one. Remembering is an individual process that follows available frames and patterns. It will not enter the public sphere automatically, therefore not every memory will become part of public or cultural memory. It takes a long selection process.[344] The Dely trial entered Hungarian cultural memory partly because of Lichter and partly because of the work of historians (like me). Without this book Dely will remain just one of the Arrow Cross women listed as executed after the Second World War.

While the survivors are still living among us – and in the case of the Csengery Street events they thankfully are – they share their memories with their contemporaries and the subsequent generations. This book shows the different sites like court, families and in the press where the survivors told their stories right after the war, and traces how their stories were gradually and selectively forgotten. In this chapter I examine the way forgetting and transformation – which Ann Rigney calls the "dynamics of memory" – worked in the case of the Csengery Street massacre.[345] Memories are not unchanging; therefore, the dynamics of memory may fundamentally affect who remembers what and how.

This mapping is particularly important in relation to the changing framework of Holocaust memorialization in Hungary and also globally. It does not matter that the second largest community of Jewish survivors in Europe lives in Hungary; due to the lack of Hungarian Holocaust researchers in the international research community, and the effect of communist memory politics, the

---

[341] Magda Kun's lecture on August 1, 2007 at the Páva Street Holocaust Memorial Center.
[342] Interview with Magda Kun, July 12, 2007.
[343] Quoted in Ann Rigney, "Portable Monuments. Literature, Cultural Memory, and the Case of Jennie Deans," *Poetics Today* 2 (2004): 363.
[344] Andrea Reiter, *Narrating the Holocaust* (London/New York: Continuum, 2000).
[345] Ann Rigney, "Plenitude, Scarcity, and the Circulation of Cultural Memory," *Journal of European Studies* 35.1 (2005): 11–28.

memory politics of the illiberal state invisibilized and framed survivors according to their political interests.[346]

9.1 Taking an inventory

By the time Andor Lichter finally returned home in February 1945 his loved ones were all long dead. His first thoughts were that this must be remembered, this must not be forgotten. Thus, Lichter started collecting information about what happened to whom. Without his lists, which played a crucial role in the People's Tribunal process, most probably there would have been no Csengery 64 trials. "What has not been counted does not count" was his principle and started to privately document the process.

The next step was the erection of the commemorative marble plaque (see appendix 6) on the first anniversary of the tragedy. There are 19 names on the plaque; 18 of them were shot on the night of October 15, 1944 while Lichter's father had a heart attack due to the effect of the events. With the installation of the plaque these names became a set of data, which later entered various official documents. The plaque was made from Lichter's own marble kitchen counter and, as it was for indoor use, it was placed in the entrance to the courtyard. The placement was symbolic because for Lichter the Csengery 64 tenants were the primary audience of the event's memory.

Through the analysis of the *yisker biher* ("tombstones of paper"), a literary genre of post-Holocaust memory culture, Nathan Wachtel shows that through these books the memory of individual tragedies claimed public form.[347] The *yisker biher* are memorial books, which listed the murdered members of Eastern European Jewish communities, thus reading it functioned as a memorial to all those who did not receive a proper burial ceremony. The tradition of memory books originates with the seventeenth-century pogroms by Cossacks in Russia, when the names of Jewish victims were read out loud on the pogrom's anniversary. The memory plaque in Csengery 64 became a place of remembrance, with a similar community shaping function; it contributes to collective memory founded on individual losses. At the same time the plaque's text inserted the events and their memory into Communist-anti-fascist discourse: "Your sacrifice shows us the way towards building a free, happy Hungary."

---

346 Andrea Pető, "The Lost and Found Library," *Memory at Stake* 9 (2019): 72–82.
347 Nathan Wachtel, "Remember and Never Forget," *History and Anthropology* 2 (1986): 307–335.

The police hearings and the people's tribunals' trials represented the next level of memory work. After Lichter had successfully reclaimed his typewriter from the Struckys he started busily corresponding with institutions that were not always responsive. This was the correspondence that was burned in a tile-stove during the 1956 events.[348] Gabriele Rosenthal showed that "[t]he mutual influence of these three components – narrability, the necessity for narration and the social function of the narrations – makes the collective thematization of historical phases possible."[349] In the case of Csengery Street, "narratability" was provided and framed by the People's Tribunal trial, and the requirement of "necessity" was fulfilled by the verdict, which also determined the "social function" of the narrative. Concerning the "mutual influence" of the three components, it is clear that the legalism of the process determined and framed the process. Consequently, the memory of the massacre remained private.

The family is also among the scenes of remembrance. The survivors told their stories to their children too. The daughter of the Rosenberg family was ten years old when her parents took her to Csengery Street to show her the memorial plaque.[350] By that time the event of the massacre was simplified into a narratable story. As Eva Hoffmann (herself the child of survivors) put it, the stories are "talismanic litanies, [...] repeated but never elaborated upon."[351] Women held key positions in these "repetitions" as they were the keepers of memory who told and retold the stories important to them.[352] In the case of the Csengery massacre as well, women survivors transmitted and preserved the memory of the event.

> I remember what my mom told me [...] because Csengery Street was always talked about. It was a central thing. [...] It was a lasting experience of our lives, of all of our lives.[353]
>
> We [the children] only knew what we overheard when the adults talked to each other. That was all we had. And then when my son was born she started to talk about it. About the details. And then when mom [...] was about 60-62, in the last five years of her life it all spilled out of her.[354]

---

348 Interview, April 1, 2005.
349 Gabriele Rosenthal, "German War Memories: Narratability and the Biographical and Social Functions of Remembering," *Oral History* 19.2 (1991): 34–41.
350 Interview with Edit Rosenberg.
351 Eva Hoffmann, *After Such Knowledge. Memory, History and the Legacy of the Holocaust* (New York: Public Affairs, 2004): 11.
352 Nechama Tec, *Resilience and Courage. Women, Men, and the Holocaust* (New Haven: Yale University Press, 2003).
353 Interview, April 1, 2005.
354 Interview, April 1, 2005.

> And then Piroska Dely dragged my mom out of the line and shoved her to the wall. And even terror has a sense of humor. I learned that from my mom. So she pushed my mom to the wall to shoot her. And then an officer of the Hungarian Royal Army walks by and stops in front of my mother, and says – that's what my mom told – to Piroska Dely "What's your plan with that woman and that child, Madame? Let me escort you home." Now this is a hilarious story. I think if I saw it in a movie I would laugh while being freaked out.[355]

During the people's tribunal trial, immediately after the happenings this story sounded very differently:

> On the evening of October 15 with several SS soldiers and if I remember correctly with two-three Arrow Cross men [Dely arrived]. Piroska Dely sent me back from the street because I had my three years old daughter on my arm.[356]

Every Holocaust survivor had to find an answer to the question why they remained alive. The story that Piroska Dely saved her life – and her child's life – did not fit the standardized narrative framework about "the Arrow Cross woman" so she transmitted another story to her family.

Memory changes all the time because its dynamics are affected by social impulses and cultural products, such as historical movies. During the interviews the survivors often said, "it was like in the movies" or "it wasn't like in the movies." Remembrance includes all that has been experienced since the event and the way newer experiences have reshaped our understanding of the event. Interestingly, canonic Hungarian Holocaust movies did not come up during the interviews. Perhaps because the memories of the Csengery Street survivors are atypical: canonic Holocaust narratives involve concentration camps, but the Csengery tenants were hiding in Budapest.[357]

9.2 In defense of the right to memory

The historical situation and with that the frames of remembrance have changed after 1989. On the one hand they became more inclusive as the survivors could finally talk about experiences that they had to silence for 45 years. For instance the battle of Budapest was never mentioned in school, only after 1989 did it be-

---

[355] Interview, March 3, 2005.
[356] BFL 19273/1949. 29.
[357] Jablonczay Tímea, "Hivatalos amnézia és az emlékezés kényszere. A traumatikus múlt női elbeszélései az 1960-as években," *Múltunk* 2 (2019): 77–110.

come a topic of discussion during class reunions.[358] In parallel, the anti-fascist discourse lost its hegemonic position, and the newly emerging revisionist history writing that labeled the People's Tribunals as "show trials," claiming that the verdicts were political and therefore unjust. With that the space of remembrance has considerably shrunk again. The House of Terror Museum on the corner of Csengery Street and Andrássy Avenue is the symbolic expression of that "shrinking": it conflates Nazism and Communism under the umbrella term of "terror."[359]

In 2004, as the Csengery 64 building underwent renovation, some tenants proposed the removal of the memory plaque in fear of reemerging anti-Semitism. From the 1990s on, more and more commemorative plaques were removed and street names were changed. The survivors, who were children in 1944, had to stand up for the plaque and they could only count on themselves – again. This is when they started to look for other survivors and to correspond with authorities. It was also around this time that the survivors entered a new life-phase in which they could devote more time to themselves and their memories. In her memoir Magda Kun writes: "These questions were important for me ever since my adolescence, but my everyday duties never let me look for answers."[360]

Perhaps my ongoing research was another catalyst of the process as I started to gather and publish testimonies already from 2003. After an article was published in the Jewish congregations' bulletin, further survivors from Israel contacted the survivors in Budapest. They agreed to an interview but wanted to remain anonymous partly because of the current Hungarian political situation and partly to protect their children.

On November 1, 2005 the sixth district's chief architect promised to put together a list of that district's commemorative plaques, which had not existed before, and to include the Csengery plaque. Apparently, the commemorative plaque was at the entrance for fifty years without any license or official recognition.

On the sixtieth anniversary of the Holocaust in Hungary the sixth district's bulletin published an article on the commemorative plaque. The text was full of mistakes, to the extent that each fact was mistaken, which is understandable since it is a complex, multilayered story and even relevant literature is rife with

---

358 Interview with Magda Kun, January 9, 2007.
359 Otto Lene, "Post-Communist Museums: Terrorspaces and Traumascapes," in *The Power of the Object. Museums and World War II*, ed., Esben Kjeldbæk (MuseumsEtc: Edinburgh, 2009): 324–360.
360 Kun Magda, *Szálasi árnyékában* (np: Manuscript, 2007). Two further stories were included in the Katalin Pécsi edited *Sós kávé* (Budapest: Novella, 2007).

factual error. The article wanted to tell a "true story" without hurting anyone's memory or feelings or without excluding important details:

> On October 15, 1944 a woman lead troop forcibly took away several man from Csengery 64, among them Miksa Eisentedter who just got over a severe surgery. The next day the troop returned for Sándor Szilágyi. His friends sought to find the troop's leader who promised to let him go for 5000 *pengős*. The money was dispatched, Sándor Szilágyi returned, but then it turned out that the person who collected the money had nothing to do with Szilágyi's escape. The troop kept on harassing and threatening the house's tenants and the Christian tenants were not allowed to communicate with the Jewish tenants.[361]

It is unclear why the journalist selected Szilágyi's story for the commemorative article. The "person who collected the money" was Nándor Szamocseta, but neither him not the janitor's family was referenced in the article. The survivors demanded a correction. A rectified version was published in the next issue, but even in that the troops were led by an "Arrow Cross woman."

A small group of survivors took on the task of protecting the memory. Lichter's stepdaughter, Magda Kun, and her husband (who was also from the house, which is where they fell in love) often participate at the Páva Street Holocaust Memorial Center's events where survivors meet schoolchildren. In the 1970s, after the "emotional turn," American pedagogy tried to personalize the historical experience of the Holocaust by focusing on individual stories and by organizing personal encounters with survivors.[362] I participated in one of these events at Páva Street, where high school pupils listened to testimonies by survivors. Lichter's stepdaughter and her husband were not trying to teach "the Holocaust" or underline their importance in the events; instead they tried to present the "truth" of the event that determined their lives. They are the "bearers of a secret" as Dori Laub calls Holocaust survivors, whose mission is to pass on "truth."[363] Both of them told the story as genuine eyewitnesses and the story they told the schoolchildren was the same story they told me during the interviews, close to verba-

---

361 A quotation from Vincellér Béla's *Sötét árny magyarhon felett. Szálasi uralma 1944. október – 1945. május* (Budapest: Makkabi 2003). 76. Quoted together with the spelling mistakes of the original.
362 See more in Wendy Lower, "Distant Encounter. An Auschwitz Survivor in the College Classroom," in *Approaching and Auschwitz Survivor. Holocaust Testimony and its Transformation*, ed., Jürgen Mattheus, 95–117 (Oxford: Oxford University Press, 2010).
363 Dori Laub: "An Event Without a Witness. Truth, Testimony and Survival," in *Testimony. Crises of Witnessing on Literature, Psychoanalysis and History*, ed., Soshana Felman and Dori Laub (New York: Routledge, 1992), 82.

tim.³⁶⁴ After this much time the narration was void of emotion, it was rather analytical and descriptive. When I showed them an earlier publication of mine that was based on the interviews I made with them,³⁶⁵ they stepped up as the owners of the memory and corrected their earlier statements in the interview because "it was not what they had said."³⁶⁶ They were reluctant to accept the uncertainty in identifying Dely as the perpetrator of the murders, and also whether Dely had been wearing an Arrow Cross armband or even a uniform. The testimonies were necessarily contradictory but the surviviors interpreted unveiling these contradictions as if this process had framed them as unreliable witnesses. They centered their identity on the concept of authentic witnessing.

Recently, scholarly literature has started to investigate the question of what will happen when the survivors die. Who will be able to authenticate a memory of an event? Will we lose the memory together with the survivors? Is a memory like a ring that can be accidentally lost? In this chapter, I analyze the different forms and practices of memorialization of the massacre in Csengery 64.

9.3 The missing dialogic collective memory

During the interviews, the survivors perceived the memory of the massacre as something that can be lost.

> I don't know much about the story of Csengery 64, I'm the last member of my family from the Holocaust generation.³⁶⁷
> I'm the only one alive from the whole story. [...] And I would like to tell my daughter and my grandchild that this was an unjust thing, and I want to give it some legal consideration whether, for instance, the perpetrator's and the victim's reaction could be measured with the same measurement.³⁶⁸

---

364 On silence, see Ronit Lentin, "Expected to Live. Women Shoah Survivors' Testimonial Silence," *Women's Studies International Forum* 23.6 (2001): 689–700.
365 Pető Andrea: "Privatised Memory? The Story of Erecting of the First 'Private' Holocaust Memorial in Budapest," in *Memory and Narrating Mass Repression*, ed., Nanci Adler, Mary Chamberlaine and Leyla Neyzi, 157–175 (New Brunswick, N.J: Transaction, 2009).
366 On this common conflict, see Katherine Borland: "'That's not What I Said.' Interpretative Conflict in Oral Narrative Research," in *The Oral History Reader*, ed., Robert Perks and Alistair Thomson, 310–321 (London: Routledge, 1998).
367 Miklós Bodor's personal letter.
368 Interview, March 3, 2005.

The survivors had every reason to trust that the Hungarian Jewish Congregation would play an active role in the shaping of memorialization practices in a way that they would feel represented, but they were bitterly disappointed. In 1990, when the Memorial Tree was created in the courtyard of the Dohány Street Great Synagogue, a silver "memory leaf" cost $125, a huge sum of money for Eastern European pockets at the time.[369] Furthermore the text of the commemorative plaque that was installed on the synagogue's wall was worded in the antifascist tradition: instead of Jewish victims it commemorated the liberating Soviet troops.[370] The congregation did nothing to protect the Csengery Street plaque, which caused bitterness among the survivors:

> And when the old man died [...] then of course Landeszmann came.[371] Then I asked Landeszmann what the congregation would do for the memory plaque in Csengery 64, so it could stay on the wall. But this was a long time ago, twenty years ago maybe. And then Landeszmann said with immense cynicism that there could be a plaque in every house. And then I told him because we were in such a relationship that I could tell him: "You know what? Shame on you!" This was all I could say. How could that be the official stance?[372]
>
> It was the fiftieth anniversary of the Holocaust. [...] And then there was nothing in the Új Élet. I mean the October 15 Új Élet. "Madame Györgyi is looking for companion" and such [were published]. I got really angry and I wrote to Kardos.[373] And I wrote that if Új Élet does not commemorate this tragedy in Budapest then how we could expect any other newspaper to remember it. And I sent the plaque and I sent the story and truly, truly shame on all of them. And then they published [...] the story of the two plaques, the one that was ours that I sent and the other was the one erected at the Military History Museum for Hungarian gendarme. And the two were put next to each other [in the paper].[374]

The exchange of memories is a key feature of community formation. It is about sharing stories through which the individual transmits their experiences in a way that seems intelligible to others. The process entails certain dangers, because if the audience cannot connect to the framework in which the experience is narrat-

---

[369] Tim Cole, *Holocaust City. The Making of a Jewish Ghetto* (London/ New York: Routledge, 2003). 241.
[370] See the memorial plaque erected on the Budapest Ghetto's wall in 1985. (Ibid., 227.)
[371] György Landeszmann, former chief rabbi of Budapest.
[372] Interview, March 3, 2005.
[373] Péter Kardos chief rabbi, the main editor of *Új Élet*, the Hungarian Jewish Congregation's bulletin.
[374] Interview, March 3, 2005

ed, they cannot identify with the memory either.[375] This meaning-making process is culturally determined and culture can never encompass all individual experiences. Cultural memory is selective, convergent, repetitive and recyclable.[376]

About the Csengery Street case the victims and the perpetrators created two, separate frameworks of interpretation which do not diverge or meet. Due to these two parallel memory cultures in his son's memory, Nándor Szamocseta became a rescuer, and in the survivors' memory Róbert Tenczer allegedly died to protect his mother.[377]

To help understand the dynamics of memory, Jan Assmann's distinction between "storage memory" (*Speichergedächtnis*) and "functional memory" (*Funktionsgedächtnis*) is useful.[378] Storage memory contains all past information unsystematically, from which functional memory selects and activates memories in accordance with socially determined frameworks. Therefore, cultural memory is a form of functional memory. In the case of Csengery Street, the structure and discourse of the people's tribunals was that framework which determined the process and also what memories were selected, narrated and made accessible from the memory storage. The narratives necessarily converged during the court process and the story became increasingly standardized through repetitions that took place on various scenes such as the trials, conversations in the corridor, family dinners, etc. Memory in Csengery Street was shaped by the People's Tribunals' press releases and other relevant articles in the press, the trials' participants' oral accounts, and the survivors' conversations. Paradoxically, the memory plaque as the first step of memorialization also contributed to forgetting, because it authenticated a list of names while there were victims who were not included on it.

The transmission of memory to those who were not present is one of the hardest tasks, especially in the case of traumatic memories. Partly, this is because there are no relevant frames within which the information could be recalled and narrated, and also because the process is affected by the space of remembrance. The procedural errors of the trials and the resentment against the People's Tribunals left their marks on the Csengery Street memory transmission process. After 1945, Jews in Hungary remained hurt, traumatized and silenced as

---

[375] Jan Assmann, *Das Kulturelle Gedächtnis: Schrift, Erinnerung und Politische Identität in frühen Hochkulturen* (Münich: C.H. Beck, 1992).
[376] Ann Rigney, "Plenitude, Scarcity, and the Circulation of Cultural Memory," *Journal of European Studies* 35.1 (2005): 16.
[377] Interviews with Nándor Szamocseta and Edit Rosenberg.
[378] Jan Assmann: *Das Kulturelle Gedächtnis: Schrift, Erinnerung und Politische Identität in frühen Hochkulturen* (Münich: C.H. Beck, 1992).

survivors found the legal system slow, sloppy and selective, while the perpetrators became convinced that they were victims of an unjust procedure and of "Stalinist Justizmord." With the collapse of Communism in 1989, the competing versions of the history of the People's Tribunals resurfaced and their legitimacy was once again questioned and muted.

This has a major importance as far as the formation of memory is concerned. Family was a crucial institution for transferring values during the period of Communism as it provided an interpretative frame which resisted both public history and more importantly, personal first-hand experiences.[379] "Family" is one of the most controversial and complex concepts, as it is a place where different power relations are constructed, acted out and performed in emotional communities. As Paul Thompson states, stories created and circulated in families about the past are signposts of remembrance and identity.[380] Family is also considered a "double wall" filtering out undesirable events and building an exterior wall, while maintaining internal cohesion.[381] The most decisive and influential unit in political socialization in politically divided communities is the family. It is the closest emotional bond that here influenced how individuals processed new, first-hand information about the controversial activity of the People's Tribunals (1945-1950). It also helped served as a "double glass" as its members saw what they wanted to see. As Chamberlain and Leydesdorff point out:

> Memories of the family (and family memories) play an important part in our perception of ourselves and others, and necessarily are implicated in the negotiations any one individual will make between cultural spheres and in the process of accommodating a new personal stability.[382]

As a result, two parellel memory cultures were formed about the same event. In the long run, the key question is whether the parallel collective memories are ca-

---

[379] See interviews with participants in the research project on People's Tribunals in Andrea Pető, "Contacting Histories: Impacts of Reading Holocaust Testimonies in Hungary," in *Jewish Studies at CEU*, ed., András Kovács, Michael Miller, and Carsten Wilke, 59–73 (Budapest: IX. Jewish Studies Project, 2020).
[380] Paul Thomson, "Family Myth, Models, and Denial in the Shaping of Individual Life Paths," in *Between Generations. Family Models, Myths, and Memories* ed., Daniel Berteux, and Paul Thomson (Oxford: Oxford University Press, 1993), 36.
[381] Katharina von Kellenbach, "Vanishing Acts: Perpetrators in Postwar Germany," *Holocaust and Genocide Studies* 17. 2 (2003): 305–329.
[382] Mary Chamberlain, Selma, Leydesdorff, "Transnational Families: Memories and Narratives," *Global Networks* 4.3 (2004): 231.

pable of interaction; in other words, will they be able to interact with other memories while acknowledging the other's framework of memory.

In the case of Csengery Street, memorialization was further complicated by the fact that it is about the memory of a site, which is a site of memory. The survivors returned to the house and lived side by side with those who allegedly robbed them or who used the apartments and belongings (undergarments, gowns, tea sets) of the victims. This helped the process of memorialization because the "site of memory" of the Budapest apartment building existed, and later the past was also present due to the memory plaque. The fact that the massacre happened in a house which survived the war intact helped structure and activate memory.

One of my book's aims is to commemorate the survivors who did and continue to do everything to prevent forgetting, as they were the ones who erected the plaque and today still follow press and research publications about October 15, and participate in "survivor conversations" in the Holocaust Memorial Center. Their testimonies are characterized by their desire to explain the past from the present. Since the events and especially during the 1990s they got access to a lot of new information. Magda Kun for instance in her memoir of the Dely case primarily connects the massacre to the Germans in order to prove that it was not a simple robbery. She learned later that on October 15, 1944 the Germans emptied several yellow star houses in order to break alleged Jewish resistance or in order to mobilize Jews to dig defense trenches in preparation for the inevitable approach of the battle for Budapest.[383]

Following Koselleck, Gábor Gyáni considers that "historical research lets past experiences take only one particular and no other discursive form."[384] It is characteristic of the Dely case that the survivors tried to influence the language used to talk about the case. Lichter appropriated the prevalent anti-fascist discourse to plead with the People's Tribunal. The memory plaque was worded within the same framework. However, the framework constantly changed as newer actors continued to contribute to the process of memorialization. The political changes during the past one and a half decades increased and strengthened fear. Still, the survivors not only practiced and stimulated memorialization by actively protecting the plaque and telling the story in their own family, but

---

383 Szita Szabolcs, *Halálerőd. A munkaszolgálat és a hadimunka történetéhez 1944–1945*, (Budapest: Kossuth, 1989).
384 Gyáni Gábor, "Történelmi esemény és struktúra. Kapcsolatuk ellentmondásossága," *Történelmi Szemle* 2 (2011): 145–162, 149.

some of them even practiced historiography: besides giving interviews, Magda Kun wrote her own reading of their story too.[385]

The survivors' goal was to create a narrative, which moves beyond the specific historical experiences of Jewry and contributes to drawing a more universal human moral conclusion. The expectations of those who stayed in Budapest and did not emmigrate to Israel failed several times. Neither the Hungarian Jewish Congregation, nor the municipal district, neither the anti-fascist Communist discourse, nor the historians, neither the Holocaust memory center nor especially not the actors of the recent memory turn were interested.

Are the survivors "agents of history"? The survivors of the Csengery Street massacre had a certain agency when they could reformulate and determine the frameworks of memory: they looked at the events as through their own kaleidoscope that emphasizes certain parts of the story and ignores or silences others, and the kaleidoscope turned in sync with political changes.

9.4 Csengery Street 64: A memorial or a monument?

Is the Csengery plaque a memorial or a monument? Arthur C. Danto holds that memorials are "meditation[s] in stone" that "ritualize remembrance" while monuments make "victories and conquests perpetually present." [386] The memorial "marks the reality of ends" and it lets us honor the dead after a completed grieving process. This is what happened in Csengery Street with the installation of the commemorative plaque. But what is the relationship between the plaque and the wider community? A memorial can turn into a monument if it can fulfill three functions for the living: 1. it acknowledges the importance of death and destruction and considers it a sacrifice; 2. claims that the sacrifice was not in vain, that there is a collective gain; 3. the victim becomes part of the collective through the logic of sacrifice.[387] By this definition the Csengery Street plaque serves as a memorial that can never turn into a monument despite the hopes of the survivors. Its text referring to the anti-fascist discourse, "your sacrifice shows us the way towards building a free, happy Hungary," applies a faulty logic. According to Freud, sacrifice is never individual, as it is the individual that is sacrificed

---

[385] Kun Magda, *Szálasi árnyékában* (np: Manuscript, 2007).
[386] Michael Rowlands, "Remembering to Forget. Sublimation as Sacrifice in War Memorials," in *The Art of Forgetting*, ed., Adrian Forty and Susanne Küchler (Oxford/New York: Berg, 1999): 130.
[387] Ibid., 144.

for the community. But what community? Hungarians? Jews? Hungarian Jews? After the Second World War the horrid massacre was explained as "the Arrow Cross' attempt to break down Jewish resistance," but after 1945 when Zionism became an ideological enemy, the Hungarian Communist Party did not want a story about Jewish resistance anymore. Moreover, because of its religious connotations the concept of "sacrifice" was not favored by the atheist Communist regime either.[388]

There was one period that the People's Tribunal did not examine during the Dely trial: the months between the November deportations and the return of the lucky few among the tenants. Budapest was already encircled by the Red Army on 25 December and liberated on 13 February. We have very little information about that period as the court did not ask any questions about this period because it found it to be irrelevant.

Luisa Passerini warned that under the effects of the Cold War a very different perception of the relationship between memory and history developed in the West and within the countries of the former Soviet bloc. While in the West remembrance was considered as spontaneous and non-reflective, in the former socialist countries, where official historiography had no space for critical reflection, unofficial memory opened the space for critical thinking.[389] "Official" historiography's position about this period hardly changed till the illiberal memory turn in the 2000s. This also means that alternative memories are shaped against and not in dialogue with each other. During the past years, several literary works were published in Hungarian about perpetrators.[390] One cannot but wonder what the effect of such books could be in a country where the government's politics is not only against the acknowledgement of the past but supports historical revisionism.

---

[388] Kovács András, "Jews and Jewishness in Post-war Hungary," *Quest. Issues in Contemporary History. Journal of the Fondazione CDEC* 1 (2010). Http://www.quest-cdecjournal.it/focus.php?id=192, accessed January 8, 2012.

[389] Luisa Passerini, "Memories of Resistance, Resistance of Memory," in *European Memories of the Second World War*, ed., Helmut Peitsch, Charles Burdett, and Claire Gorrara (New York/ Oxford: Berghahn Books, 1999), 288–296, 289.

[390] Zoltán Gábor, *Orgia* (Budapest: Libri, 2016), Jonathan Littell, *The Kindly Ones: A Novel* (New York, Harper., 2009), Sacha Batthányi, *És nekem mi közöm ehhez* (Budapest: Helikon, 2016).

10 Conclusion

Jürgen Habermas in his seminal essay "On How Postwar Germany Has Faced Its Recent Past" uses Hermann Lübbe's concept of "communicative silencing" *(kommunikatives Beschweigen)*. In Habermas' definition, communicative silencing is "meant to describe a situation in which a tacitly acknowledged moral asymmetry between offender and victim is kept tactfully hidden beneath the surface of proceedings that pretend to business as usual."[391] Lübbe's example was the following: in the 1950s a freshly returned German immigrant became the rector of a West German university, the exact same university from where he was expelled in 1933, and where he had to work together again with those silent colleagues who had opportunistically blended in after 1933. In the Hungarian case "communicative silencing" – as well as its four phases that Habermas identified in order to understand the post-war justice process in East and West German comparison – took place within one country. The anti-fascist rhetoric imported by the Soviet occupiers, as mentioned in the chapter on the People's Tribunals, was received with much reluctance by the survivors who nevertheless adopted it, and this fundamentally influenced the way the recent past was remembered and narrated. After 1989, the returning Hungarian immigrants of 1945 and 1956 further strengthened the anti-Communist interpretative framework, while the immigrant German intellectuals returning after 1945 were anti-fascist social democrats or leftists.[392]

"Communicative silencing" is also an applicable concept in the Hungarian case because it entails the society's pillarization, which in Hungarian society formed along the lines of victim versus perpetrator, and was manifested in rejection versus (critical) acceptance of the People's Tribunals' process. The questioning of the tribunals' legitimacy became a constitutive element of right-wing identity politics, and it remained so as families constructed it, sustained it and passed their version of these past events down.[393]

My book examines the intersection of law, justice and social peace. Using the case of Austria, Anton Pelinka showed that the sidelining of law and justice in

---

[391] Jürgen Habermas, "On How Postwar Germany Has Faced Its Recent Past," *Common Knowledge* 5.2 (1996): 1–13, 6.
[392] On the Netherlands, see Jolande Withuis, "Das Kriegstrauma in den Niederlanden," in *Europapolitik seit 1945. Die Niederlande und Deutschland im Vergleich*, ed., Friso Wielenga and Loek Geereadts (Jahrbuch des Zentrums für Niederlande-Studien, 15.), 153–161 (Münster: Aschendorf, 2004).
[393] For more, see Mary Fulbrook, *German National Identity after the Holocaust* (Cambridge, UK: Polity Press, 1999).

exchange for social peace could contribute to short-term reconciliation, but in the long run social reconciliation would suffer.[394] The Hungarian case differs from the Austrian in so far as Hungarian state rhetoric emphasized the responsibility of war criminals and the crimes were publicized – and that did not contribute to reconciliation either.

There are two standpoints concerning the impact of court trials. Hannah Arendt considered trials to have but one task, to find out the truth in the case of each distinct crime.[395] Lawrence Douglas holds that court trials are "didactic trials" that have to prove the normative working of law not independently from the social context of the trial. According to Douglas the "didactic trial" allows space for victims and survivors to construct memories through testimonies, but at the same time it acts as a history class too.[396] On the one hand, survivors have the right to know who committed what against them; on the other hand stories are requisites of healing and reconciliation. Furthermore, transparent discussions about the past contribute to the building of a strong democratic culture.

In the Dely–Szamocseta case, discussions about the past happened in a controversial way and thus did not serve reconciliation. Neither the court testimonies nor oral history interviews revealed who did what when, but this painful hiatus could have been compensated for by a discerning court decision or by public recognition. But in post-war Hungary no other frame was available for public dialogue but the legal, which was necessarily overburdened by sometimes conflicting expectations. Therefore, the practice and process of democracy was not established, instead rival memory cultures were silenced and rendered taboo. Piroska Dely stood in front of the court as a solitary perpetrator, and, relatedly, the court process did not strive to understand the deeper structural reasons behind Hungarian perpetrators, especially female perpetrators.[397]

What could a trial accomplish among those frameworks and limitations? The success of legal stories depends on their social acceptance – if legal frameworks fail, they fail socially.[398] Dely's legal story is also a failed story. Despite all their

---

394 Anton Pelinka, "Justice, Truth and Peace," in *Justice and Memory. Confronting Traumatic Pasts. An International Comparison*, ed., Ruth Wodak and Gertraud Auer Borea, 49–65 (Vienna: Passen, 2009).
395 Hannah Arendt, *Eichmann in Jerusalem. A Report on the Banality of Evil* (London/New York: Penguin Books/Viking Press, 1994).
396 Lawrence Douglas, "The Didactic Trial. Filtering History and Memory in the Courtroom," *European Review* 14.4 (2006): 513–522.
397 For more, see Andrea Pető, *Invisible Women in the Arrow Cross Party* (London: Palgrave Macmillan, 2020).
398 Devin O. Pendas, *The Frankfurt Auschwitz Trial, 1963–1965. Genocide, History and the Limits of Law* (New York: Cambridge University Press, 2006), 301–302.

efforts, a "simple" legal sentence could not satisfy the survivor's desire for justice. They initiated the Szamocseta-trial too, but as far as political, emotional or material compensations are concerned it did not provide a straightforward solution either. Although the survivors played an active role in retribution, they were not at all satisfied with the results.

The period after 1945 was characterized by forgetting and silencing, which led to selective invisibility. The history of the Csengery Street massacre remained an enigma: it is still unknown who was killed and who was deported, and no one knows where the victims were buried. The victims' relatives did not apply for death certificates until the 1970s, and then they did so only because they needed them for administrative purposes.[399] Lastly in 2004 the survivors and relatives found out that the victims were probably buried in the Kerepesi Cemetery's Parcel of Martyrs, that is parcel 5c. In 1962, the daughter of a victim requested an official transcript of the people's tribunals' trial documents to prove that her relative was a "victim," but her request was rejected by the Ministry of Internal Affairs. At the end in 1972 she received a certificate which stated that her relative participated in the "resistance" and SS soldiers (not the Arrow Cross!) sought weapons in the Csengery Street house. The official certificate that a dutiful clerk at the Ministry of Justice prepared contained that section of Dely's testimony in which she claimed that "the soldiers gathered a whole basketful of firearms" in the house.[400] The lie with which Dely wanted to convince the court that she followed orders gave legitimacy to the victims' burial in the Parcel of Martyrs. Dely's testimony created a Csengery Street "resistance group," a set of heroic anti-fascists out of mercilessly and senselessly slaughtered and robbed civilians.

The process of remembrance is always hard and painful, and it is determined by systems of power. In times when cultural codes are uncertain remembrance becomes even more challenging: previous political frameworks weaken or disappear, and earlier systems of reference lose their meaning. The family remains the only framework of memory which offers some sort of autonomous stability. In the case of Csengery Street, "private memories" remained the only accessible forms of memory. The People's Tribunals worked slowly and incorrectly, the Jewish Congregation was not interested in the case, journalists were superficial and hasty, and historians aimed at simplification. Thus far.

In order to understand the complexity of the history of Csengery Street, I suggest using the distinction between memory and remembrance. Memory marks a

---

[399] Interview, March 3, 2005.
[400] BFL 2442/1947. 65.

deliberate and selective interpretation of the past that yields to the future, while remembrance is an inescapable process, which evokes past events without conscious selection. The construction of the historical canon should encompass both; both should be part of it. With a sole focus on "memory," that is on particular historical facts, events, and experiences, it is not possible to shake off the traditional positivist epistemology of "history" which only allows for one, "definite" interpretation of the "truth."

German research exposed a marked tendency in the intergenerational memory process. The third generation, i.e. the grandchildren interpreted their parents' and grandparents' lives in the Third Reich within the frameworks of resistance and suffering.[401] Hungarian memory follows a similar route. Jewish Hungarian citizens were silent after 1945 because they were not included in the anti-fascist canon, while the perpetrators were convinced – as the Szamocseta-monologue evidenced – that they had fallen victim to the injustice of a Stalinist type people's court system. After the collapse of Communism, the competition between antagonistic interpretations about Second World War events in Hungary commenced, including the night of October 15, 1944 in Budapest's Csengery Street 64.[402]

Despite his immense resourcefulness and committed struggle, Andor Lichter could not really influence how the perpetrators were thinking about their role and responsibility. Not even with his masterfully maneuvering amidst the otherwise chaotic operation of the post-war justice. Lichter trusted the justness of law and that the People's Tribunal would administer justice – if urged to. Survivors slowly leave, and the task remains to understand how this polarized memory culture was born. The survivors had a distinct sense of what was good and bad in the last months of the war, but the clarity of their discernment fades through mediation.

"Transitional justice is the legal and administrative process carried out after a political transition, for the purpose of addressing the wrongdoings of the previous regime."[403] The new system decides what it considers unjust, how it punishes the culprits, what counts as suffering and how to compensate the victims. After the Second World War in Hungary just like in every European country, jus-

---

[401] Harald Welzer, Sabine Moller, and Karoline Tschuggnall, *"Opa war kein Nazi." Nationalsozialismus und Holocaust im Familiengedächtnis* (Frankfurt: Fischer Verlag, 2002).

[402] For a Croatian example, see Mila Dragojevic and Vjeran Pavlakovic "Local Memories of Wartime Violence: Commemorating World War Two," *Gospić* 8.1 (2016): 66–87.

[403] Jon Elster, "Memory and Transitional Justice." Unpublished paper prepared for the "Memory of war" workshop, MIT January 2003:1, Http://web.mit.edu/rpeters/papers/elster_memory.pdf.

tice was urgent and politically defined. In this volume, I demonstrate that in order to understand the motivations, interests and conduct of the actors we need to deploy a multifocal lens, while the analysis of emotions can be an additional asset in understanding this common heritage.

Piroska Dely's case is unique but not singular. For instance, there are similarities between Dely's Teople's tribunal case and Mrs. Gyula László's case. Mrs. László was the Budapest ninth district Arrow Cross section leader who raided and plundered in a green shirt and with an armband. On first being tried Mrs. László was sentenced to death, later the verdict was changed to life imprisonment, which in 1948 was again changed to ten years imprisonment. Her daughter, who actively participated in Arrow Cross Party recruitment and wrote reports on social affairs (judging which deprived persons were truly worthy of support) disappeared from the internment camp and the police could not find her at her state of residence either. She lived undisturbed in Debrecen where she died on August 9, 1950. However, three years later she was still wanted by the police.[404] Possibly if Dely had been more cautious and had not returned to the crime scene she could also have avoided the process. On the other hand, unlike Dely, Mrs. László had a paid lawyer and there was no Andor Lichter-like figure in the case's background. We could also compare Dely's case to Géza Lőrinczi's who was indicted for an eerily similar case: for participation in a raid and the forcible taking away of Jews on October 15, 1944. Lőrinczi was at first sentenced to death on October 19, 1945. However, he had a clever and committed sister who brought fake witnesses and achieved a much lighter sentence of five years imprisonment. Supposedly she declared, "[f]or a hundred dollars I can save anyone even from the gallows."[405]

Collective memory is a controversial analytical category but it can be instructive when examining the way a country faces its past.[406] In West Germany the justice system blamed all crimes on a small group, the Nazi party elite, and under the Cold War circumstances the search for further perpetrators hardly progressed. Thus, for West Germans the war became an "accident, tragic fate, nat-

---

404 ÁBTL V 102304.
405 MOL I-E-17. On April 25, 1946, the Népszava published an article on the case, which drew the attention of the Ministry of Justice's section on People's Tribunals.
406 On stories of suffering, see Natan Sznaider, "Suffering as a Universal Frame for Understanding Memory Politics," in *Clashes in European Memory. The Case of Communist Repression and the Holocaust*, ed., Muriel Blaive, Christian Gerbel and Thomas Lindenberger, 239–255 (Innsbruck/Vienna/Bozen, Studienverlag, 2011).

ural disaster."[407] Memory is foundational for communities: through their shared stories of suffering, people construct a common identity. West German identity was based on the idea and practice of *Lastenausgleich*, the common sacrifice during the Second World War that requires an equivalent compensation. Their collective memory represented a morally acceptable community, which created a sense of belonging. The myth of the *Stunde Null*, which in the post-war period (and especially today) looked dubious, in the long run opened up space for democratization, and the possibility of slowly coming to terms with the past. In the meantime, in France the "spontaneous" justice executed by the government in exile and the resistance primarily hit collaborating women. The mythic cleansing of the France that was "in bed" with the Germans restored male power. While Maurice Papon and other Vichy officials were honored members of French society, women, who were less culpable but physically and socially more vulnerable, were stigmatized, which contributed to the development of the "Vichy syndrome."[408]

Hungary took a different route. Although the people's tribunals identified "Arrow Cross people" and punished them for their crimes, because of the controversial operation of the People's Tribunals' (as analyzed in this book) and the Soviet occupation, it was not perceived as "justice." As a result after the postwar justice process, Hungarian society was just as divided as beforehand, with further sources of conflicts added to existing ones, such as collaboration with the Soviets.[409] It is a miracle that during the revolution of 1956, which was a civil war, even more blood was not spilt when all the tensions within Hungarian society exploded.[410]

According to Michael Rothberg's theoretical concept of "multidimensional memory," memories are framed not as competitive phenomena in a closed public arena but rather are "subject to ongoing negotiation, cross-referencing and borrowing."[411] Rothberg quotes Richard Terdiman: "[M]emory is the past made

---

[407] Sabine Behrenbeck is quoted in Michael L. Hughes, "'Through No Fault of Our Own.' West Germans Remember Their War Losses," *German History* 2 (2000): 209.

[408] Alison M. Moore, "History, Memory and Trauma in Photography of the Tondues. Visuality of the Vichy Past through the Silent Images of Women," *Gender and History* 5 (2005): 657–681.

[409] For more, see Andrea Pető and Patricia Chiantera-Stutte, "Populist Use of Memory and Constitutionalism. Two Comments," *German Law Journal* 2 (2005): 165–175. http://www.germanlawjournal.com/article.php?id=564

[410] On the 1956 revolution, see János M. Rainer, *Imre Nagy. A Biography* (London/New York: Tauris, 2009).

[411] Michael Rothberg, *Multidirectional Memory. Remembering the Holocaust in the Age of Decolonisation* (Stanford, CA: Stanford University Press, 2009), 3.

present,"[412] with which he emphasizes the importance of temporality as well as agency, for according to him memory is "made." This normative intentionality informs his definition of the concept of "multidirectional memory" too: "Memories are not owned by groups – nor groups 'owned' by memories."[413] This might be the case in academic discussion but, as demonstrated by this book, in people's lives and discourses the situation is different as certain memories have memory owners.

"Welcome to the memory industry!" thus commences Kerwin Lee Klein's article in which he scrutinizes the concept of memory.[414] Klein agrees with Charles Maier that "memory appeals to us because it lends itself to the articulation of ethnoracial nationalisms that turn away from the cosmopolitan discourses of history."[415] According to Klein, memory research is a response to the challenge of a postmodernism that lost its intellectual radicalism, this is why the vocabulary of "memory industry" is a quasi-religious vocabulary: trauma, grief, healing, testimony, identity.[416] This book offered an introduction to life stories of survivors and perpetrators who were using, adapting and shaping this vocabulary. The actions and activity of Lichter were in line with the suggestion by Hartman that the proper treatment of extremes requires an extreme representation.[417] But in the case of Csengery 64, Lichter's private commemoration – the erection of the first Holocaust plaque in Budapest – proved insufficient to prevent the construction of a divided and dichotomized memory of the massacre. He believed that after the war justice could be done by means of the available legal instruments, such as the People's Court. That this turned out to be an illusion is not his fault. It is now our responsibility to understand the consequences of a lack of consensual "sites of remembering" for Holocaust victims. It is high time to do so because we need to think about alternative forms of commemoration – ones that last longer than the lifespan of survivors' "private memories" and that indicate what was "right" and what was "wrong" during the fateful final years of World War Two in Hungary. The present illiberal turn in memory politics also calls for 'extreme' innovative approaches in order to rethink structural causes of selective forgetting.

---

412 Ibid., 3.
413 Ibid., 5.
414 Kerwin Lee Klein, "On the Emergence of Memory in Historical Discourse," *Representations* 69 (2000): 127–150.
415 Ibid.,143.
416 Ibid., 145.
417 Geoffrey Hartman, *The Longest Shadow: The Aftermath of the Holocaust* (Bloomington: Indiana University Press, 1996), 157.

References

Ádám, Pál István. *Budapest Building Managers and the Holocaust in Hungary*. London: Palgrave, 2017.

Albrich, Thomas, Winfried R Garscha, and Martin Polaschek, ed. *Holocaust und Kriegsverbrechen vor Gericht. Der Fall Österreich*. Innsbruck/Vienna/Bozen: Studienverlag, 2006.

Aleksiun, Natalia. "Intimate Violence: Jewish Testimonies on Victims and Perpetrators in Eastern Galicia." *Holocaust Studies* 1-2.23 (2017): 17–33. DOI: 10.1080/17504902.2016.1209833

Aleksiun, Natalia. "Organizing for Justice: Jewish Leadership in Poland and the Trial of the Nazi War Criminals at Nuremberg." In *Beyond Camps and Forced Labour. Current International Research on Survivors of Nazi Persecution*, edited by Johannes-Dieter Steinert and Inge Weber-Newth. Osnabruck, Germany: Secolo, 2006.

Arendt, Hannah. *Eichmann in Jerusalem. A Report on the Banality of Evil*. London/New York: Penguin Classics, 2006.

Assmann, Jan. *Das Kulturelle Gedächtnis: Schrift, Erinnerung und Politische Identität in frühen Hochkulturen*. Munich: Verlag C.H. Beck. 1992.

Auslander, Leora. "Coming Home? Jews in Postwar Paris." *Journal of Contemporary History* 40.2 (2005): 237–259.

Balla, Erzsébet. *József körút 79. Dokumentum-regény a pesti Holocaustról*. Tel-Aviv: Új Kelet, 1974.

Barna, Ildikó, and Andrea Pető. *Political Justice in Post War Budapest*. Budapest: CEU Press, 2015.

Bar-On, Dan. *Legacy of Silence. Encounters with Children of the Third Reich*. Cambridge, Mass.: Harvard University Press, 1989.

Batthányi, Sacha. *És nekem mi közöm ehhez*, Budapest: Helikon, 2016.

Bauer, Yehuda. *Flight and Rescue*. New York: Random House, 1970.

Bernstein, Richard J. *Hannah Arendt and the Jewish Question*. Cambridge: Polity Press, 1996.

Bitunjac, Martina. *Verwicklung. Beteiligung. Unrecht. Frauen und die Ustaša-Bewegung* [Involvement, Participation, Injustice. Women in the Ustasha Movement]. Berlin: Duncker&Humblot, 2018.

Bloxham, Donald. *Genocide on Trial. War Crimes Trials and the Formation of Holocaust History and Memory*. Oxford: Oxford University Press, 2001.

Booth, W. James. "The Unforgotten. Memories of Justice." *The American Political Science Review* 4 (2001): 777–791.

Borland, Katherine. "That's not What I Said." Interpretative Conflict in Oral Narrative Research. In *The Oral History Reader*, edited by Robert Perks and Alistair Thomson. London: Routledge, 1998.

Braham, Randolph. Rescue Operations in Hungary: Myths and Realities, *East European Quarterly* 38.2 (2004): 173–203.

Braham, Randolph L. and Attila Pók, ed. *The Holocaust in Hungary. Fifty Years Later*. New York: Columbia University Press, 1997.

Braham, Randolph L.. *Politics of Genocide: The Holocaust in Hungary*. Detroit: Wayne State University Press, 2000.

Browning, Christopher R.. *Ordinary Men. Reserve Police Battalion 101 and the Final Solution in Poland.* New York: HarperCollins, 1992.

Burke, Peter. *Eyewitnessing. The Uses of Images as Historical Evidence.* London: Reaktion Press, 2001.

Cesarini, David, ed. *Genocide and Rescue. The Holocaust in Hungary.* London/New York: Berg, 1997.

Chamberlain, Mary, and Selma Leydesdorff. "Transnational Families: Memories and Narratives." *Global Networks* 4.3 (2004): 227–241.

Cohen, Asher. *The Halutz Resistance in Hungary 1942–1944.* Boulder CO: East European Monographs, 1986.

Cole, Tim. "Constructing the 'Jew.' Writing the Holocaust. Hungary 1920–1945," *Patterns of Prejudice* 33.3 (1999): 19–27.

Cole, Tim. *Holocaust City. The Making of a Jewish Ghetto.* London: Routledge, 2003.

Connerton, Paul. "Seven Types of Forgetting." *Memory Studies* 1.1 (2008): 60–61.

Dagnino, Jorge, Matthew Feldman, and Paul Stocker, ed. *The "New Man" in Radical Right Ideology and Practice, 1919-1945.* London: Bloomsbury 2018.

Diner, Dan and Joel Golb. "Source on Guilt Discourse and Other Narratives: Epistemological Observations regarding the Holocaust." *History and Memory* 9.1-2 (1997): 301–320.

Dolapchiev, Nikola. "Law and Human Rights in Bulgaria." *International Affairs* 29.1 (1953): 59–68.

Dondi, Mirco. *La lunga liberazione. Giustizia e violenza nel dopoguerra italiano.* Rome: Riuniti, 2004.

Douglas, Lawrence. *The Memory Judgement. Making Law and History in the Trials of the Holocaust.* New Haven/London: Yale University Press, 2001.

Douglas, Lawrence. "The Didactic Trial. Filtering History and Memory in the Courtroom." *European Review* 14.4 (2006): 513–522.

Dragojevic, Mila and Vjeran Pavlakovic. "Local Memories of Wartime Violence: Commemorating World War Two." *Gospić, suvremene TEME* 8.1 (2016): 66–87.

Elster, Jon. "Memory and Transitional Justice." Unpublished paper. Prepared for the "Memory of war" workshop, MIT January 2003. Http://web.mit.edu/rpeters/papers/elster_memory.pdf.

Engel, David. *Historians of the Jews and the Holocaust.* Stanford: Stanford University Press, 2010.

Érdi-Krausz, György. "Márványtábla a kapu alatt." *Terézváros* (May-June, 2004).

Eschenbach, Insa. "Gespaltene Frauenbilder: Geschlechterdramatugien im juristischen Diskurs ostdeutscher Gerichte." In *"Bestien" und "Befehlsempfänger". Frauen und Männer in NS-Prozessen nach 1945,* edited by Ulrike Weckel and Edgar Wolfrum. Göttingen: Vandenhoeck & Ruprecht, 2003.

Ezekiel, Raphael S.. *The Racist Mind. Portraits of American Neo-Nazis and Klansmen.* New York: Viking, 1995.

Felman, Shoshana. "Theater of Justice. Arendt in Jerusalem, the Eichmann Trial, and the Redefinition of Legal Meaning in the Wake of the Holocaust." *Critical Inquiry* 27.2 (2007): 201–238.

Frei, Norbert, Dirk van Laak, and Michael Stolleis, ed. *Geschichte vor Gericht. Historiker, Richter und die Suche nach Gerechtigkeit.* München, Beck, 2000,

Friedländer, Saul. "History, Memory and the Historian. Dilemmas and Responsabilities." *New German Critique* 80 (Spring-Summer, 2000): 3–15.
Friedländer, Saul. *Memory, History, and the Extermination of the Jews of Europe.* Bloomington: Indiana University Press, 1993.
Frojimovics, Kinga. "Different Interprerations of Reconstructions. The AJDC and the WJC in Hungary after the Holocaust." In *The Jews Are Coming Back. The Return of the Jews to Their Countries of Origin after WWII*, edited by David Bankier. Jerusalem: Yad Vashem, 2005.
Frydel, Tomasz. "The Pazifizierungsaktion as a Catalyst of Anti-Jewish Violence. A Study in the Social Dynamics of Fear." In *The Holocaust and European Societies, The Holocaust and its Contexts*, edited by Frank Bajohr and Andrea Löw. London: Palgrave, 2016.
Fulbrook, Mary. *German national identity after the Holocaust.* Cambridge, UK: Polity Press, 1999.
Grabowski, Jan. *Rescue for Money. Paid Helpers in Poland. 1939–1945.* Jerusalem: Yad Vashem, 2008.
Gradvohl, Paul. Magyarországi deportálások: az észlelés rétegei, *Kultúra és Közösség* 5.4 (2014): 33–58.
Gross, Jan. *Neighbors: The Destruction of the Jewish Community in Jedwabne, Poland.* Princeton: Princeton University Press, 2001.
Gyáni, Gábor. "Történelmi esemény és struktúra. Kapcsolatuk ellentmondásossága." *Történelmi Szemle* 2 (2011): 145–161.
Habermas, Jürgen. "On How Postwar Germany Has Faced Its Recent Past." *Common Knowledge* 5.2 (1996): 1–13.
Hagemann, Karen. "Mobilizing Women for War: The History, Historiography, and Memory of German Women's War Service in the Two World Wars." *Journal of Military History* 75.3 (2011): 1055–1093.
Hilberg, Raul. *The Destruction of the European Jews.* Chicago: Quadrangle Books, 1961.
Hoffmann, Eva. *After Such Knowledge. Memory, History and the Legacy of the Holocaust.* New York: Public Affairs, 2004.
Horváth, Cecília. *A magyar zsidóság és a holokauszt.* Budapest: Új Palatinus, 2004.
Hughes, Michael L. "'Through No Fault of Our Own.' West Germans Remember Their War Losses." *German History* 2 (2000): 193–213.
Jablonczay, Tímea. "Hivatalos amnézia és az emlékezés kényszere. A traumatikus múlt női elbeszélései az 1960-as években." *Múltunk* 2 (2019): 77-110.
Kádár, Gábor, and Zoltán Vági. *Aranyvonat. Fejezetek a zsidóvagyon történetéből.* Budapest: Osiris, 2001.
Kádár, Gábor, and Zoltán Vági. *Hullarablás. A magyar zsidók gazdasági megsemmisítése.* Budapest: Jaffa, 2005.
Karády, Viktor. "Szociológiai kísérlet a magyar zsidóság 1945–1956 közötti helyzetének elemzésére." In *Zsidóság az 1945 utáni Magyarországon*, edited by Péter Kende. Párizs: Magyar Füzetek, 1984.
Karády, Viktor. *Túlélők és újrakezdők.* Budapest, Múlt és Jövő, 2002.
Karsai, Elek, ed. *"Fegyvertelen álltak az aknamezőkön..." I–II. Dokumentumok a munkaszolgálat történetéhez Magyarországon.* Budapest: Hungarian Izraeliták Országos Képviselete, 1962.

Karsai, László. "Shylock is Whetting his Blade." Fear of the Jews' Revenge in Hungary during World War II." In *The Jews Are Coming Back. The Return of the Jews to Their Countries of Origin after WWII*, edited by David Bankier. Jerusalem: Yad Vashem, 2005.
Karsai, László. *Holocaust*. Budapest: Pannonica, 2001.
Karsai, László. "The People's Court and Revolutionary Justice in Hungary, 1945-1946." In *The Politics of Retribution in Europe. World War II and its Aftermath*, edited by István Deák, Jan T. Gross, and Tony Judt. Princeton: Princeton University Press, 2000.
Kasekamp, Andres. "Radical Right-Wing Movements in the North-East Baltic." *Journal of Contemporary History*. 4.34 (1999): 587–600.
Katzburg, Nathaniel. *Zsidópolitika Magyarországon, 1919–1943*. Budapest: Bábel, 2002.
Kellenbach, Katharina von. "Vanishing Acts: Perpetrators in Postwar Germany." *Holocaust and Genocide Studies* 17.2 (2003): 305–329.
Kende, Péter. *Védtelen igazság. Röpirat a bíróságról és ítéletekről*. Budapest: Hibiszkusz, 2007.
Kis, Oksana. "National Femininity Used and Contested: Women's Participation in the Nationalist Underground in Western Ukraine during the 1940s–50s." *East/West: Journal of Ukrainian Studies* 2.2 (2015): 53–82.
Klacsmann, Borbála. "Abandoned, Confiscated, and Stolen Property: Jewish–Gentile Relations in Hungary as Reflected in Restitution Letters." *Holocaust Studies* 1-2.23 (2017): 133–148.
Klein, Kerwin Lee. "On the Emergence of Memory in Historical Discourse." *Representations* 69 (2000): 127–150.
Kopstein, Jeffrey S., and Jason Wittenberg. *Intimate Violence. Anti-Jewish Pogroms on the Eve of the Holocaust*. Ithaca, NY: Cornell University Press, 2018.
Korb, Alexander. "The disposal of corpses in an ethnicized civil war: Croatia, 1941–45." *Human remains and mass violence*. March 31, 2017. DOI: https://doi.org/10.7765/9781526125026.00010.
Kovács, András. "Jews and Jewishness in Post-war Hungary." *Quest. Issues in Contemporary History. Journal of the Fondazione CDEC* 1 (2010). Http://www.quest-cdecjournal.it/focus.php?id=192.
Kovács, M. Mária. "The Numerus Clausus in Hungary, 1920-1945." In *Alma mater antisemitica: Akademisches Milieu, Juden und Antisemitismus an den Universitäten Europas zwischen 1918 und 1939*, edited by Regina Fritz, Grzegorz Rossolinski-Liebe, and Jana Starek. Vienna: New Academic Press, 2016.
Kreutzmüller, Christoph, and Jonathan R. Zatlin, ed. *Dispossession: Plundering German Jewry, 1933-1953*. Ann Arbor: University of Michigan Press, 2020.
Kubicki, Leszek. "Zbrodnie wojenne w swietle prawa polskiego" [War Crimes in the Mirror of Polish Laws]. Warszawa: PWN, 1963.
Kulcsár, István. "A maradék zsidóság lelki keresztmetszete 1946-ban." *Thalassa* 1-2 (1994): 334–336.
Kuretsidis-Haider, Claudia, and Winfried R. Garscha, ed. *Keine "Abrechnung". NS-Verbrechen, Justiz und Gesellschaft in Europa nach 1945*. Leipzig: AVA/Vienna: DÖW, 1998.
Laczó, Ferenc. "The foundational dilemmas of Jenő Lévai: On the birth of Hungarian Holocaust historiography in the 1940s." *Holocaust Studies*, 21.1-2 (2015): 93–119.

Lagrou, Pierre. "Return to a Vanished World. European Societies and the Remnants of their Jewish Communities." In *The Jews Are Coming Back. The Return of the Jews to Their Countries of Origin after WWII*, edited by David Bankier. Jerusalem: Yad Vashem, 2005.

Laky, Dezső. "A háztulajdon alakulása Budapesten." *Statisztikai Közlemények* 66.1 (1932): 89–99.

Laub, Dori. "An Event Without a Witness: Truth, Testimony and Survival." In *Testimony. Crises of Witnessing on Literature, Psychoanalysis and History*, edited by Shoshana Felman and Dori Laub. New York: Routledge, 1992.

Lene, Otto. "Post-Communist Museums: Terrorspaces and Traumascapes." In *The Power of the Object. Museums and World War II*, edited by Esben Kjeldbæk. Edinburgh: MuseumsEtc, 2009.

Lentin, Ronit. "Expected to Live. Women Shoah Survivors' Testimonies Silence." *Women's Studies International Forum* 23.6 (2001): 689–700.

Lévai, Jenő. *A pesti gettó csodálatos megmenekülésének hiteles története*. Budapest: Officina, 1946.

Lévai, Jenő. *Fekete könyv a magyar zsidóság szenvedéseiről*. Budapest: Officina, 1946.

Lévai, Jenő. *Zsidósors Magyarországon. Az üldözés kora*. Budapest: Magyar Téka, 1948.

Lim, Jie-Hyun. "Afterword: Entangled Memories of the Second World War." In *Remembering the Second World War*, edited by Patrick Finney. London/New York: Routledge, 2018.

Littel, Jonathan. *The Kindly Ones: A Novel*. New York: Harper, 2009.

Lower, Wendy. *Hitler's Furies. German Women at the Nazi Killing Fields*. NY: Houghton Mifflin Harcourt, 2013.

Lower, Wendy. "Distant Encounter. An Auschwitz Survivor in the College Classroom." In *Approaching and Auschwitz Survivor. Holocaust Testimony and its Transformation*, edited by Jürgen Mattheus. Oxford: Oxford University Press, 2010.

Lower, Wendy. "Male and Female Holocaust Perpetrators and the East German Approach to Justice 1949-1963." *Holocaust and Genocide Studies* 24.1 (2010): 56–84.

Lugosi, András. "'Sztalin főhercege': Kohn báró vacsorái a Falk Miksa utcában a fajgyalázási törvény idején." *Fons* 17.4 (2010): 527–576.

Mahmood, Saba. "Feminist Theory, Agency, and the Liberatory Subject: Some Reflections on the Islamic Revival in Egypt." *Temenos* 1.42 (2006): 31–71.

Major, Ákos. *Népbíráskodás. Forradami törvényesség*. Budapest: Minerva, 1988.

Mälksoo, Maria. "Memory must be Defended: Beyond the Politics of Mnemonical Security." *Security Dialogue* 46.3 (2015): 221–237.

Margalit, Avishai. *The Ethics of Memory*. Cambridge, Mass.: Harvard University Press, 2002.

Markovits, Inga. "How the Law Affects what we Remember and Forget about the Past. The Case of East Germany." *Law and Society Review* 35.3 (2001): 513–563.

Mátraházi, Ferenc, ed. *Szemelvények a magyarországi zsidóság életét korlátozó törvényekből és rendeletekből*. L. n., P. n., 2004.

May, Larry. *Crimes Against Humanity. A Normative Account*. Cambridge: Cambridge University Press, 2005.

Minow, Martha. *Between Vengeance and Forgiveness. Facing History after Genocide and Mass Violence*. Boston: Beacon Press, 1998.

Moore, Alison M. "History, Memory and Trauma in Photography of the Tondues. Visuality of the Vichy Past through the Silent Images of Women." *Gender and History* 3 (2005): 657–681.

Nagy, Ágnes. "Hatalom – lakásrendszer – társadalom Egy lipótvárosi bérház lakói 1941 és 1960 között." *Korall* 17 (2004): 138–166.
Naimark, Norman. *Fires of Hatred. Ethnic Cleansing in Twentieth-Century Europe*. Harvard, Mass.: Harvard University Press, 2001.
Nánási, László. *A magyarországi népbíróság joganyaga 1945-1950, Pártatlan igazságszolgáltatás vagy megtorlás*? Bács Kiskun Megyei Önkormányzat Levéltára. Kecskemét 2011.
Nino, Carlos Santiago. *Radical Evil on Trial*. New Haven/London: Yale University Press, 1996.
Nora, Pierre, "Between Memory and History: Les Lieux de Mémoire." *Representations* 26 (1989): 7–24.
Novák, Attila. "Resistance or Saving One's Skin? Notes to the Problem of 1944's Hungarian Zionist Resistance." In *State and Equality*, edited by Attila Károly Molnár and Milán Pap. Budapest: Dialog Campus, 2018.
Passerini, Luisa. "Memories of Resistance, Resistance of Memory." In *European Memories of the Second World War*, edited by Helmut Peitsch, Charles Burdett and Claire Gorrara. New York/Oxford: Berghahn Books, 1999.
Passerini, Luisa. *Torino operaia e fascismo*. Rome: Laterza, 1984.
Payne, Leigh A.. *Unsettling Accounts. Neither Truth nor Reconciliation in Confessions of State Violence*. Durham/London: Duke University Press, 2008.
Pelinka, Anton. "Justice, Truth and Peace." In *Justice and Memory. Confronting Traumatic Pasts. An International Comparison*, edited by Ruth Wodak and Gertraud Auer Borea. Vienna: Passen, 2009.
Pelle, János. "A nyilasterror Budán." *Valóság* 10 (2015): 65–87.
Pendas, Devin O. "Eichmann in Jerusalem, Arendt in Frankfurt. The Eichmann Trial, the Auschwitz Trial, and the Banality of Justice." *New German Critique* 34.1 (2007): 77–109.
Pendas, Devin O. *The Frankfurt Auschwitz Trial. 1963–1965. Genocide, History and the Limits of Law*. New York: Cambridge University Press, 2006.
Penter, Tanja. "Local Collaborators on Trial." *Cahier du Monde Russe* 49.2–3 (2008): 341–364.
Pető, Andrea, and Patricia Chiantera-Stutte. "Populist Use of Memory and Constitutionalism. Two Comments." *German Law Journal* 2 (2005): 165–175.
Pető, Andrea, and Klaartje Schrijvers. "The Theatre of Historical Sources. Some Methodological Problems in Analyzing post-WWII Extreme Right Movements in Belgium and in Hungary." In *Professions and Social Identity. New European Historical Research on Work, Gender and Society*, edited by Berteke Waaldijk. Pisa: Edizioni Plus/University of Pisa Press, 2006.
Pető, Andrea. "Digitalized Memories of the Holocaust in Hungary in the Visual History Archive." In *Holocaust in Hungary 70 years after*, edited by Randolph Braham and András Kovács. CEU Press, Budapest, 2016.
Pető, Andrea. *Geschlecht, Politik und Stalinismus in Ungarn. Eine Biographie von Júlia Rajk*. Gabriele Schäfer Verlag, 2007.
Pető, Andrea. "Privatised Memory? The Story of Erecting of the First 'Private' Holocaust Memorial in Budapest." In *Memory and Narrating Mass Repression*, edited by Nanci Adler, Mary Chamberlaine and Leyla Neyzi. New Brunswick, N.J: Transaction, 2009.

Pető, Andrea. "Problems of Transitional Justice in Hungary. An Analysis of the People's Tribunals in Post-War Hungary and the Treatment of Female Perpetrators." *Zeitgeschichte* 2007.34 (2007): 335–349.

Pető, Andrea. *Rajk Júlia*. Budapest: Balassi, 2001.

Pető, Andrea. "Roots of Illiberal Memory Politics: Remembering Women in the 1956 Hungarian Revolution." *Baltic Worlds* 10.4 (2017): 42–58.

Pető, Andrea. "Contacting Histories: Impacts of Reading Holocaust Testimonies in Hungary." In *Jewish Studies at CEU*, edited by András Kovács, Michael Miller, and Carsten Wilke. Budapest: IX. Jewish Studies Project, 2020.

Pető, Andrea. "Revisionist Histories, 'Future Memories': Far-Right Memorialization Practices in Hungary." *European Politics and Society* 1.18 (2017): 41–51.

Pető, Andrea. "Historicizing Hate: Testimonies and Photos about the Holocaust Trauma during the Hungarian post-WWII Trials." In *Tapestry of Memory. Evidence and Testimony in Life Story Narratives*, edited by Nanci Adler and Selma Leydesdorff. New York/London: Transaction Publishers, 2013.

Pető, Andrea. "A magyar büntetőjog szovjetizálása: egyéni közvetítők és intézmények (1945–1961)." *Aetas* 33.2 (2018): 69–82.

Pető, Andrea. "Hungary's Illiberal Polypore State." *European Politics and Society Newsletter* 21.4 (2017): 18–21.

Pető, Andrea. "The Lost and Found Library." *Memory at Stake* 9 (2019): 72–82.

Pető, Andrea. *Women of the Arrow Cross Party*, London: Palgrave MacMillan, 2020.

Petrenko, Olena. "Frauen als 'Verräterinnen.' Ukrainische Nationalistinnen im Konflikt mit den kommunistischen Sicherheitsorganen und dem eigenen Geheimdienst" [Women as Perpetrators. Ukrainian Nationalist in Conflict with the Communist Security Organizations and their own Security Services]. In *"Frauen im Kommunismus." Jahrbuch für Historische Kommunismusforschung* [Women in Communism. Yearbook of Research on Communism], edited by Ulrich Mählert, Jörg Baberowski, Bernhard H. Bayerlein et al. Berlin: Metropol Verlag, 2015.

Prusin, Alexander Victor. "Fascist Criminals to the Gallows. The Holocaust and the Soviet War Crimes Trials December 1945–February 1946." *Holocaust and Genocide Studies* 1.17 (2003): 1–30.

Rainer, János M. *Imre Nagy. A Biography*. London/New York: Tauris, 2009.

Reiter, Andrea. *Narrating the Holocaust*. London/New York: Continuum, 2000.

Reiter, Margit. *Die Generation danach. Der Nationalsozialismus im Famielengedächtnis*. Vienna/Innsbruck/Bozen: Studienverlag, 2006.

Rigney, Ann. "Plenitude, Scarcity, and the Circulation of Cultural Memory." *Journal of European Studies* 35.1 (2005): 11–28.

Rigney, Ann. "Portable Monuments. Literature, Cultural Memory, and the Case of Jennie Deans." *Poetics Today* 2 (2004): 361–396.

Rigó, Róbert. "A zsidóvagyon sorsa Kecskeméten." *Forrás* 40.9 (2008): 42-80.

Rosen, Alan. "Autobiography from the Other Side. The Reading of Nazi Memoirs and Confessional Ambiguity." *Biography. An Interdisciplinary Quarterly* 24.3 (2001): 553–570.

Rosenthsal, Gabriele, and Dan Bar-On. "A Biographical Case Study of a Victimizer's Daughter." *Journal of Narrative and Life History* 2.2 (1992): 105–127.

Rosenthal, Gabriele, ed. *"Als der Krieg kam, hatte ich mit Hitler nichts mehr zu tun". Zur Gegenwärtigkeit des "Dritten Reiches" in erzählten Lebensgeschichten.* Opladen: Leske - Budrich, 1990.
Rosenthal, Gabriele ed. *Der Holocaust im Leben von drei Generationen. Familien von Überlebenden der Shoah und von Nazi-Tätern.* Gießen: Psychosozial Verlag, 1997.
Rosenthal, Gabriele, ed. *The Holocaust in Three-Generations. Families of Victims and Perpetrators of the Nazi-Regime.* London: Continuum, 1998.
Rosenthal, Gabriele. *"Wenn alles in Scherben fällt..." Von Leben und Sinnwelt der Kriegsgeneration.* Opladen: Leske - Budrich, 1987.
Rosenthal, Gabriele. *Erlebte und erzählte Lebensgeschichte. Gestalt und Struktur biographischer Selbstbeschreibungen.* Frankfurt am Main: Campus, 1995.
Rosenthal, Gabriele. "German War Memories. Narrability and the Biographical and Social Functions of Remembering." *Oral History* 19.2 (1991): 34–41.
Rosenthal, Gabriele, ed. Klaus Hurrelmann. *Interpretative Sozialforschung.* Weinheim – München, Juventa, 2005.
Rosenthal, Gabriele. "Reconstruction of Life Stories. Principles of Selection in Generating Stories for Narrative Biographical Interviews." *The Narrative Study of Lives* 1.1 (1993): 59–91.
Rosenthal, Gabriele. "The Healing Effects of Storytelling. On the Conditions of Curative Storytelling in the Context of Research and Counseling." *Qualitative Inquiry* 9.6 (2003): 915–933.
Rosenwein, Barbara. "Worrying about Emotions in History," *American Historical Review* 3.107 (2002): 821–845.
Rowlands, Michael. "Remembering to Forget. Sublimation as Sacrifice in War Memorials." In *The Art of Forgetting*, edited by Adrian Forty and Susanne Küchler. Oxford/New York: Berg, 1999.
Sandulescu, Valentin. "Fascism and its Quest for the 'New Man.' The Case of the Romanian Legionary Movement." *Studia Hebraica* 4 (2004): 349–361.
Sauerland, Karol. *Dreissig Silberlinge. Denunziation in Gegenwart und Geschichte.* Berlin: Volk und Welt Verlag, 2000.
Schacter, Daniel L., ed. *Memory Distortion. How Minds, Brains and Societies Reconstruct the Past.* Cambridge, Mass.: Harvard University Press, 1994.
Schiavo, Gianluca. 2016. "The Italian Civil War in the Memoirs of Female Fascist Soldiers." In *Gendered Wars, Gendered Memories. Feminist Conversations on War, Genocide and Political Violence*, edited by Ayşe Gül Altınay and Andrea Pető. London: Routledge, 2016.
Schmidt, Sibylle. "Perpetrators' Knowledge: What and How Can we Learn from Perpetrator Testimony?" *Journal of Perpetrator Research* 1.1 (2017): 85–104.
Simpson, David. "Naming the Dead." *London Review of Books* 23.22 (2001): 3-7.
Sipos, Balázs. *Women and Politics: Nationalism and Femininity in Interwar Hungary.* Trondheim: Studies on East European Cultures & Societies, 2019.
Stark, Tamás. *Zsidóság a vészkorszakban és a felszabadulás után (1935–1955).* Budapest: MTA Történettudományi Intézet – História Alapítvány, 1995.
Sturken, Marita. "The Remembering of Forgetting. Recovered Memory and the Question of Experience." *Social Text* 57 (1998): 103–125.
Szarka, László ed. *Jogfosztó jogszabályok Csehszlovákiában, 1944–1949.* Komárom: Kecskés László Társ, 2005.

Székely, Gábor and Robert Vértes, ed. *Magyarországi zsidótörvények és rendeletek, 1938–1945.* Budapest: Polgár Kiadó, 1997.

Szita, Szabolcs. *Haláleröd. A munkaszolgálat és a hadimunka történetéhez 1944–1945.* Budapest: Kossuth, 1989.

Szita, Szabolcs. *Utak a pokolból. Magyar deportáltak az annektált Ausztriában 1944-1945* [Roads from Hell. Hungarian deportees in occupied Austria]. Budapest: Metalon Manager Iroda KFT, 1991.

Szívós, Erika. "Bonds Tried by Hard Times: Jews and Christians on Klauzál tér, Budapest, 1938–1945." *Hungarian Historical Review* 1–2.1 (2012): 166–199. Https://www.ceeol.com/search/article-detail?id=253807.

Sznaider, Natan. "Suffering as a Universal Frame for Understanding Memory Politics." In *Clashes in European Memory. The Case of Communist Repression and the Holocaust*, edited by Muriel Blaive, Christian Gerbel and Thomas Lindenberger. Innsbruck/Vienna/Bozen: Studienverlag, 2011.

Tec, Nechama. *Resilience and Courage. Women, Men, and the Holocaust.* New Haven, Yale University Press, 2003.

Thomson, Paul. "Family Myth, Models, and Denial in the Shaping of Individual Life Paths." In *Between Generations. Family Models, Myths, and Memories*, edited by Daniel Berteux and Paul Thomson. Oxford: Oxford University Press, 1993.

Tilkovszky, Lóránt. "Vád, védelem, valóság. Basch Ferenc a népbíróság előtt." *Századok* 6 (1996): 1393–1450.

Tokarska-Bakir, Joanna. "The Unrighteous Righteous and the Righteous Unrighteous." *Dapim: Studies on the Holocaust* 1.24 (2010): 11–63.

Treize, Thomas. "Between History and Psychoanalyses. A Case Study in the Reception of Holocaust Survivor Testimony." *History and Memory* 1 (2008): 7–47.

Veszprémy, László Bernát. "Népirtás és mozgástér. A magyar közigazgatás felelőssége az 1944-es deportálásokban és a nyilas terrorban." *Archivnet* 2.18 (2008).

Vincellér, Béla. *Sötét árny magyarhon felett. Szálasi uralma 1944. október – 1945. május.* Budapest: Makkabi 2003.

Wachtel, Nathan. "Remember and Never Forget." *History and Anthropology 2* (1986): 307–335.

Welzer, Harald, S. Moller, and K. Tschuggnall. *"Opa war kein Nazi". Nationalsozialismus und Holocaust im Familiengedächtnis.* Frankfurt am Main: Fischer Verlag, 2002.

Wierzcholska, Agnieszka. "Helping, Denouncing, and Profiteering: a Process-Oriented Approach to Jewish–Gentile Relations in Occupied Poland from a Microhistorical Perspective." *Holocaust Studies* 1-2.23 (2016): 34–58.

Wieviorka, Annette. "From Survivor to Witness. Voices from the Shoah." In *War and Remembrance in the Twentieth Century*, edited by Jay Winter and Emmanuel Sivan. Cambridge: Cambridge University Press, 1999.

Withuis, Jolande. "Das Kriegstrauma in den Niederlanden." In *Europapolitik seit 1945. Die Niederlande und Deutschland im Vergleich*, edited by Friso Wielenga and Loek Geereadts. Münster: Aschendorf, 2004.

Wodak, Ruth. *"Wir sind alle unschuldige Täter". Diskurshistorische Studien zum Nachkriegsantisemitismus.* Frankfurt am Main: Suhrkamp, 1990.

Yeomans, Rory. "Militant Women, Warrior Men and Revolutionary Personae: The New Ustasha Man and Woman." *The Slavonic and East European Review* 4.83 (2005): 720–721.

Zavacká, Marína. "Crossing Sisters: Patterns of Protest in the Journal of the Catholic Union of Slovak Women during the Second World War." *Social History* 4.37 (2012): 425–451. DOI: 10.1080/03071022.2012.733509.

Zinner, Tibor. "Háborús bűnösök perei. Internálások, kitelepítések és igazoló eljárások 1945–1949." *Történelmi Szemle* 1 (1985): 118–140.

Zoltán, Gábor. *Orgia*. Budapest: Libri, 2016.

Archival Sources

Historical Archives of the Hungarian State Security Services
(*Állambiztonsági Szolgálatok Történeti Levéltára*)
    Piroska Dely V 48889
Budapest City Archives
(*Budapest Főváros Levéltára*)
    XVII. 2. 19. Committee for the Investigation of Nazi and Arrow Cross Atrocities
    XXV. 1. a. (Budapest People's Tribunal, criminal trial records)
    Dely Piroska 2442/1947
    Szamocseta Nándor 19273/1949 (1746/1947, V 119019)
The Archive of the Budapest Bar Association
(*Budapesti Ügyvédi Kamara Irattára*)
    4770 Jobbágy Lajos
    7573 Surányi Dezső
Hungarian National Archives
(*Magyar Országos Levéltár*)
    XIX-E-1-L Tank-2000-1946 Piroska Dely
    XIX-E-1-L Ministry of Justice Department of People's Tribunals, box 2. 3. 13.
    XIX-J-1-q Hungarian Ministry of Foreign Affairs, Department of Prisoners of War 8/1945, 15/1946, 23/1947, 26/1948.
    I-E-17
    I-F-24

List of Interviews

Magda Kun, Zsuzsa Forgács, János Kun
    March 3, 2005
    March 22, 2005
    April 1, 2005
Magda Kun
    October 5, 2005
    January 9, 2007
    July 27, 2007
Piroska Döme March 22, 2005
György Kálmán March 22, 2005
Holocaust Memorial Center, District 6 Local History Class. Lecture by Magda Kun and János Kun August 1, 2007
Iván Svéd August 6, 2007
Róbert Morton. August 9, 2007
Mrs. Károly Petőcz née Edit Rosenberg August 13, 2007
Nándor Szamocseta
    July 27, 2007
    August 4, 2007
György Bárándy August 23, 2007

Manuscripts

Miklós Bodor's letter to Magda Kun and János Kun. n.d.
Miklós Bodor's letter to Andrea Pető. August 7, 2007
Hungarian Prison Service, Department of Detention Cases, Miklós Sárdi deputy department head, June 27, 2005. Records on Piroska Dely.
Joseph Morton's email to Andrea Pető. August 15, 2007
Magda Kun: *Szálasi árnyékban* [Szálasi in Shade]. Manuscript, 2007
Response of László Mihályfi chief architect, November 1, 2005. ref. 696-2005.
The letter of eight survivors to the National Heritage Committee (*Nemzeti Kegyeleti Bizottság*). February, 2004
Erika Gabányi's email to Andrea Pető. June 19, 2019
János Polgár's Facebook message to Andrea Pető. June 20, 2019

Appendix 1
The chronology of Piroska Dely's trial, its background and afterlife

1939
Piroska Dely works in the Svábhegy Sanatorium (Buda).

1944
March 19
Dely gets an Arrow Cross armband and badge from an Arrow Cross man called Horváth: "I wore them but I was not a member."

October 8
Piroska Dely meets Pista, the finance guard who gives her an Arrow Cross badge.

Sometime during October, on a Saturday
The Nagyatádi (Kertész) Street events: "robbery and plunder" committed by Piroska Dely and Arrow Cross and German soldiers.

October 15
Pál Laub's (engineer, Csengery Street 47) testimony: Piroska Dely allegedly cursed the Jewish men in front of Csengery Street 45.
(For a reconstruction of the October 15 events, see appendix 3)

1945
February 7
Mrs. Károly Tóth denounces Piroska Dely, Dob Street 74 third floor 32/b who was active under the pseudonyms Etel Simon and/or Eta Pap: "[O]n her command a mother was taken away from her children and deported ... [she wore an] Arrow Cross badge and green shirt."

Note: Based on the People's Tribunal's documentation.

Appendix 1 The chronology of Piroska Dely's trial, its background and afterlife — 131

February 9
Piroska Dely goes into in pre-trial detention. According to the emergency group's report she denied being an Arrow Cross member. During the house search, several suitcases were confiscated but these were not mentioned later. "Her real name and her role in the Hársfa Street 57 deportation should be clarified."

February 10 and 13
Piroska Dely's interrogated by Justice Endre Szebenyi.

February 12
The Hungarian State Police's (HSP – *Magyar Állami Rendőrség*) Political Security Bureau's detective house-searched Dely's Dob Street 74 groundfloor apartment, and reported on the results. Testimonies by Mrs. Dezső Hajós, Mrs. Sándor Waldman, Mrs. Lajos Engel, Mrs. Béla Ruttkay, Mrs. Jenő Rosenthal, interrogation of Simon Zweig.

February 26
Piroska Dely interrogated in the presence of László Bajor people's prosecutor. Dely goes into pre-trial detention.

February 27
Dely indicted with illicit traficking (Hungarian Criminal Code 370/1) in the Hársfa Street case.

February 28
Szamocseta and János Pál janitors "voluntarily" return the stolen goods to Csengery Street 64's tenants. Piroska Dely interrogated by the People's Tribunal based on Law 1945/81 Act 13.2, and BTK 370/1, that is illicit trafficking, in the presence of Justice Ernő Fogas. She claims to be pregnant, last sexual intercourse December 23, last period December 18. "I regret my partial culpability and I want to fully reimburse for all damage."

March 5
Piroska Dely's People's Tribunal trial in the Hársfa Street case. Andor Lichter's testimony changes the course of events.

March 6
Based on Andor Lichter and Mrs. Béla Krámer's testimonies, the people's prosecutor requests a separate case and the repeated interrogation of Piroska Dely.

March 12
Mrs. Ervin Gábor arrived late to the Political Security Bureau and is told that she can give her testimony during the next day's People's Tribunal trial instead.

March 13
The HSP Political Security Bureau's investigation files were forwarded due to Andor Lichter and Mrs. Béla Krámer's testimonies. Mrs. Ervin Gábor goes to Piroska Dely people's tribunal trial and recognizes the woman in the black coat with the Arrow Cross armband.
Testimonies by Piroska Dely, Mrs. András Veréb, Mrs. József Strucky are given at the Hungarian State Police's Political Security Bureau. Sándor Steiner also present a testimony concerning Csengery Street 45.

March 14
The Budapest People's Tribunal's 1945/81 public trial presided over by Justice Béla Pálosi. Witnesses: Simon Zweig, Mrs. Sándor Waldman, Mrs. Lajos Engel, Mrs. Jenő Rosenthal, Mrs. Károly Spiegel; Mrs. Béla Ruttkay and Mrs. Dezső Hajós did not come forward. Dely claims that she is not pregnant and speaks no German. Because of the investigation files that belatedly arrived from the HSP Political Security Bureau, the two cases are united and the trial is postponed.

March 16
József Strucky's testimony at the HSP Political Security Bureau.

March 17
Mrs. Ervin Gábor's testimony at the HSP Political Security Bureau and Pál Laub's letter to László Bajor people's prosecutor.

March 24
Mrs. Andor Steiner's testimony at the HSP Political Security Bureau.

March 26
Mrs. Lajos Steiner née Olga Mitzaki's testimony at the HSP Political Security Bureau.

March 27
Piroska Dely's indictment.

Appendix 1 The chronology of Piroska Dely's trial, its background and afterlife — **133**

March 29
The additional investigation's protocol is completed.

April 6
The trial date is set for April 25.

April 25
Budapest people's prosecutor's trial is presided over by Justice Béla Pálosi. The final judgement establishes that Dely participated in the following atrocities: rounded up Jews, plundered apartments in Nagyatádi (Kertész) Street, led SS soldiers into Csengery Street with a pistol in her hand, and ordered them to fire. The body searching and torturing of Csengery Street 45 Jewish tenants was proven. In Hársfa Street 57 she kicked a child, she took children away from their mothers, she purchased a fur coat and a golden ring from the Arrow Cross. Witnesses: Simon Zweig, Mrs. Gábor Waldman, Mrs. Lajos Engel, Mrs. Jenő Rosenthal, Mrs. Károly Spiegel, Mrs. Ervin Gábor, József Strucky, Mrs. Béla Krámer, Mrs. Lajos Steiner née Olga Mitzaki, Mrs. Andor Steiner, Mrs. Miksa Tenczer, Mrs. András Veréb, Sándor Steiner, Pál Laub, Mrs. Samu Forgács; Mrs. Gábor Waldman did not come forward. Dely says that she was a nurse at the Svábhegy Sanatorium and as such she was under the command of the German Headquarters. Piroska Dely is sentenced to death. She claims to be four months pregnant. She files a clemency appeal. The closed clemency trial supports her appeal because of her two children and pregnant state.

May 8
László Kerekes MD prison physician diagnoses that Dely is six months pregnant. According to the Budapest People's Tribunal's council records, her appeal was rejected, i.e. the death sentence could be enforced.

May 22
The High National Council (*Nemzeti Főtanács*) submits Dely's clemency appeal to the People's Tribunals' section leader.

May 24
The National Council of People's Tribunals (NOT) reaches a decision about Piroska Dely's clemency appeal: "[T]he verdict is suspended until [Dely's] accouchement." The case is forwarded to the Ministry of Justice.

June 1
The NOT rejects Dely's clemency appeal "because of her extremely severe actions and her brutal demeanor while performing those actions." Only one council member was in favor of clemency because of Dely's pregnancy.

June 2
The NOT submits the verdict for approval to the Minister of Justice.

June 4
The High National Council in its response to the verdict – "as a pregnant woman in need of special care [...] which the state may terminate at any time" – proposes the postponement of the execution.

June 7
The High National Council's three members agree that the decision about the clemency appeal should be suspended until accouchement.

June 15
The State Secretary of Justice's letter to the Budapest People's Tribunal: "[U]ntil her accouchement the documents should be filed. Should the accouchement occur report it and send the documents back without delay."

July 24
Justice Béla Pálosi's letter to György Temesvári prison physician inquires after the due date of the accouchement.

September 17
Another letter to the physician like the first received no response.

October 8
According to the prison physician the accouchement is to be expected between October 25 and 30.

December 18
The People's Tribunal's judge's handwritten note to the prison physician: "Has she given birth and is the child alive?"

1946

January 9
At the request of the Budapest People's Tribunal Piroska Dely states that her last period was in December 1944, she feels no fetal motion, she does not feel pregnant, and she has abdominal pain. Diagnosis: cysta ovarii.

January 10
The prison physician's report: the tumor could be perceived as an enlarged uterus. The medical report is submitted to the High National Council.

January 16
Upon receiving the prison physician's diagnosis, the High National Council rejects the clemency appeal.

January 23
Minister of Justice István Ries requests that "against Piroska Dely justice should ensue without hindrance."

January 30
László Rajk, Ferenc Nagy, Zoltán Tildy (members of the High National Council): "[W]e agree that against Piroska Dely justice should ensue without hindrance."

February 1
Andor Lichter's letter to President of the Republic Zoltán Tildy urging him to reject the clemency appeal.

February 4
The High National Council's resolution submitted to the National Council of People's Tribunals (NOT): "[W]e agree that against Piroska Dely justice should ensue without hindrance."

March 22
The National Council of People's Tribunals submits the High National Council's resolution to the President of the Budapest People's Tribunals' National Council.

March 23
Execution supervised by Viktor Zucker people's prosecutor.

June 1
The people's prosecutor requests the bill of costs.

1947

February 18

The Budapest People's Tribunal failed to deal with the *corpus delicti* (gold necklace with cross), therefore it should take action.

March 17

The People's Tribunal cannot act because the list of *corpora delicti* got lost from among the trial documents.

April 30

The Budapest people's prosecutor submits the list of *corpora delicti* to the Budapest people's tribunal.

1948

May 29

Róbert Apor people's prosecutor requests information about the resolution concerning the *corpus delicti*.

October 6

Róbert Apor people's prosecutor repeatedly requests information.

November 4

The HSP Budapest Police Headquarters investigates whether Sándor Temesvári is Piroska Dely's lawful heir.

December 14

Róbert Apor people's prosecutor repeatedly requests information.

December 29

The Budapest People's Tribunal's announcement: Sándor Temesvári should come forward for a gold necklace with cross.

1949

April 21

The people's prosecutor's letter to the People's Tribunal: no one has come forward for the object.

Appendix 1 The chronology of Piroska Dely's trial, its background and afterlife

May 9
The Budapest People's Tribunal auctions off the gold necklace with cross (*corpus delicti*) because came forward after 30 days.

May 31
Estimated value of the necklace with cross: 2.5 grams, 90 forints.

May 24
Pál Solt people's prosecutor reminds the Budapest People's Tribunal about the case.

July 11
The gold necklace with cross gets auctioned off in the state loan office.

November 11
The Hungarian National Bank sends the gold necklace with cross back because it was sent there by mistake.

November 30
The Budapest criminal court is ordered to issue the cross to the Hungarian National Bank.

December 24
The Metropolitan Financial Authority requests the Budapest People's Tribunal to forward the verdict.

1950

January 5
The Budapest People's Tribunal forwards the requested verdict.

February 20
The necklace was sold for 17 forints and 60 fillérs; the money is transferred to the Hungarian National Bank's Metropolitan Financial Directorate's account.

1962
March 22
Tibor Lukács, the President of Chamber at the Budapest Metropolitan Court submits a transcript without a procedural document, therefore the court has no right to start the process of selling the necklace.

1972
March 28
Mrs. Károly Sziklai née Ilona Steiner requests the Metropolitan Funerary Institute issue the court records of Piroska Dely, the murderer of Béla Steiner and István Steiner, who suffered martyrdom. Their names are on the commemorative plaque.

March 28
The Budapest Metropolitan Court requests the files from the Registrar of the Ministry of Internal Affairs because "the case requires action."

April 13
The file is returned.

May 10
From Tibor Lukács's letter concerning the victims' placement in the Kerepesi Cemetery's Parcel of Martyrs: "From the testimony of the accused person [Piroska Dely] it is apparent that the German SS troops went to the house to search for ammunition and weapons and to collect those who resisted [...] From an upper floor of the house someone shot at the intruding SS, the Germans went upstairs and opened fire. The Germans collected firearms from the house and from elsewhere too. During the trial it was established that someone shot at passing Germans from Csengery 64's windows. [...] In the house several people were shot dead, others got deported. The members of the Steiner family were among those attacked. I am sending this notification per the request of Mrs. Károly Sziklai concerning the dispute around the tombs of Béla Steiner and István Steiner in the Kerepesi Cemetery."

Appendix 2
The Chronology of the Szamocseta Case

February 9, 1919
Nándor Szamocseta is born in Rákospalota.

January 1937 – February 1938
Nándor Szamocseta attends the Aszód Reformatory.

November 1, 1937
György Szamocseta rents a tailor shop at Csengery Street 64.

1939
Easter
Nándor Szamocseta works at his father's shop. From 1938 he works in Germany, then from 1941 at the Ajax Concern, then at the Győr Aeroplane Factory.

Easter to December
Nándor Szamocseta works at the Uhry Brothers Car-body and Vehicle factory Ltd.

1940
February 6
Nándor Szamocseta tries to flee to Germany because on seeing a poster advertising German factory jobs. He gets caught on the Slovakian border and returns.

Spring
To escape the military draft, Nándor Szamocseta flees to Germany and spends 18 months there.

September
Nándor Szamocseta works with Polish forest loggers till March 1941.

Note: Based on BFL 19273/1949, 1746 / 47 and ÁBTL V 119019.

1941
March
Nándor Szamocseta works as a mechanic in a car shop till May 1942.

1942
May
Szamocseta gets drafted, works for the Rába Services, finishes a three-month long training period at the Győr Aeroplane Factory.

November
Nándor Szamocseta's wedding.

December
Nándor Szamocseta works for the Csepel Aeroplane Factory until Christmas, then in a war plant until September 1943. At first he works in the Győr Aeroplane Factory, then in the Csepel Aeroplane Factory until September 1943.

1944
January
Nándor Szamocseta is a driver at the Kálmán Tisza (later: *Köztársaság tér*, i.e. Republic Square, today: Pope John Paul II) Square Volksbund-house, then he "volunteered to or got ordered to" the Svábhegy German Headquarters.

February
Szamocseta becomes a driver at Kálmán Tisza Square, because they did not check employment records.

February 17
Following Albert Binder's advice, Szamocseta applies for the position of Polish translator at the Svábhegy German Headquarters.

After March 19
Nándor Szamocseta is in Nagyvárad (Oradea, Romania).

April 12
Nándor Szamocseta is transferred from Kálmán Tisza Square to Svábhegy (Buda).

Appendix 2 The Chronology of the Szamocseta Case

April 18
A German car stops in front of his house and Szamocseta is kidnapped. He is in captivity for two weeks then is employed as a translator. According to his father, around this time she worked as a projectionist and Polish translator on the Svábhegy.

April 27
Imre Bodor, the son of Ilona Bodor the house owner is taken by the Gestapo from Csengery Street 64 to the Svábhegy. Strucky offers Szamocseta's help; he looks into Bodor's file and finds that he is in Matthausen. Nándor Szamocseta offers his services: Since he is often sent to Wien he can bring a letter from Matthausen.

Summer
The Struckys' Alsógöd house is mortgaged.

June 19
Mrs. György Szamocseta is the air raid shelter commander of Csengery Street 64, but later the family moves to Csengery Street 62.

June 25
Csengery Street 64 becomes a designated yellow Star of David house. György Szamocseta switches apartments with László Rózsa from 62/a: "He gave a furnished room and the dining room's equipment to my daughter. Rózsa put this all on paper."

Summer
Nándor Szamocseta acquires the Csengery Street 55 groundfloor apartment.

July
Mária Veres is the Szamocseta's lodger for a month. She visits the upstairs Jewish tenants. Mrs. Szamocseta warned her not to do so because she would get interned. Mrs. Szamocseta in the air raid shelter cellar separates Jewish and non-Jewish tenants.

October 7
Mrs. Krámer meets Nándor Szamocseta, who tells her that "much sorrow awaits the Jews." According to Szamocseta it was October 13.

October 14
Katalin Kurcweil and Széplaki (Szedlacsek) are the only Christian tenants at Csengery Street 64.
(For the chronology of October 15 events see appendix 3)

1945
January 20
Nándor Szamocseta receives a *Persilschein* from the tenants (see appendix 4).

January
When the Russians are in Csengery Street, Szamocseta says, "the Jews should have been all destroyed because they will come back and take revenge on us."

1946
January 6
Interrogation of Mrs. János Pál née Oravetz Erzsébet, janitor of Csengery Street 64 from December 1, 1944, at the HSP Budapest Police Headquarters' Political Security Bureau.

January 24
Interrogation of Mrs. Andor Steiner, Ernő Sárdi, and Mrs. Lajos Steiner née Olga Mitzaki at the HSP Budapest Police Headquarters' Political Security Bureau.

January 25
Interrogation of Ernő Sárdi, Mrs. Ervin Gábor née Magdolna Lichter, Mrs. Béla Krámer née Irén Schlesinger, Mrs. Miksa Tenczer, Mrs. Izsák Grünfeld née Irma Stoller, Mrs. László Propper née Lívia Klein, Mrs. Ernő Grünberger née Sári Müller, Andor Lichter, Mrs. András Veréb née Zsófia Vágási, and Sándor Steiner at the HSP Budapest Police Headquarters' Political Security Bureau. Mrs. Strucky is taken to the Political Security Bureau.

January 26
Mrs. Sándor Temesvári née Piroska Dely's interrogation at the HSP Budapest Police Headquarters' Political Security Bureau. Marital status: widow.
Sándor Steiner's interrogation at the HSP Budapest Police Headquarters' Political Security Bureau.

January 28
Mrs. Ernő Sárdi née Katalin Berkovits' interrogation at the HSP Budapest Police Headquarters' Political Security Bureau.

January 29
Interrogation of László Bodor, Mrs. Miklós Rosenberg née Margit Klein, and György Berkovits Barát at the HSP Budapest Police Headquarters' Political Security Bureau.

January 30
The HSP Budapest Police Headquarters' Political Security Bureau files a report on József Strucky, Mrs. Strucky, and Nándor Szamocseta. Interrogation of Mrs. Miksa Eisenstadter née Elza Schwartz, Mrs. József Strucky, Mrs. János Pál née Erzsébet Oravetz at the HSP Budapest Police Headquarters' Political Security Bureau.

January 31
Interrogation of György Szamocseta, Nándor Szamocseta, and József Strucky at the HSP Budapest Police Headquarters' Political Security Bureau.

February 15
József Strucky and Mrs. József Strucky are taken into pre-trial detention, placed in a prison (*toloncház*), then in the Buda-Dél internment camp. Strucky remains under arrest until August 21, 1947, Mrs. Strucky until November 28, 1948.

September 30
Andor Lichter's denouncement letter to the Hungarian State Police's Political Security Bureau against József Strucky and his wife, Nándor Szamocseta, György Szamocseta and his wife, and István Kiss.

December 27
Interrogation of Mrs. Béla Krámer née Irén Schlesinger, Mrs. Gábor Singer née Ilona Horschowsky, Mrs. Miklós Faragó née Elza Goldfinger, Andor Lichter, Mrs. Jakab Schwartz née Etel Zelinger, Ilona Bodor, Mrs. Viktor Aupek née Teréz Glück, Mrs. Ernő Grünberger née Sári Müller, Mrs. Ervin Gábor née Magdolna Lichter at the HSP Budapest Police Headquartersá Political Security Bureau.

December 28
Interrogation of Andor Lichter, Mária Szabó (Csengery Street 62), and Nándor Hahn (Csengery Street 55) at the HSP Budapest Police Headquarters' Political Security Bureau.

1947
January 2
Interrogation of Mrs. Rezső Braun née Szidónia Fischer at the HSP Budapest Police Headquarters' Political Security Bureau. Nándor Szamocseta's interrogation (to be continued on January 15). He is the Allied Commission's (SZEB) driver. Interrogation of Mrs. József Steffen née Anna Petzinger (Csengery Street 55) at the HSP Budapest Police Headquarters' Political Security Bureau.

January
Mrs. Strucky is in pre-trial detention in the Markó Street.

January 8
The ÁVO's people's prosecutor's department starts an investigation against Nándor Szamocseta.

January 9
Nándor Szamocseta is arrested.

January 16
Interrogation of Pál Kádár people's prosecutor at the HSP Budapest Police Headquarters' Political Security Bureau.

January 28
Mrs. József Strucky declares that she was abused during her testimony; her hand was hit with a stick.

February 20
Budapest people's prosecutor's records. Pál Kádár people's prosecutor interrogates Mrs. Aladár Bydeskuti.

March 10
The ÁVO's people's prosecutor's department interrogates Mrs. György Szamocseta. Her earlier testimonies and the records of the cross-examinations were lost from the file.

May 3
The Szamocseta-case's indictment is completed.

May 10
Mrs. Miklós Rosenberg's interrogation at the HSP Budapest Police Headquarters' Political Security Bureau.

May 29
József Strucky receives the indictment. He does not require an appointed lawyer.

June 23
The Budapest People's Tribunal's public trial led by Justice Gusztáv Tutsek in the case of Nándor Szamocseta, József Strucky, Mrs. József Strucky, György Szamocseta, Mrs. György Szamocseta. Witnesses: Pál Kádár, Mrs. Miklós Rosenberg, Mrs. Aladár Bydeskuti, Ilona Bodor, Mrs. Miklós Faragó, Mrs. Béla Krámer, Andor Lichter, Mrs. Ernő Grünberger, Mrs. Viktor Aupek, Mrs. László István Várnai, Mrs. Ernő Sárdi, Sándor Steiner, Mrs. Gábor Zinger, Mrs. András Veréb. Mrs. Miksa Tenczer, Mrs. Andor Steiner, and Mrs. Sándor Temesvári (!) were not present. It is on record that she did not come forward as a witness, i.e. they did not work out that Mrs. Sándor Temesvári was the married name of the executed Piroska Dely.
The court orders György Szamocseta and Mrs. Szamocseta's pre-trial detention.

After June 23
György Szedlacsek's letter to the people's tribunal requests the tribunal to terminate the procedure against his son, György (Széplaki) Szedlacsek.

August 17
Mrs. Richter's statement enforces György (Széplaki) Szedlacsek's alibi.

August 21
The Budapest People's Tribunal led by Justice Gusztáv Tutsek delivers its judgement: Nándor Szamocseta receives ten years forced labor, József Strucky one year imprisonment, Mrs. József Strucky née Emília Kalliszta three years imprisonment, György Szamocseta one year imprisonment, Mrs. György Szamocseta née Mária Kalliszta one year imprisonment and confiscation of assets from the Strucky-Szamocseta family's Szentes and Budapest apartments. Mrs. Strucky's release was suggested but rejected. The court reads out loud the testimonies of Pál Kádár, Mrs. Miklós Rosenberg née Margit Kelin, Andor Lichter, Mrs. Krámer, Mrs. Jakab Schwartz, Mária Verebes, Mrs. István Steiner née Erzsébet Faragó,

Mrs. Endre Szász née Katalin Steinic, Gyula Pap (Csengery 62). Witnesses Mrs. Miksa Stender and Mrs. László Germanh did not come forward.
József Strucky is released.

November 15
The National Council of People's Tribunals sentences Nándor Szamocseta to ten years forced labor, József Strucky gets three years imprisonment, Mrs. Strucky née Emília Kalliszta four years imprisonment, György Szamocseta one year imprisonment, Mrs. Szamocseta née Mária Kalliszta one year imprisonment.

1948
April 9
The release appeal is rejected.

April 25
Éva Strucky's letter to the Minister of Justice requests her mother be released because of her poor health and her paralysed arm.

June 17
Széplaki cannot be accused of war crimes, so the indictment is withdrawn. József Strucky's release appeal is rejected.

August 21
The Budapest People's Tribunal's final verdict in the case of Nándor Szamocseta, Strucky, Mrs. Strucky and Mrs. Szamocseta.

November 15
Nándor Szamocseta's sentence is reinforced by the second instance court led by Justice Péter Jankó, the NOT Council President.
Mrs. Strucky is under arrest until this day.

1949
January 5
The verdict of Nándor Szamocseta, József Strucky, Mrs. József Strucky née Emília Kalliszta, György Szamocseta, Mrs. György Szamocseta née Mária Kalliszta is final and executable. In the case of József Strucky and Mrs. Strucky, the time spent arrested and in the internment camp is taken into account. The Budapest

Metropolitan Financial Authority cannot confiscate György Szamocseta and his companion's assets because of administrative errors.

1950
February 15
Mrs. József Strucky gets provisionally released from the Márianosztra Women's Penitentiary.

August 5
The Szamocsetas file for divorce. Their appointed lawyer, Lajos Lengyel gets access to their files.

1956
March 16
Mrs. József Strucky's clemency appeal on behalf of Nándor Szamocseta is rejected by the Budapest Metropolitan Court.

1957
November 22
Nándor Szamocseta is provisionally released.

December 18
The ten years of forced labor are suspended for three years.

Appendix 3
The story of the Csengery Street massacre

1944
October 15 (Sunday)
Nándor Szamocseta moves into a Csengery Street 55 apartment that the Gestapo required for the German Police.

Late morning
Horthy's radio proclamation had a very different effect on the Jewish tenants and the janitors. According to Mrs. Lajos Steiner née Olga Mitzaki's testimony, Mrs. Strucky started to cry: "[T]he janitor woman and her daughter cried and they said that they would have rather endured the bombings than the Russians."
 The Jewish tenants decided to keep guard, and according to Miklós Bodor "a former army officer had a sword and someone else had a bayonet but these were long gone before the Germans arrived."

Late afternoon
Mrs. Miksa Eisenstadter said that when a little boy told to Éva Strucky that "now it will be better for us," Éva Strucky slapped him. Mrs. Eisenstadter also claimed that Mrs. Strucky or Széplaki made a phone call that started the events. She also heard that the Struckys' medical student lodger [Széplaki?] said that he would take care of the Jews.
 At this time Piroska Dely was, according to one of her testimonies, at another house, but later said: "I went out with the SS soldiers [to Csengery 64], and the janitor greeted us with 'Persistence! Long live Szálasi!' After that I had a feeling that the person belongs with us. As I found out, he actually did, because I saw him in the stairwell in conversation with the Arrow Cross Horváth and with Stefan Müller, and I heard him saying that they are not at home around this time. He meant the Christian tenants. The janitor said that they, the Christians, hid Jews [...] so we had to go out the next day again. When I went out the next day with the SS and the Arrow Cross we took away the people that the janitor mentioned, they could be 3 or 4."
 Mrs. Grünfeld said that on her way home she saw that in Eötvös Street a yellow star had been removed. At Csengery 64 she asked the janitor why he had not

---

Note: Based on BFL 19273/1949, 1746 / 47 and ÁBTL V 119019 and witness testimonies.

taken off the star from the house yet. "Mrs. Strucky said that I should take it off because she wouldn't." Two tenants remove the star.

When the Horthy-proclamation was cut off, Nándor Szamocseta arrived and told Mrs. Lichter to "stay put and go to the air raid shelter and take food with you!" He told Mrs. Grünberger that he just came from the Castle and the battle had just begun.

Early evening (according to Sándor Steiner at 9 pm)
Piroska Dely and seven SS-soldiers arrive at Csengery Street 45. According to Lajos Steiner eight tenants kept guard at the gateway waiting for the soldiers who were supposed to come and protect the house. When the bell rang, the tenants opened the gate thinking that the soldiers arrived. "Then a woman in black dress jumped through the gate, later I learned that she was Piroska Dely. She shouted 'Hende Hoch!'. 3-4 SS soldiers followed her. They started to body search people in the gateway." Dely held a pistol and she had an Arrow Cross armband. The Germans fired and Dely shouted "Hands up!" then she ordered the body searching of the tenants. Mrs. András Veres, the janitor tells Dely that she was not Mrs. Szabó. Dely's bullet missed her. Rónai and Schwartz and the others beat up two men. In the dark, Steiner hid in the cellar. They took away seven men, Gruber tried to escape, got beaten to death or shot.

21:30
The armed men knocked on the gate of Csengery Street 62 but the janitor, Gyula Pap tells them "you can shoot me but I will bring out no Jews because in our house there is none."

From her window Mrs. Krámer saw that "several people were knocking on the gate of 62 and I heard heavy bootsteps. They were sent away from there and over to the next house, that is 64. After a few minutes I heard that they rattled our gate, I heard gunshots and that several people entered the house. Two German SS soldiers told us to leave our apartments and go under the gateway and from there we were led by Piroska Dely to the Kertész Street school." Through the window she also saw that the Szamocseta family went over from 62 to 64 into the tailor shop where "they were enthusiastically celebrating Szálasi. [...] From the window I clearly saw everything and heard that the boots were approaching on the pavement, and I saw uniformed men stop in front of 62a or 62b. They rattled the gate, and then they asked if this was 64. When they got the information they immediately came to our gate and shot out the light in front."

Dely commanded with a pistol in her hand, she took the house keys, and the SS soldiers started shooting. (According to Mrs. Ervin Gábor there were three shots, but Mrs. Lajos Steiner née Olga Mitzaki said that "we heard many shots."

Dely remembered two warning shots.) The tenants were rounded up. In the Steiner-apartment Dely ordered body searches and took their gold and other assets. Lajos Steiner, Andor Steiner, and the 15-year old Róbert Tenczer were shoved in the bathroom, witnesses heard Dely's voice as she ordered fire. Mrs. Grünberger, her husband and their two daughters ran down in the cellar and stayed there till October 19 without food and water.

21:45

György Szamocseta's testimony: "We heard many gunshots. We left the tailor shop and ran home" to Csengery Street 62/a. He went back on October 17, he disapproved of the massacre, heard from his sister-in-law that there were Jews hiding in the cellar, but allegedly he did not make a remark about opening the gas taps.

Strucky's version: "[A]t 21:45 I heard that someone forcefully rattled the gate. I went out to open it but as soon as I put the key into the lock someone shoved the gate open and Piroska Dely and several SS and Arrow Cross soldiers entered. [...] I did not greet them with 'Perseverance! Long live Szálasi!' [...] Piroska Dely asked me if I was Jewish. I told her that I was Christian and I am the janitor." Dely locked him into his apartment together with his wife and their Christian lodger, and gave the key to an SS soldier.

Mrs. Henrik Bodor, the owner of the house hears the rattling and immediately takes her family in the coal cellar from the second floor. Her mother's ankle got sprained so her father and Laci took her downstairs. Miklós Bodor stayed. After the first transport the owner of the house brings Miklós downstairs. When the Germans return "the shooting and the killing began. Four of our neighbors were taken to the anteroom and shot. Unfortunately I don't remember their names, they were not old time residents, they moved into the yellow star house. When the shooting stopped the police and the Arrow Cross rounded up everyone else and took us into an empty apartment."

22:00

According to Mrs. Steiner, "the whole house was dead silent. We were about to go to bed when Piroska Deli and three SS soldiers showed up. She had a weapon in her hand."

Mrs. Miklós Faragó is hiding in the cellar.

22:00–23:00

Mrs. Propper and her husband hide underneath the mangle, then in Strucky's apartment, then they run away from Csengery Street.

"Through the stairwell side door they brought many elderly and children into the [Strucky] apartment, there were altogether 30 of us. I don't know how long it took but before Dely and the others left they called me and told me to turn off the lights and to not speak anyone about the happenings." Strucky added: "Dely warned me not to be shocked by the sight in the apartments."

23:00
The house was quiet again. There were 18 dead and Izrael Lichter who died of a heart attack.

Strucky followed "the order" together with Katalin Kurcweil, the local administrator of the house (*házgondnoknő*), and Széplaki: "When I went upstairs I told several tenants to come downstairs and stay there." Széplaki's active role during the raid was later omitted from the story.

24:00
The first transport started towards Nagyatádi (Kertész) Street: 70 Jews were taken to the Nagyatádi Street school where they were tortured. Mrs. Ervin Gábor stated that the noise of army boots and shooting lasted for another hour.

October 16 (Monday)
1–1:30am
Piroska Dely checks the headcount in the janitor apartment where 20 to 25 people were crammed together, among them elderly, women and children. She tells the janitor that he is responsible for keeping them in the apartment. According to Mrs. Ervin Gábor's testimony, Strucky promised a house search that morning: "[H]e yelled that we should know that Szálasi seized power and everything will happen the way he wants it."

2–3:00am
The armed men search through the attic.

The deportation happens in three transports. Mrs. Ervin Gábor is sent back, according to her testimony: "Between Csengery 64 and Andrássy Avenue the woman in Arrow Cross uniform took me out of the line and sent me back in the house."

5:00am
Mrs. Andor Steiner climbs out from underneath the bed where she lay wounded. The local administrator of the house, Katalin Kurzweil tends to her wounds but she was not let back into her apartment because of Piroska Dely's command.

Mária Verebes looks for the Lichter family, Strucky tells her that "[t]he old Lichter died, Mrs. Gábor is here but the rest were taken."

8:00am
Strucky enters second floor 1 and finds the body of Sándor Takács, the old lodger of Grünberger. In the bathroom of third floor 1 he finds Ignác Stern, Mrs. Ignác Stern, and Mrs. Artúr Braun from first floor 2/a. In second floor 2, the previous night, he found István Faragó the owner, but now he finds István Faragó's lodger, István Faragó. The third body is the Grünberger girl in second floor 1. (see appendix 9)

Morning
Strucky: "Next day the Arrow Cross returned. I was in the gate when they arrived and I went inside and waited in the courtyard for them to enter and they entered indeed [...]."

Piroska Dely returned with two SS soldiers to Csengery Street 64. According to Strucky, Dely asked him if there were any more Jewish tenants "to which I answered that only those whom you left yesterday." Mrs. Gábor said that Dely took away three more persons from Csengery Street 64: Szegő, Biró, and Szilágyi. Piroska Dely let the women and children take a walk on the courtyard, but when Mrs. Ervin Gábor asks her to let her old mother back [from Nagyatádi] Dely rebuffs: "Shut up and be glad that I let you back."

Late morning
Strucky lets Mrs Bydeskuti out of the house although he knows that she has forged papers.

Mrs. Grünberger climbed out of the lightwell and asked Strucky to search the pockets of her dead relatives, Vimos, Margit, and Ilona Grünberger (second floor 2) and gather their personal belongings. The janitor responded that he had already examined the bodies and "found nothing valuable on them" and returned an empty wallet.

Afternoon
When Nándor Szamocseta arrived and sent the two Arrow Cross guards away the corpses were still in the building. The Struckys told everyone to go into the air raid shelter and collect money for their protection; still, on October 17 everyone was taken into Nagyatádi Street. "György Szamocseta told the Jewish tenants to go to the air raid shelter, and that he would guarantee their safety. While we were in the shelter our apartments were searched through." In the air raid shelter, Nándor Szamocseta gives a speech: "Following the order from Eastern Comer-

ades (*Keleti Arcvonal Bajtársi Szövetség*, paramilitary group formed in 1944 from former soldiers who served on the Eastern Front) will hold a house search and those who remained will suffer no harm. Of course, in the meantime we were locked into the air raid shelter and the corpses were laying in the apartments." According to Ilona Bodor they put together 1000 *pengős*. Mrs. Bydeskuti also gathered money to give it to Szamocseta "who would protect the house in exchange [...] he would make it sure that the remining approx. 60 people suffered no harm." Strucky takes half of the sum. After the money was collected the tenants were allowed back in their apartments.

Mrs. Bydeskuti said that she and her niece, Mrs. Dénes Bíró gathered the money, which was several thousand *pengős* because the tenants gave 150 banknotes. The following morning they ran away from the house. They say that the incident in the shelter happened on October 17 because they already wanted to leave on October 16 but Nándor Szamocseta did not let them out.

László Bodor says that he wanted to leave the house but Strucky did not allow it although there were no Arrow Cross or SS in the vicinity.

Mária Verebes came to ask about the events again but Strucky sent her away.

Evening
Piroska Dely returned to Csengery Street 45 together with 16 SS soldiers (according to Steiner's testimony): "The SS soldiers were Hungarian Schwab people from Jánoshalma or elsewhere from Bácska."

In the ground floor Schwartz-apartment, "during the house search Nándor Szamocseta told Mrs. Ervin Gábor that 'only the Germans can win, you, Jews, have to accept that, national socialism is the most amazing, majestic state formation and only you Jews dislike it, everyone else welcomes it joyfully.'"

October 16 or 17
In the evening Szedlacsek (Széplaki) and his relative, József Fuchs flee to Bocskay Avenue for the night.

October 17 (Tuesday)
0:30
Two German soldiers come, so the collected money was in vain. They hold a house search and steal every valuable item.

At dawn
The Arrow Cross returns and takes Mrs. Schwartz to Nagyatádi (Kertész) Street.

5:00am
From Nagyatádi Street 40 and 44 to 46 armed people plunder all valuables.

5:30am
Mária Verebes lets Andor Lichter know that according to Strucky in Csengery Street 64 "there are no more Lichters."

The tenants start to demolish the cellar wall *(see appendix 5)* in order to get through to 66: "[T]he most practical would be to open the water and gas taps," says Szamocseta upon hearing the noise.

3:00pm
The women and the children are let home from Nagyatádi Street.

Afternoon
According to Mrs. Grünfeld "Strucky said that from next week on this house would be a Christian house."

Around 11pm
Mrs. Grünfeld is taken.

1am
SS soldiers take away Mrs. Grünberger: "they snatched our remaining assets." A policeman, an Arrow Cross and an SS soldier "took all Jews from the house to Nagyatádi Street and let them home after two days."

The Bodor family returns after two days of captivity.

October 18
Mrs. Propper returns from her hideout. Mrs. Strucky tells her that Piroska Dely and her company arrived with a prepared tenant list.

Strucky says that two detectives came to the house but by mistake they brought the files of another case and with that they left never to return. A police committee arrives to investigate the massacre because it was an "individual action." They make a list of the dead; they indicate the cause of death as by "gunshot wound." (Mrs. Steiner's testimony.)

October 18 or 19
The deported tenants return from Nagyatádi Street.

October 19 (Thursday)

Szilágyi returns to Csengery Street 64. It turns out that he was in Nagyatádi and Rumbach Streets, although Nándor Szamocseta collected money with the promise that he would bring him back from Svábhegy.

According to Mrs. Aupek: "Nándor Szamocseta said that if the Germans lost the war he would go on the street with five bullets, fire four times and put the last one in his head [...] he mentioned that on Friday they would take the men from the yellow star houses and on Monday the women. Truly, the men were taken on Friday and the women on Monday. So he had accurate information about their plans." The deported people return from Rumbach Street. "Strucky was horrified by the events and told me that one of the SS soldiers had a list and the first name on it was my husband's [Aupek]."

Those who were taken on Sunday return in the evening.

October 20 (Friday)

Mrs. Krámer returns from Nagyatádi (Kertész) Street. Strucky tells her "we should accept that we are his captives and he forbids us to leave our apartments, to visit each other." According to his testimony Nándor Szamocseta runs away from the Gestapo.

October 21 (Saturday)

A new regulation allows the opening of the yellow star houses' gates. According to Mrs. Gábor, Strucky was aware of this since he had a radio, but he did not open the gate. In his testimony Strucky denied knowing about the new regulation.

October 22 (Sunday)

According to another testimony this is the day when Nándor Szamocseta ran away from the Gestapo.

October 23 (Monday)

Mrs. Ervin Gábor claimed that according to a new decree those women of Jewish faith whose husbands were on the battlefield did not have to stay inside, but still Strucky insisted.

November 5 (Saturday)
5:15pm
Another deportation. Miksa Eisenstadter gets deported because Strucky does not confirm his illness to the Arrow Cross soldiers. According to Mrs. Eisenstadter's testimony: "Strucky said that he did not know [if he was sick] and that he should step in the line. I want to add that after the surgery Strucky carried my husband up and down in the elevator so he was very much aware that he was ill, still, he deliberately claimed the opposite."

Six more people are taken, Pál Kádár escapes from the brick factory with two men, the others never return.

November 7 (Monday)
Pál Kádár returns home as a forced labor service man. Mrs. Krámer says about her apartment, "the janitor family moved into the house's nicest apartment [the Krámer's]. My pantry stored the food supplies of four families and the Struckys took it all. Mrs. Aupek saw Strucky leaving my apartment with a huge sack of sugar."

November 13 (Sunday)
In her testimony Mrs. Gábor recalls that she wanted to go for a medical check up but she was afraid to cross Klauzál Square because allegedly they were "catching Jews" there, to which "Mrs. Strucky said that if I was so worried I should take a change of underwear and some food with me."

November 1944 – mid-February 1945
Éva Strucky gave the Krámers' apartment to the Struckys. Mrs. Krámer said that "apart from the furniture hardly anything remained in my apartment, they took away everything [...] they took my curtains too in November 1944." The curtains and the undergarments were later returned.

November 15, 1944
Strucky does not let Mrs. Grünberger and her sister, Mrs. István Várnai László out although they were officially enlisted as battle debris cleaners (*romeltakarító igazolvány*). Strucky knew that there would be checks, but still did not let them out, hence they were taken to the Óbuda brick factory and subsequently deported.

Mrs. Andor Lichter was deported to Bergen Belsen.

November 20
The deportation of all Csengery Street 64 tenants. Mrs. Gábor gave her apartment keys, her father's chrome pocket watch and chrome nickel watch to Strucky for safeguarding but she did not get them back upon her return.

December 1
Mrs. János Pál becomes the new janitor.

Mid-December
Mrs. Krámer says that she was hiding at the Szamocseta's for a week ("of course I paid a substantial price"), but he kicked her out at midnight and threatened her "to leave or else there would be trouble. [...] I had to return from my hideout out early December because no one took me and my little daughter without papers. I tearfully pleaded with Mrs. György Szamocseta to take me into their apartment. I spent 8-9 days at their place and paid for the food that they took from my own pantry, and when I wanted to change our underwear she did not let me use my own that she hid in her wardrobe, I had to steal back my belongings when they were away. Their wardrobes were stuffed with clothing items, for instance I recognized my husband's silk neckties and my daughter's little dresses. While I was there they had plenty of food, which was not at all the case earlier. [...] Strucky warned me to leave the apartment because otherwise he would denounce each of them, the whole family he meant [...] he yelled that they stole everything from the Jews. I came back a few days later from Buda, where we hid, for some bedding, but Mrs. Strucky refused to give me any, although after liberation I found that it was all in their possession."

1945
End of January
Lichter returns: "[A]s the house overseer I urged the Csengery Street 64 tenants to return the illicitly acquired Jewish possessions."

January
Miklós Bodor, his brother and his aunt return. Mrs. Strucky welcomes them in Bodor's aunt's gown and serves tea using their tea set.

End of February
Mrs. Strucky returns Lichter's wife's gown but there is no trace of the other assets.

Beginning of April
Mrs. Strucky returns Andor Lichter's typewriter, a crocheted table cloth and a duvet cover.

In November
Szamocseta tells Mrs. Krámer that in Alsógödön there are two suitcases, which are hers.

1946
February
Andor Lichter testifies at the police that he recognized his wife's gown on Mrs. Strucky.

Appendix 4
Persilschein

For his honor Nándor Szamocseta, Budapest VI. Csengery Street 62.[421]

Events fade with time. In order to save them for posterity we will put down those happenings of the last several months during which You aided us, and we hereby express our sincere and deepest gratitude for your help.

On the year's October 16 Arrow Cross men armed with hand grenades came to Csengery Street 64. Your aunt Mrs Strucky called for You and You personally prevented that the Arrow Cross would access the air raid cellar where approx. 70 Jewish people were hiding.

The following day Arrow Cross and Death Skull soldiers came to the house and You again stopped them before they reached the shelter because You personally assured their leader that there were no Jews in the cellar.

On the night of October 18 German soldiers came to the house. Once again You prevented their ascending into the apartments with what you prevented further atrocities.

Besides these actions there were countless instances when You demonstrated that You are a true, sympathetic, helping friend of the house's tenants.

Budapest, January 20, 1945

Özv. Horschawsky Sándorné
Singer Gáborné
Özv. Szegő Albertné
Szegő Ármin
Gábor Ervin
Özv. Lichter Izraelné
Róth József
Biró Dénesné
R. Pauncz Erzsébet
Özv. Ippi Bydeskuti Aladárné
Özv. Hidvéger Miklosné
Özv. Weisz Andorné
Pauner Ferencné
Dr. Popper Lászlóné

---

421 BFL 19273/1949. 279. transcript of the handwritten text.

Klein Ernő
Klein Ernőné
Klein Ibolya [These three with the same handwriting.]
Spitzer Ernőné
Várnai L. Istvánné
Glückkron Ernőné.

Appendix 5
Tenant registry

Csengery Street 64

	1941	Occupation	Moved in	Reconstruction of October 15, 1944 state of affairs	1945	Occupation	Moved in
GF							
1	József Strucky 1895
Mrs. Strucky 1901
Éva Strucky 1926	file cutter	1929	József Strucky
Mrs. Strucky
Éva Strucky
Lodger:
György Széplaki (Szedlacsek)	János Pál 1907
Mrs. Pál 1915
Erzsébet Pál 1934
Éva Pál 1940
Co-tenants:
Mihály Sáska 1912
Mrs. Sáska 1918
László Sáska 1941	file cutter underworker employed at the Beszkárt	1944 December
1945 January
2	Mrs. Izsák Grünberger née Sári Müller 1903	trader	1937	Ernő Grünberger
Mrs. István Várnai
Izsák Grünberger
Mrs. Izsák Grünberger
Mrs. Grossmann née Olga Grünberger
Ilona Grünberger
Margit Grünberger
Vilmos Grünberger	Ernő Grünberger 1903
Mrs. István Várnai 1896		1944
2a	Alfréd Köszler 1893
Mrs. Köszler 1891
Their child 1927	pressman	1937	Mrs. Miklós Rosenberg
Magda Rosenberg
Edit Rosenberg	Miklós Rosenberg 1905
Mrs. Rosenberg 1929
Magda Rosenberg 1929
Edit Rosenberg 1931	tinker	1942 September

Note: Reconstruction based on the court testimonies and the interviews. The victims' names are with bold.

Continued

	1941	Occupation	Moved in	Reconstruction of October 15, 1944 state of affairs	1945	Occupation	Moved in
GF							
3	Jakab Schwartz 1883 Mrs. Jakab Schwartz 1894 László Schwartz 1921	turner	1934	Mrs. Jakab Schwartz László Schwartz Mrs. Miksa Eisenstadter née Elza Schwartz Miksa Eisenstadter	Mrs. Jakab Schwartz 1894 László Schwartz 1921		
4	Miksa Lichtman 1892 Mrs. Miksa Lichtman 1891 Mihály Lichtman 1930	stock trader	1937	Mrs. Miksa Lichtman Mihály Lichtman	Mrs. Miksa Lichtman 1891 Mihály Lichtman 1910 Co-tenant: Mrs. Adolf Pálmai 1897		1945
5	Géza Hámori 1905 Mrs. Hámori 1907 Éva Hámori 1932 Béla Hámori 1937	post officer			Mrs. Ármin Lichtenstein 1895 Olga Gradt 1916 Györgyi Hade 1940 Co-tenants: Mrs. Weisz 1899 Rózsi Weisz 1831		June 1944
	Ede Hartrick 1893 Mrs. Ede Hartrick 1875	vice janitor	1921		Mrs. Ede Hartrick 1875		
8	György Szamocseta 1891 Mrs. György Szamocseta 1900 Lenke Szamocseta 1926	tailor	1937				

Continued

	1941	Occupation	Moved in	Reconstruction of October 15, 1944 state of affairs	1945	Occupation	Moved in
GF							
1st floor							
1	Béla Krámer Mrs. Béla Krámer Magda Krámer 1932 Maid: Erzsébet Torma 1893	butcher	1938 1941	Béla Krámer Samu Éber Mrs. Béla Krámer née Irén Schlesinger Magda Krámer Gábor Éber Mrs. Jenő Éber Bora Donáth Ágnes Éber Mrs. Pál Beck Julia Schlesinger Vera Beck Ernő Blitz Mrs. Blitz	Béla Krámer Mrs. Béla Krámer 1910 Ilona Krámer 1932 Lodger: József Krámer 1907	homemaker	
1a	János Jellinek 1870	physician	1938	János Jellinek Mrs. János Jellinek Kamillo Jellinek	Mrs. János Jellinek 1881 Lodgers: Mrs. Miksa Bodor 1892 Mrs. Jakab Stein 1964	homemaker	1945
2	Mrs. Henrik Bodor 1869 Maid: Katalin Révész	house owner	1940		Ilona Bodor Lodgers: Miklós Bodor 1932 László Bodor 1928 Ármin Leindhofer 1895 Mrs. Ármin Leindhofer 1895 András Leindhofer 1916 Tamás Leindhofer 1942		1945
2a	Asztrik Braun 1892 Mrs. Asztrik Braun 1920	oil merchant	1938	**Remembered as Elza Braun but actually Erzsébet;** probably Mrs. Rezső Braun and her two sons	Pál Hegyi 1899 Mrs. Pál Hegyi 1920 Lodgers: Katalin Kurcweil 1916 László Kurcweil 1932	retired auditor	November 1944 January 1945

Continued

	1941	Occupation	Moved in	Reconstruction of October 15, 1944 state of affairs	1945	Occupation	Moved in
GF							
3	Izsák Grünfeld 1883 Mrs. Izsák Grünfeld 1892	jeweller	1928	Izsák Grünfeld Mrs. Izsák Grünfeld	Károly Fok 1903 Mrs. Károly Fok 1903 Lodgers: Károly Fogl 1895 Mrs. Fogl 1893	Beszkárt driver jeweller	December 1944
4	Ernő Spitzer 1901 Miksa Spitzer 1872	central heating technician	1936	Ernő Spitzer (Sárdi) Mrs. Spitzer née Kató Berkovits Mrs. Ickovits Ágnes Ickovits Tibor Ickovits	Ernő Spitzer Mrs. Ernő Spitzer 1910		
5	Mrs. Ignác Reiner Ernő (Ödön) Singer 1884 Mrs. Zoltán Kahn née Róza Stern 1899 István Ehlich 1909	tradesman	1936	Ödön Singer Mrs. Ödön Singer Her sister-in-law **Ernő Singer**	Mrs. Ignác Reiner Rózsa Singer 1874 Co-tenant: Ödön Singer 1886 Ödön Singer 1887 Lodger: Sándor Sebők 1909		1945
6	Ervin Gábor 1903	tradesman	1939	**Izidor (Izrael) Lichter** Mrs. Izidor Lichter Mrs. Andor Lichter née Halász Irén György Lichter Mrs. Ervin Gábor née Magda Lichter Zsuzsa Gábor Mrs. Bierman	Mrs. Ervin Gábor née Magda Lichter 1908 Zsuzsa Gábor 1940 Mrs. Izrael Lichter 1874 Andor Lichter 1890	clerk at a publishing house	
2nd floor							
1	Mrs. Mózes Rubinyi née Ilona Bodor 1924 Mrs. György Rejtő 1915		1924	Mrs. Mózes Rubinyi née Ilona Bodor	Pál Gráber 1898 Mrs. Pál Gráber 1904 Hedvig Gráber 1925 Mária Gráber 1932 Co-tenant: Mrs. Mór Rajna 1875	auditor	1945
2	István Faragó 1898 Mrs. Faragó née Júlia Frankl 1906	bank clerk, Hungarian Credit Bank	1939	**István Faragó** **Mrs. István Faragó** **Lajos (István) Faragó** **lodger**	Imre Frankl 1907 Lodger: Mrs. Solf	lawyer	

Continued

	1941	Occupation	Moved in	Reconstruction of October 15, 1944 state of affairs	1945	Occupation	Moved in
GF							
3	Béla Bodor 1895 Mrs. Béla Bodor 1904 László Bodor 1928 Miklós Bodor 1932 Katalin Bodor 1914	Hungarian bank clerk	1929	Béla Bodor Mrs. Béla Bodor László Bodor Miklós Bodor Katalin Bodor	Béla Czóbel 1904 Mrs. Béla Czóbel 1908 Mária Czóbel 1930 Márta Czóbel 1930 Margit Czóbel 1933 Béla Czóbel 1935 Emília Czóbel 1937 Gábor Czóbel 1939 Co-tenant: the maid	municipal clerk	December 1944
4	Ernő Léderer 1882 István Léderer 1912 Lodgers: Anna Bitter 1913 Rózsa Bitter 1909	textile trader	1912	Mrs. Ernő Léderer née Gizella Scheffer	Mrs. Ernő Léderer née Gizella Scheffer 1888 Lodgers: Mrs. Ernő Török 1893 Emma Léderer 1888	homemaker	
5	Zsuzsa Steiner 1918 Endre Steiner 1920	textile trader employee	1936	Mrs. Ármin Steiner Mrs. Somogyi née Zsuzsa Steiner Dezső Somogyi **Andor (Endre) Steiner** Mrs. Andor Steiner **István Steiner** **Lajos Steiner** Mrs. Lajos Steiner née Olga Mitzaki **Béla Steiner** Mrs. Miksa Tenczer **Tenczer Róbert** **Ernő Singer** Two unknown men: **Faragó, Faragó**	Mrs. Ármin Steiner née Ilona Fürst 1932 Mrs. Dávid Predberger 1915 András Predberger 1943	nurse	

Continued

	1941	Occupation	Moved in	Reconstruction of October 15, 1944 state of affairs	1945	Occupation	Moved in
GF							
6	Zsigmond Kanitz 1861	clerk	1935		Mrs. Zsigmond Kanitz née Erzsébet Haas 1870 <u>Co-tenants:</u> Albert Dunai 1914 Mrs. Albert Dunai 1914 Albert Dunai Jr 1941	homemaker	
7	Ignác Steinicz 1897 Mrs. Ignác Steinicz née Paula Neufeld 1884 Endre Szász 1898 Mrs. Szász née Katalin Steincz 1914	shopclerk clerk	1934 1939	Károly Réti Mrs. Károly Réti her two sisters and a nephew	András Marosvölgyi 1901 Mrs. Marosvölgyi 1907 Erzsébet Marosvölgyi 1918 Piroska Marosvölgyi 1931 <u>Co-tenant:</u> Kálmán Szalay 1903 Mrs. Szalay 1904 Mrs. András Marcsa 1878	Beszkárt officer handyman	December 1944
3rd floor							
1	Mrs. Ignác Stern 1884 <u>Lodgers:</u> Irén Rédecsi 1920 Karl Kurt Shobez 1913	cooperative society clerk	1920	**Ignác Stern Mrs. Ignác Stern**	Endre István Tóth MD 1919	physician	December 1944
2	Gyula Porderák 1899 Mrs. Porderák née Sarolta Bossényi 1899 Henrik Jáger 1870 Maid: Lídia Bede 1920	cooperative society clerk	1939		József Strucky[418] 1895 Mrs. József Strucky 1901 Éva Strucky 1926		February 1945

---

[418] The Struckys moved here after Mrs. Krámer had succefully reclaimed her 1st floor apartment.

Continued

1941	Occupation	Moved in	Reconstruction of October 15, 1944 state of affairs	1945	Occupation	Moved in
GF						
3 Gábor Kardos 1881 László Kardos 1918 Maid: Erzsébet Nyitári 1919	trader, salesman	1937	Adolf Klein Mrs. Adolf Klein Ilona Klein her sister Babi László Propper lawyer Mrs. László Propper (Lili)	Mrs. László Kardos née Éva Szász 1922 Mrs. Pryna 1903 Mrs. Ernő Rácz 1897 Irén Szász 1928 Ferenc Braun 1972 Co-tenants: Mrs. László Propper 1913 Ernő Klein 1886 Mrs. Ernő Klein 1886 Lujza Klein 1910	women's tailor teacher milliner	1937
4 Mrs. Pál Boller 1895	dresser	1929		Mrs. Pál Boller 1894 Co-tenants: Herbert Kollina 1902 Mrs. Kollina 1916	homemaker auditor clerk	1929 1944
5 Mrs. Andor Balázs née Margit Treitsch 1903 Andor Balázs 1896	clerk	1938		Jenő Stern 1906 Mrs. Jenő Stern 1910 Iván Tibor 1937 Lodger: Erzsébet Kornhauser 1915	technician	1945
6 Mrs. Sándor Horschavszky (Lina) Her daughter: Mrs. Gábor Simor		1915		Mrs. Gábor Singer 1896 Mrs. Lina Horschavszy 1867 Mrs. Berkovits 1864 Lodgers: Mrs. Albert Szabó 1868 Mrs. Szegő 1891	clerk cleaner	1915

Continued

	1941	Occupation	Moved in	Reconstruction of October 15, 1944 state of affairs	1945	Occupation	Moved in
GF							
7	Miklós Schneider 1898 Mrs. Schneider 1897 Mária Gyekits	women's tailor	1936		Mrs. Sándor Réti née Margit Amstein 1902 Róbert László Réti 1927 Erzsébet Amstein 1904 Co-tenants: Károly Raffman 1906 Mrs. Károly Raffman 1905 András Raffman 1942	clerk book seller	June 1944
4th floor							
1	Zsigmond Schillinger 1903 Maid: Krisztina Nyekő 1922	locksmith	1930	Zsigmond Schillinger Mrs. László Polgár Lili Schillinger Endre Polgár Adolf Kohn, his mother: Mrs. Kohn, his brother: Aladár Kohn			
2	Endre Uprimny 1903 Mária and Edit Uprimny 1905 Maid: Anna Varga 1920	owner of a machine shop	1933	Endre Uprimny Edit Uprimny Mrs. Imre Kun née Lili Uprimny János Kun Teréz Fischer Mrs. Geiger Mrs. Loránt Morton née Erzsébet Neuwirth Mrs. Neuwrith Róbert Morton Éva Morton	Miklós Kis 1903 Mrs. Miklós Kis 1904 Co-tenants: János Kun 1930 Teréz Fischer 1877	bank clerk	June 22, 1944
3	n. a.			Grandpa Róth Grandma Róth Márta Róth and brother			
4	Miklós Barabás 1887 Mrs. Barabás 1885	assistant clerk	1935	Mrs. Tenczer **Róbert Tenczer**	Mrs. Lajos Steiner née Olga Mitzaki 1892	papermaker	June 1944

Continued

	1941	Occupation	Moved in	Reconstruction of October 15, 1944 state of affairs	1945	Occupation	Moved in
GF							
7	Mihály Nyikolits 1913 Mrs. Nyikolits 1915	clerk	1939		Jenő Spitz 1884 Mrs. Jenő Spitz 1896 Co-tenant: Mrs. Ferenc Kertész	salesman	June 1944
storefront							
2	György Szamocseta	tailor	1937		György Szamocseta	tailor	1937
3	Andor Borson	bookbinder	1910				
5	Vilmos Kőmüves (Klein) 1873 Mrs. Klein 1874	shoemaker	1930		György Szamocseta	tailor	1937
6	Péter Bakonyi	waiter	1926		Péter Bakonyi	waiter	1926
7	n. a.				Hajdu		
8	József Eisler	chandler	1908		József Eisler	chandler	1908
	n. a.				Mrs. Kálmán Polgár		
	n. a.				Ignác Róth		
	n. a.				Mrs. Miksa Eisentadter		
	n. a.				Iván Ámbori		

Appendix 6
The text of the memory plaque

In eternal memory of our fellow humans who fell victim to fascist persecution on October 15, 1944

Braun Arthurné [Braun Asztrikné]
Faragó István
Faragó Istvánné
Faragó Lajos [correctly: István]
Grossmann Olga
Grünberger Ilona
Grünberger Margit
Grünberger Vilmos
Lichter Izrael
Mann Vilma
Singer Ernő
Steiner Andor
Steiner Béla
Steiner István
Steiner Lajos
Stern Ignác
Stern Ignácné
Takács Sándor
Tenczer Robert

Your sacrifice shows us the way towards building a free, happy Hungary.
The tenants of the house.

Appendix 7
The victims of the Csengery Street massacre

	Commemorative plaque	Strucky when...	With whom...	Where he found them...	Apartment of residence
1	Mrs. Arthur Braun	Morning	Ignác Stern Mrs. Ignác Stern	3rd floor 1 (bathroom)	1st floor 2/a.
2	István Faragó	Evening	alone	2nd floor 2	2nd floor 2
3	Mrs. István Faragó	Evening	Béla Bodor the 2 Grünberger girls Vilma Mann	2nd floor 3.	2nd floor 2
4	Lajos Faragó (correctly István)	Morning	Landlord – evening, tenant - morning	2nd floor 2	2nd floor 2
5	Olga Grossmann (the third Grünberger-girl)	Morning	Sándor Takács Vilmos Grünberger	2nd floor 1	GF 2
6	Ilona Grünberger	Evening	Béla Bodor Margit Grünberger Mrs. István Faragó Vilma Mann	2nd floor 3	GF 2
7	Margit Grünberger	Evening	Béla Bodor Ilona Grünberger Mrs. István Faragó Vilma Mann	2nd floor 3	GF 2
8	Vilmos Grünberger	Morning	Sándor Takács Olga Grossmann	2nd floor 1	GF 2
9	Izidor Lichter				1st floor 6
10	Vilma Mann	Evening	Béla Bodor The two Grünberger girls Mrs. István Faragó	2nd floor 3	
11	Ernő Singer	Evening	István and Béla Steiner, Lajos Steiner, Róbert Tenczer	4th floor 4	1st floor 5
12	Andor Steiner	Evening	István Steiner and Lajos, Róbert Tenczer	1st floor 5	2nd floor 5

Note: Based on people's tribunals's trial records and testimonies.

https://doi.org/10.1515/9783110687552-021

Continued

	Commemorative plaque	Strucky when...	With whom...	Where he found them...	Apartment of residence
13	Béla Steiner	Evening	Ernő Singer, István Steiner, Lajos Steiner, Róbert Tenczer	4th floor 4	3rd floor 1
14	István Steiner	Evening	Andor Steiner, Róbert Tenczer	1st floor 5	2nd floor 5
15	Lajos Steiner	Evening	István and Béla Steiner, Ernő Singer and Róbert Tenczer	4th floor 4	
16	Ignác Stern	Morning	Mrs. Ignác Stern Mrs. Arthur Braun	3rd floor 1 (bathroom)	3rd floor 1
17	Mrs. Ignác Stern	Morning	Ignác Stern Mrs. Arthur Braun	3rd floor 1 (bathroom)	3rd floor 1
18	Sándor Takács	Morning	Vilmos Grünberger Olga Grossmann	2nd floor 1	
19	Róbert Tenczer	evening	István Steiner Andor Steiner	1st floor 5	4th floor 4
	Béla Bodor (missing form the plaque)	Evening	Vilma Mann two Grünberger girls Mrs. István Faragó	2nd floor 3	2nd floor 3

Based on the reconstruction in further sources, the victims on the plaque and the places they were found are as follows:

Braun Arthurné [Mrs. Braun]
Faragó István 2/2
Faragó Istvánné 2/3
Faragó Lajos [correctly István] 2/3
Grossmann Olga [the "third Grünberger-girl" in the testimonies]
Grünberger Ilona 2/2
Grünberger Margit 2/3
Grünberger Vilmos 2/3
Lichter Izrael
Mann Vilma
Singer Ernő
Andor Steiner 1/5
Steiner Béla
Steiner István

Lajos Steiner
Stern Ignác [Steiner]
Stern Ignácné [Steiner]
Takács Sándor
Tenczer Róbert 1/5
Béla Bodor 2/3 [name missing from the plaque]

Appendix 8
Petition for the Csengery Street commemorative plaque

National Heritage Committee
1205 Budapest P.O. Box 19

Dear Mrs. Katalin Fogarasi-Radnai!
We turn to You and the National Heritage Committee with a request in the matter of the protection of a Budapest commemorative plaque. The plaque was erected by the tenants of District 6 Csengery Street 64, that is our parents, immediately after the Second World War, to commemorate our 19 innocent relatives and neighbors who were murdered by fascist German soldiers and their Arrow Cross companions who intruded into the house on October 15, 1944, the day Szálasi came to power. They yelled for firearms but they were aware that there had been no weapons hidden in the house. By that time working age men were all taken away, only the frightened elderly, the crippled, the women and the children remained – not the most combattant populace. We were 5-16 years old children then and the bloody tragedy took place right in front of our eyes. On the approaching 60th anniversary of the Holocaust we would like to commemorate our deads together with our children and grandchildren at the plaque. Please provide official protection to the plaque so it does not become a chance victim of the soon beginning house renovation. For many years now the house stores the trashbins right underneath the plaque. What a shameful and unworthy surrounding! If this is within your remit please let us place the plaque on the street wall or in the courtyard. On our part we are ready to provide all help. We hope that our request would be received with understanding and we are looking forward to your viewpoint and assistance. In support of our statements here are the signatures of the eyewitnesses in accordance with the Hungarian State Archives' 94/945 court documents. (This trial was a 1945 People's Tribunal trial against those Arrow Cross people who "suggested" our house to the Germans and accompanied them.)

Forgács Antalné Gábor Zsuzsa
Radványi Pálné Beck Vera
Petőcz Károlyné Rosenberg Edit
Kun Jánosné Krámer Ilona
Kun János
Ickovits Tibor

https://doi.org/10.1515/9783110687552-022

Ickovits Ágnes
Dr. Morton József

Appendix 9
Interview with the son of Nándor Szamocseta

"Those were messy affairs. My father didn't like to talk about it, his sister told me those things because he never talked much about it. He was a liaison between the German and the Hungarian army; he worked for the German intelligence. He was in Germany, he learned his craft, he got military training, [he had] perfect German, 30 years later he was a technical translator. He worked as a translator in the army. There was a conversation that I heard, that's how I got to know that he was trained in Germany. He went there following an advertisement, but I don't know what kind of training he received exactly. He got specialized. He was not politically aware.

My grandfather was a gentleman's tailor; he worked for famous people. The family had a shop that was nationalized. He was arrested and terribly beaten up on the Andrássy Avenue. He got home and soon he died. This happened in '45-'46. I don't know when he died. He was severely beaten, that's why he died. Grandmother said that he was taken to Andrássy Avenue where he was beaten and probably got an internal issue. He was released and soon died. I think he got kidney injuries. In 1946 my father's sister and my grandmother had no more ties here. They went abroad. Father was in prison for ten years they didn't wait for him. He didn't leave in 1956, he met my mother and he didn't go to the West.

Father started a new life and a family. His wife died earlier, his parents died. My sister was born in 1957. From my mother's side, I'm from Nógrád and Vác, that's where my father was imprisoned. That's where he was released, that's where they met. I don't know how they met. Me and my sister grew up in Vác. I don't have many memories about father.

My father died in 1982, he suffered a lot. He was so quiet about his time in prison that I was 18 when I got to know. He didn't want me to have a problem. He didn't want that to be a bother in Communism. In the army the political officer said that the children shouldn't suffer for the deeds of the fathers. I was a photographer. I had a camera in the barracks. There was a sign: be alert. The political officer was the real boss. I was in the army in 1984.

He didn't say anything about the time before the war. Grandmother was an active member of the church. She got papers for Jewish acquaintances. My father got certificates of baptism for Jews in the house.

My father had hip problems. In the prisoners' camp they worked waist-deep in water. That's why. I have fragmented memories. Socialism was in full force when I was a child. My father didn't want me to feel ashamed. During the war they went to visit Auntie Emmi [Mrs. Strucky] to Göd. Éva Strucky died, her daughter is a teacher. Where she lives today I don't know. When we were still in contact I was 6-7 years old. Then Auntie Emmi died. The family ties loosened.

My father told me nothing. I was a member of the Communist Youth Alliance. He didn't mind that I lived in harmony with the expectations of those times. [...] My political views started to clear up in 1985-86. Then I started to see things more clearly. I grew up in the system. My father was an educated man, he spoke five languages, Slavic languages. Grandfather was Serb, perfect in German, then in the prison he learned English, Russian. He read and did crosswords. He was technically well trained. I learned a lot from him. As a kid I considered him smart. Every kid looks up to his father. I didn't know what he was accused of, I don't know what he did only that he was in prison for war crimes. I don't like to trouble myself with that but I'm curious. It would be better to give it a wide berth. If I had been my father and if I had done something that put me to prison for ten years, I wouldn't have talked about it either. Back then everyone was sentenced for war crimes, I assume for political reasons."

Appendix 10
List of illustrations

Figure 1: Map of Budapest, 20.
Figure 2: House, 21.
Figure 3: Map of the cellar, 22.
Figure 4: The janitor's apartment, 24
Figure 5: The commemorative plaque, 52.

Index of Names

Arendt, Hannah   9f., 14, 95, 112
Assmann, Jan   4, 106
Aupek, Viktor, Mrs (née Teréz Glück)   71, 74, 143, 145, 155f.

Balla, Erzsébet   10
Bán, Sándor   86
Bauer, Mrs.   56, 71
Bodor, Henrik, Mrs   141, 150, 157, 163, 165, 171–173
Bodor, Ilona (Mrs. Mózes Rubinyi)   21, 72, 88, 141, 143, 145, 150, 153, 157, 163, 164, 165, 171–173
Bodor, Imre   141, 150, 157, 163, 165, 171–173
Bodor, László   141, 143, 150, 153, 157, 163, 165, 171–173
Bodor, Miklós   63, 82, 104, 141, 150, 157, 163, 165, 171–173 148, 150, 157, 163, 165
Bodor family   154
Booth, W. James   90, 93
Browning, Christopher   9, 47
Bydeskuti, Aladár, Mrs   68, 73, 144f., 152f., 159

Chamberlain, Mary   35, 104, 107
Chambers, Ross   18

Danto, Arthur C.   109
Dely, Piroska (see in Index of Terms)   1, 3f., 11, 13–15, 19, 23, 26–28, 32, 35–51, 54, 56, 58f., 62, 65f., 70, 79, 93f., 98, 101, 104, 112–113 115, 130–133, 135f., 138, 142, 145, 148–154
Dely, Terézia   15, 26f., 36–51, 56, 58–63, 66, 70, 98, 101, 104, 113, 115, 130–133, 149–152
Diner, Dan   79
Douglas, Lawrence   80, 112

Eichmann, Adolf   9f., 14, 95, 112

Eisenstadter, Miksa   55, 66, 143, 148, 156, 162
Eisenstadter, Miksa, Mrs   66f., 73f., 148, 156
Endre, László   77, 131, 146, 165f., 168
Erdélyi, Lujza, MD   54, 64

Faragó, István (lodger)   39, 59, 60, 70, 87, 143, 145, 150, 152, 164f., 170–172
Faragó, István (owner)   39, 59, 70, 87, 143, 145, 150, 152, 164f., 170–172
Faragó, Miklós, Mrs   39, 70, 87, 143, 145, 150, 164f., 170–172
Friedländer, Saul   18, 77

Gábor, Ervin, Mrs   15, 46, 60f., 67, 69, 71, 82, 85, 88, 108, 110, 132f., 142f., 145, 149, 151–153, 155–157, 159, 163–165, 167, 174
Golb, Joel   79
Göth, Amon   77
Gruber, Ernő   42, 149
Grünberger, Ilona   60, 67, 142f., 145, 149f., 152, 154, 156, 161, 170–172
Grünberger, Margit   60, 67, 142f., 145, 149f., 152, 154, 156, 161, 170–172
Grünberger, Vilmos, Mrs   60, 67, 142f., 145, 149f., 152, 154, 156, 161, 170–172
Grünberger, Vilmos   60, 67, 142f., 145, 149f., 152, 154, 156, 161, 170–172
Grünberger girl   59f., 152, 171f.
Grünfeld, Izsák Mrs   148, 154
Gyáni, Gábor   108

Habermas, Jürgen   111
Hoffman, Eva   100
Horthy, Miklós   2, 15, 18, 21, 29, 79, 149
Huizinga, Johan   98

Jelin, Elizabeth   93
Jellinek family   84

Kádár, Pál, Dr   13, 15, 69, 74, 82, 91 f., 144 f., 156
Kalliszta, Emília (Mrs. József Strucky)   66 f., 145 f.
Kalliszta, Mária (Mrs. György Szamocseta)   66, 145 f.
Kalliszta sisters   65
Karády, Katalin   70, 95
Kardos, Péter   105, 167
Kiss, István   45, 65, 94, 143
Klein, Kerwin Lee   117, 142 f., 160, 167, 169
Krámer, Béla, Mrs   69, 75, 86 f., 89, 131–133, 141–143, 145, 149, 155–158, 163, 166, 174
Kulcsár, István   97
Kun, János   1, 23, 55, 102, 109, 168, 174
Kun, Magda   23, 39, 87, 90, 98, 102 f., 108 f., 168, 174

Lagrou, Pierre   95
Landeszmann, György   105
László, Gyula, Mrs.   11, 15 f., 29 f., 57, 96, 115, 131–133, 141 f., 145 f., 156, 161–163, 167 f.
Laub, Dor   44, 94, 103
Laub, Pál   44, 94, 130, 132 f.
Leydesdorff, Selma   90, 107
Lichter, Andor   19, 26, 36 f., 40, 44, 49–52, 54, 55 f., 58, 64–66, 68–70, 73, 77, 83, 85–87, 90, 92–100, 103, 114 f., 117, 131 f., 135, 142–145, 152, 154, 156, 157, 158, 159, 164, 170–172
Lichter, Andor, Mrs   9, 26, 36–38, 44, 46, 51, 54, 65, 68–70, 77, 85–87, 90, 92–100, 108, 114, 117, 142 f., 149, 152, 157, 159, 164, 170–172
Lichter, Izrael   9, 26, 36–38, 44, 46, 51, 54, 64, 65, 68–70, 77, 85–87, 90, 92–100, 108, 114, 117, 142 f., 151, 152, 157, 159, 164, 170–172
Lőrinczi, Géza   115
Lübbe, Hermann   111

Mahmood, Saba   8
Maier, Charles   117
Margalit, Avishai   92 f., 95
Mezey, Mrs   54

Nora, Pierre   13 f., 78
Pál, János, Mrs   3, 65, 69, 74, 83, 85, 86, 87, 91 f., 137, 144 f., 156, 161, 163 f., 167
Pál, János   3, 65, 69, 74, 83, 85, 86, 87, 91 f., 131, 137, 142 f., 144 f., 156, 157, 161, 163 f.
Pap, Etel   26, 43, 56, 130, 146, 149
Passerini, Luisa   80, 110
Payne, Leigh A.   40, 93
Pelinka, Anton   111 f.
Propper, László, Mrs, dr.   45, 87, 142, 150, 154, 167

Rajk, László   30, 135
Reiter, Margit   76, 78–80, 98
Rigney, Ann   98, 106
Rosenberg, Edit   39, 57 f., 64, 75, 88 f., 94, 100, 106, 143, 145, 161, 174
Rosenthal, Gabriele   78 f., 81 f., 100, 131–133
Rothberg, Michael   116
Rózsa, László, Mrs   67, 141, 164 f.
Rubinyi Mózes Mrs (née Ilona Bodor)   21, 164

Salzer, Vilmos, Mrs (née Lujza Háy)   26
Sárdi, Jenő, Mrs   56, 87, 142 f., 145, 164
Schillinger, Livia   54, 168
Schwartz, Jakab, Mrs   72, 88, 143, 145, 149, 153, 162
Simon, Etel   42 f., 130
Singer, Ernő   53 f., 61 f., 72, 84, 143, 159, 164 f., 167, 170–172
Steiner, Alajos, Mrs   23, 42, 44, 47, 49, 51, 54, 61–63, 65, 132 f., 138, 142, 145, 149 f., 153, 165, 170–173
Steiner, Andor, Mrs   23, 42, 44, 47, 49, 51, 54, 61–63, 65, 83, 132 f., 138, 142, 145, 149 f., 153, 154, 165, 170–173
Steiner, Andor   23, 42, 44, 47, 49, 51, 54, 58 f., 61–63, 65, 83, 132 f., 138, 142, 145, 149 f., 153, 165, 170–173
Steiner, Lajos, Mrs   23, 42, 44, 47, 49, 51, 54, 61–63, 65, 83, 132 f., 138, 142, 145, 149 f., 153 f., 165, 170–173

Index of Names — **181**

Steiner, Lajos   23, 42, 44, 47, 49, 51, 54, 61–63, 65, 132f., 138, 142, 145, 148–150, 153, 165, 168, 170–173
Stern, Ignác   67f., 75, 85f., 152, 166, 171f.
Stern, Ignác, Mrs   164, 167, 170, 173
Stern, Ignác   164, 167, 170, 173
Stongl Mrs   67
Strucky, Éva   21, 23, 37, 45f., 51, 53, 58–61, 63f., 66–68, 73, 75, 81f., 84–88, 141, 143, 146, 148, 151–157, 171f., 177
Strucky, József   16, 21, 23, 25, 37, 45f., 51, 53, 57, 59–61, 63, 65–-68, 7375, 81f., 84–88, 132f., 141, 143–147, 151–157, 161, 166, 171f.
Strucky, József, Mrs (née Kalliszta, Emília)   21, 23, 37, 45f., 47, 49, 51, 53, 59–61, 63f., 66–68, 71, 73–76, 81f., 84–88, 141–146,, 151–157, 161, 171f.
Strucky family   17, 21, 25, 39, 41, 56, 58f., 64–69, 75f., 82–89, 94f., 100, 141, 148, 150, 152, 156, 166
Strucky-Szamocseta family   2, 4, 5,, 25, 65–66, 71, 76, 80, 96, 145
Svéd, Iván   96
Szabó, Margit   28, 45, 149, 167
Szabó, Mária   28, 45, 70, 72, 144, 149, 167
Szakasits, Árpád   92
Szálasi, Ferenc   3, 85, 102f., 109, 148–151, 174
Szamocseta, György, Mrs (née Kalliszta, Mária)   44, 65, 68, 69, 70–72, 74–76, 78, 80–82, 84, 85, 88, 96, 114, 131, 139–142, 145f.,149, 153f., 158, 162, 169
Szamocseta, György   21, 44, 46, 65f., 68f., 70–72, 74–76, 78, 80–82, 84, 88f., 95, 114, 131, 139–142, 143–147, 150, 152, 153f., 157, 158, 162, 169
Szamocseta, Nándor   41, 44, 65, 68–76, 78, 80–82, 84, 86, 103, 106, 114, 131, 139–149, 152f., 155, 158–159, 162, 169, 176
Széplaki, (Szedlacsek) György, Sr   55, 57f., 67
Szilágyi, Sándor   103, 152, 155

Temesvári, Sándor, Mrs (Dely, Piroska)   27, 66, 134
Temesvári, Sándor   27, 134, 136, 142, 145
Tenczer, Miksa   42f., 133, 142, 145, 165, 168, 170, 173
Tenczer, Róbert   61f., 106, 150, 165, 168, 170, 171f., 173
Terdiman, Richard   116
Tildy, Zoltán   26, 50, 92, 135
Toronyi, Zsuzsa   77

Uprimny, Endre   72, 74, 168

Varga, Béla   58, 77, 91, 168
Veréb, András   42, 46, 132f., 142, 145
Veréb, András, Mrs   42, 132f.
Verebes, Mária   51, 95, 145, 152–154

Wachtel, Nathan   99
Welzer, Harald   78, 114
Werner, Alexander   48
Wieviorka, Annette   92
Willinger, Otto (Wildinger, Otto)   40

Zweig, Simon   26, 131–133

Index of Subjects

abettor 51, 58
accomplice 36, 48, 60, 62
accusation 33, 51, 56, 66f., 70
– accuse 31f., 37, 41, 44, 54, 65–68, 94, 146, 177
– accused person 66, 74, 138
agency 8, 15, 109, 117
air raid shelter 58, 69, 72, 84, 141, 149, 152f.
– air raid shelter commander 69, 76, 141
amnesty 35, 65, 90
Andrássy Avenue 43, 45, 60, 71, 102, 151, 176
Andrássy Avenue 60 20, 44, 58
anti-communism 7
– anti-communist 15
anti-fascist 5, 7f., 35, 77, 80, 96, 99, 102, 105, 108f., 111, 113f.
– anti-fascist rhetoric 7, 111
Anti-Jewish Laws 1f., 7, 18, 79
anti-Semite 68
– anti-Semitic 10, 18, 32, 66
– anti-Semitism 5, 18, 56, 96, 102
appeal 33, 73f., 117, 133–135, 146f.
armband 38f., 43, 45f., 48f., 72, 115
armed forces 1
armed intruder 3, 14, 16, 21, 23, 38, 42, 45, 47f., 53, 57–61, 73, 83, 85, 149, 151, 154
armed robbery 4, 16, 52
armistice 2, 29
arrest 57, 66, 68, 70, 143f., 146, 176
Arrow Cross 4, 13f., 19f., 25f., 32, 37–39, 42–46, 48, 53–55, 57f., 61, 64, 66f., 69f., 75, 82, 86, 88, 91f., 94, 110, 113, 115f., 133, 148, 150, 152–154, 159, 174
– Arrow Cross and German soldier 43, 59, 84, 130, 150
– Arrow Cross badge 41, 69, 130
– Arrow Cross armband 38, 42, 46, 61, 104, 132, 149
– Arrow Cross coup 19, 52
– Arrow Cross house 26, 44, 69

– Arrow Cross man 38f., 42–44, 47, 52, 62, 66f., 70, 76, 91, 101, 130, 159
– Arrow Cross member 4, 13, 30, 34, 46f., 50, 54, 68, 75, 131
– Arrow Cross Party 2f., 14f., 24, 26, 67, 115
– Arrow Cross rule 8, 16, 25, 75, 91
– Arrow Cross soldier 72, 156
– Arrow Cross takeover 10, 25, 48, 70
– Arrow Cross uniform 37–39, 151
– Arrow Cross woman 1, 4, 13, 15, 26, 43, 45–47, 49, 61, 66, 91, 98, 101, 103
asset 15f., 25, 36f., 56, 60, 67, 74, 76, 82f., 85–88, 115, 145, 147, 150, 154, 158
atrocity 4, 18, 51, 91, 133, 159
audience 5, 11, 17f., 77, 90, 99, 105
ÁVO 30, 144

belongings 15, 21, 35, 38, 45, 60, 67, 70, 75f., 83, 85–88, 108, 152, 157
benevolence 65f., 71, 75, 84
blackmail 25, 74
body 51, 54, 59f., 63f., 139, 152
– body search 61, 133, 149f.
Budapest 1–6, 10f., 13, 15f., 19–30, 32f., 35f., 40f., 51–53, 55–57, 65, 67, 70f., 82f., 87, 90f., 95f., 101–105, 107–110, 114f., 117, 133, 136–138, 143–147, 159, 174, 178
– battle of Budapest 10, 101
bury 53, 64, 95, 113

captivity 58, 141, 154
carpet 63, 82, 85f., 88
casualty 60, 63
Christian 2, 20, 23, 25, 32, 51, 82f., 95f., 115, 148, 150, 154
Christian janitor 3, 16, 18, 59, 84
civilian 2, 4, 28, 47, 49, 53, 58, 72, 113
clothing items 85, 88, 157
Cold War 7, 110, 115

https://doi.org/10.1515/9783110687552-026

Index of Subjects

collaborate   41, 45, 69, 85 f., 92, 116
– collaborator   4, 33 f., 95
collective memory   4, 6, 99, 104, 107, 115 f.
command   26, 37, 41, 46–48, 61, 86, 130, 133, 149, 151
commander   40, 56
commemorate   51, 105, 108, 174
commemorative plaque   5, 19, 51 f., 54, 61, 77, 99, 102, 105 f., 108 f., 138, 170–174, 178
Committee for the Investigation of Nazi and Arrow Cross Atrocities   13, 91
common offence   52, 73
communicative memory   4, 6
communism   8 f., 80, 102, 107, 176
– collapse of communism   107, 114
– communist   7 f., 29, 35, 56, 77, 79 f., 92, 96, 98 f., 102, 109–111, 115, 177
– Communist Party   30 f., 35, 56, 80, 91, 110
– communist police   47, 56
concentration and death camp   6, 10, 14, 101
confiscate   38, 68, 82, 86, 131, 145, 147
conspiracy   45, 55, 79
corpse   51, 53, 59 f., 63 f., 85, 152 f.
court   15, 17, 27, 29, 31–35, 37, 42, 45, 49, 51, 58, 68 f., 74 f., 90, 98, 110, 112–114, 117, 137 f., 145, 147, 174
– court process   27, 32, 65, 76, 82, 95, 106, 112
– court records   32 f., 49, 66, 94, 138, 171
crime   3, 8, 11, 16, 27 f., 32, 35 f., 41 f., 45, 48, 56, 64, 70, 77, 81, 93, 95, 112, 115 f.
– crime against people   11, 29, 35, 66, 73, 112
– crimes against humanity   28 f.
– crimes against property   18, 74
– crime scene   19, 37 f., 46, 48, 52, 115
criminal   7, 26 f., 29 f., 34, 90 f., 131, 137
Csengery Street   2, 5, 19, 26, 37, 41, 43 f., 49, 53–55, 65, 70, 79, 88 f., 91, 93–96, 98, 100–102, 106, 108 f., 113, 130, 133, 142, 150, 174
– Csengery 64 tenant   16, 23, 55, 83, 99
– Csengery 64 trials   92, 99

– Csengery Street 45   42, 44, 46, 48, 51, 58, 130, 132 f., 149, 153
– Csengery Street 55   70, 141, 144, 148
– Csengery Street 62   58, 141, 144, 146, 149 f., 159
– Csengery Street 64   2–5, 13–18, 20, 22 f., 26, 29, 37–39, 42, 44, 46–49, 51, 53–58, 63, 66, 69 f., 81 f., 85 f., 91, 99, 102–105, 109, 114, 117, 131, 138 f., 141 f., 148, 151 f., 154 f., 157, 159, 161, 174
– Csengery Street case   11, 38, 65, 106
– Csengery Street house   45, 113
– Csengery Street massacre   1, 8, 13 f., 19, 36 f., 48, 52 f., 57, 61, 77, 79, 94, 98, 104, 109, 113, 148, 171
culpable   76, 116
culprit   6, 36, 43, 64, 69, 114
cultural memory   98, 106
curse   32, 44, 75, 130

dead   3, 13, 45, 47, 49, 51, 53 f., 58, 60 f., 63 f., 66, 84, 91, 96, 99, 109, 150–152, 154, 174
death penalty   26, 36, 96
death sentence   1, 11, 14, 46, 49, 115, 133
deceased   54, 62, 67, 75
decree   2, 22, 28–30, 155
defendant   31–33
defense   32, 41, 54, 69, 74, 101, 108
Dely case   4, 6, 9, 11, 34 f., 37, 66, 70, 77, 108, 115
– Dely-razzia   53
– Dely's testimony   41, 55, 66, 113
– Dely-Szamocseta case   112
– Dely trial   26, 30 f., 60, 70, 82, 85, 89, 98, 110
denounce   35, 65 f., 74, 130, 157
– denouncement   35, 45, 52, 90, 94, 143
– denouncer   91
– denunciation letter   17, 36, 58
deport   2, 23, 26, 36 f., 45, 54, 56, 59, 68, 76, 84, 86–88, 92, 113, 130, 138, 154–156

Index of Subjects

deportation   3, 6, 15–17, 22 f., 36 f., 42, 49, 54 f., 60, 66 f., 75, 77, 83, 85, 88, 110, 131, 151, 156 f.
– mass deportation   2
deprivation of rights   30
– deprived   15, 115
detective   64, 131, 154
dispossession   15, 82, 84
"double occupation"   8, 11
drive away   47, 49, 59
dynamics of memory   98, 106

escape   23, 32, 42 f., 55, 60, 90 f., 103, 139, 149, 156
evidence   16, 33, 44, 47, 90 f., 114
evil   9, 40, 68 f., 80, 93, 95, 112
execute   1, 4, 10, 26, 36, 50 f., 66, 82, 91, 98, 116, 145
execution   37, 45, 50 f., 66, 90, 134 f.
executive power   26, 47, 61
eyewitness   26, 36–39, 42, 44, 54, 64, 94 f., 103, 174

far right   2, 6, 8, 15, 45
fascist   9, 34, 74, 80, 92, 170, 174
financial gain   3, 25, 74, 81
financial loss   82, 89
fire   18, 55, 82, 133, 138, 149, 155
firearm (see also: gun, pistol, revolver, weapon)   46, 55, 113, 138, 174
fire order   49, 51, 54, 62, 150
First World War   1, 15, 27
food supply   75, 87, 89, 156
forced labor   35 f., 80, 145–147
– forced laborer   14, 28
– forced labor service   23, 26, 42, 74, 156
forcible relocation   2, 22
forcibly taken away   26, 42, 49, 60, 64, 74, 115
forged documents   68, 91, 152
forgetfulness   91, 95
forgetting   6–9, 11 f., 19, 56, 78, 90, 93–95, 98, 106, 108 f., 113
– selective forgetting   6, 19, 117
forgiveness   90, 94 f.
forgiving   94 f.
forgotten   6, 11, 27, 98 f.

forsaken apartment   76, 86
functional memory   106
furniture   62, 86–88, 156

gender   4, 9, 17, 27, 32, 40, 46, 116
German   1 f., 6, 8–10, 12, 15, 26, 28, 32–34, 37–46, 48, 51, 55, 61 f., 68–72, 74, 76–82, 85, 95, 100, 108, 111, 114–116, 132, 138 f., 141, 148–150, 153, 155, 174, 176 f.
German soldier   52, 59, 68, 153, 159, 174
Germany   1 f., 17, 37, 70, 107, 111, 139, 176
– West Germany   80, 115
Gestapo   26, 40, 50, 63, 68, 70–72, 74, 141, 148, 155
gold   38, 42 f., 61, 133, 136 f., 150
government   1, 6, 11, 29, 34, 64, 77, 110, 116
greed   6, 16, 44, 66, 82
guilt   79
– guilty   33, 36, 40
gun (see also: firearms, pistol, revolver, weapon)   47, 67

Hársfa Street   37, 41
– Hársfa Street 57   38, 42 f., 51, 131, 133
– Hársfa Street case   37, 131
– Hársfa Street robbery   36 f., 44
headquarters   20, 56
– German headquarters   43 f., 48, 55, 133, 140
– HSP Budapest Police Headquarters   136, 142–145
hearing   42 f., 49, 58, 82, 154
hiding   7, 11, 42, 54, 58, 60, 63, 69, 84, 89, 101, 150, 157, 159
hiding Jews   17, 54, 76
high-profile court case   19, 35
historical framework   10, 78
historiography   4 f., 11, 17, 26, 28, 35, 67, 98, 109 f.
Holocaust   3–8, 10 f., 14, 16, 18–20, 34, 36, 65, 67, 73, 76–80, 86, 90, 94, 96, 98, 100–105, 107, 109, 111, 114–117, 174
– Holocaust memorial   5, 19, 29, 35, 104
– Holocaust Memorial Center   98, 103, 108

- Holocaust memorialization   7, 98
- Holocaust research   4, 6, 11, 98
Horthy proclamation   3, 55, 84, 148
House of Faith (Andrássy Avenue Arrow Cross Headquarter)   20, 43, 57
House Office responsible for the redistribution of Jewish property   68, 85f.
house overseer   37, 85, 87f., 157
house search   72, 88, 131, 151, 153
Hungarian   1f., 4–17, 19f., 24, 28–37, 47, 50, 53f., 56–59, 63, 67f., 72, 77, 79f., 90f., 96–98, 101f., 105, 109–112, 114, 116, 131, 137, 153, 164f., 174, 176
- Hungarian citizen   7, 10, 74
- Hungarian Jews   2, 15, 110
1956 Hungarian Revolution   13, 24, 30, 35, 116
Hungarian State Police (HSP)   131f., 143
Hungary   1–4, 6–8, 11, 13–15, 17, 24, 28f., 34f., 38, 40, 46, 56, 65, 71, 77, 82, 86, 90–92, 94–96, 98f., 102, 106f., 109, 114, 116f., 170

ignorance of sin   95
illiberal   13, 34f., 99, 110, 117
imprison   34, 115, 145f., 176
indict   27, 32, 48, 51, 66f., 70, 74, 115, 131f., 145f.
intern   96, 141
internment   69
- internment camp   96, 115, 143, 146
interpret   40, 64, 78, 94, 104, 114
- interpretation   5, 11, 17f., 23, 29, 47, 106, 114
interrogate   65, 131, 144
interview   5, 9, 16–19, 22f., 31, 36, 39, 47, 49, 55f., 64, 75, 78–80, 87–90, 92, 94, 96, 98, 100–107, 109, 113, 128, 161, 176
- interviewee   5, 39, 81
intimacy   14, 83, 87
- intimate murder   14, 52
- intimate violence   6, 19, 36
intrude   3, 13, 85, 174
inventory   86, 99

investigate   64, 91, 104, 136, 154
- investigation   31, 37, 42, 45, 51, 74, 91, 132f., 144
invisibility   4, 6, 113
- invisibilize   8, 11, 47, 99
- invisible   1, 4, 18, 20, 94, 112

janitor   2f., 5, 16f., 21, 23–25, 37, 41–46, 48, 51, 53f., 58–60, 63, 65–68, 75, 79, 82–89, 103, 131, 142, 148–152, 156f., 162
jeweler   3, 23, 44, 54
Jewish   6, 8–10, 16, 18f., 32, 36, 53, 55f., 68, 70, 73, 75–77, 86, 96–99, 105, 107, 141, 150, 155, 157, 176
- Jewish Acts   10, 84
- Jewish children   41f.
- Jewish citizen   1f., 15, 20, 114
- Jewish community   2, 10, 14, 95, 99
- Jewish congregation   5, 102, 105, 109, 113
- Jewish family   19, 22–24
- Jewish owner   24f., 83
- Jewish resident   22f.
- Jewish tenant   2f., 16–18, 21, 23, 25, 37, 41, 56, 58, 60, 66–69, 72, 74f., 84, 103, 133, 141, 148, 152
- Jewish woman   24, 43, 47
- Jewry   2, 6, 10, 75, 82, 95–97, 109
- Hungarian Jewry   2, 15, 82, 95, 97
Jews   2f., 5, 7, 10, 13, 15f., 18–20, 22, 28, 34f., 38, 42, 44, 47f., 52, 55, 67, 71f., 76, 80, 82, 86f., 95–97, 106, 108, 110, 115, 130, 133, 141f., 148–151, 153f., 156f., 159, 176
judge   5, 30–33, 41, 134
judicial process   30f., 91f.
justice system   31–34, 46, 50, 56, 63, 115

Kerepesi Cemetery's Parcel of Martyrs   53, 113, 138
kill   6, 10, 26, 36, 42, 46, 50, 52f., 55, 57, 61–63, 87, 92, 113
killing   8, 14, 26, 47, 91, 150
- mass killing   19, 52

lawyer   31–33, 70, 73, 115, 164, 167
- appointed lawyer   32, 145, 147

Index of Subjects

legal   6, 11, 14, 17f., 23, 25, 27–33, 35, 37, 67, 82, 104, 112–114, 117
– legal framework   6, 29, 112
– legal process   9, 80
– legal system   30, 33–35, 65, 107
liberation   3, 19, 21, 64, 68, 70f., 76, 82, 86–88, 157
local administrator of the house   59, 151
lodger   24, 41, 67, 84, 141, 148, 150, 152, 161, 163–167
loot   4, 47, 84

massacre   3–5, 7, 11, 13f., 16, 19f., 26, 36f., 45, 47, 49, 51–54, 57, 60, 64, 66, 74f., 77, 94, 100, 104, 108, 110, 117, 150, 154
mass deportation   2
mass grave   53, 64
mass murderer   9, 91
memorial   5, 99f., 105, 109
– memorialization   6, 19, 104–106, 108
memory   1, 4–9, 11, 17–19, 28, 33, 35, 47, 64, 76–81, 90, 92–110, 112–117, 170, 176
– memory culture   6, 8, 19, 98f., 106f., 112, 114
– memory entrepreneur   93
– "memory industry"   117
– memory militant   93
– memory of truth (memory-truth)   93
– memory owner   117
– memory politics   4–8, 13, 34f., 77, 93, 98f., 115, 117
– memory turn   109f.
military   1, 14, 23, 27–29, 33, 40, 55, 69f., 76, 105, 139, 176
Ministry of Internal Affairs   2, 96, 113, 138
Ministry of Justice   31, 34, 91, 113, 115, 133
monument   5, 98, 109
MÜNE   32f.
murder (see also: killing)   3, 5, 14f., 18, 19, 26, 46f., 49, 51, 53–55, 57–58, 62, 64f 82f., 86, 99, 104, 174
– murderer   13, 36, 62, 138

Nagyatádi (Kertész) Street   37, 43, 48f., 51, 54f., 130, 133, 151–155

narratability   79, 100
– narratable   13, 19, 89, 100
– narration   17, 26, 100, 104
– narrative   5, 7, 11, 14, 17, 41, 43, 46, 54–56, 63, 78–80, 90, 100f., 104, 106f., 109
Nazi   1f., 8, 35–37, 65, 77–79, 91, 95, 114f.
neighbor   14, 51, 65, 150, 174
– neighborhood   19, 43f., 86
non-Jewish   2, 10, 141
NOT30f., 73, 133–135, 146

occupation
– double occupation   7
– German occupation   7, 16, 18, 24, 40
occupy   2, 6, 8, 14, 16, 24, 41, 71, 73
– occupying German forces   20, 69
October 15, 1944   2f., 5, 13f., 16f., 19, 21–23, 26, 36, 44, 47f., 51, 53, 55, 58f., 64, 67, 73, 84, 93f., 99, 101, 103, 105, 108, 114f., 130, 142, 148, 161–170, 174
October 16   52, 60, 63, 89, 151, 153, 159
offence   29, 34, 44
officer   39, 56, 59, 72, 74, 77, 101, 162, 166, 176
– army officer   56, 148
– German officer   40f.
oral history interviews   2, 17, 38, 112

party delegate   31, 33
penal action   45
penal squad   44f.
people's judge   32, 91f.
people's prosecutor 34, 36, 69, 91f., 131f., 135–137, 144
– people's prosecutor's office   31, 35, 91
people's tribunal   1, 3–6, 8, 11, 14f., 17f., 23, 28–36, 40f., 43, 49, 51, 54, 57f., 66, 69, 73–76, 79, 89, 91, 94, 96f., 100, 102, 106–108, 110f., 113–116, 130f., 133–136, 145f., 171
– Budapest people's tribunal   13, 28, 30, 35, 73, 132–137, 145f.
– people's tribunal process   31, 34, 74, 77, 99

Index of Subjects

- people's tribunals' press releases   36, 45, 106
- people's tribunal trial   1, 4, 13, 42, 65, 100 f., 131 f., 174
perpetrator   4–10, 13 f., 16–19, 28, 36 f., 40, 43, 45, 48 f., 52 f., 55, 61, 65, 76–80, 91, 94, 104, 106 f., 110–112, 114 f., 117
- female perpetrator   4, 14 f., 32, 112
- Hungarian perpetrator   6, 8, 112
- ordinary perpetrator   9, 47, 78
persecute   7, 74, 79, 83, 88
- persecuted people   71, 73–76
- persecution   7, 37, 170
Persilschein   16, 74, 142, 159
personal items   17, 83
pistol (see also firearms, revolver, gun, weapon)   48 f., 133, 149
plotted political penal action   52
plunder   15 f., 18, 26, 44, 58, 67, 72, 82, 115, 130, 133, 154
police   9, 16 f., 26 f., 30, 35–37, 40, 42, 46 f., 49, 51 f., 57–59, 64, 68 f., 76, 84, 115, 143, 148, 150, 154, 158
- police hearing   4, 17, 27, 37, 42, 47, 62, 72, 100
- police investigator   16, 51 f.
- political police   64, 91
possession   2, 44, 61, 76, 85, 157
post-Holocaust   28 f., 99
post-war Hungary   94, 110, 112
post-war justice   1, 11, 13, 15, 34 f., 90, 111, 114, 116
prison (see also: imprison)   3, 25, 34, 50, 57, 74, 84, 133–135, 143, 176 f.
"private memory"   113, 117
prosecutor   30 f., 49
punish   33, 41, 53, 64, 114, 116
- punishment   36, 41, 60, 73, 80, 90 f.

racist   7, 75, 78
reclaim   29, 35, 88, 100, 166
reconciliation   40, 93, 112
recovered memory   78
Red Army   2, 16, 30, 110
religion   7, 18, 93
- religious   56, 96, 110, 117

remember   8, 17, 22 f., 38 f., 49, 55, 63 f., 68, 70, 78–80, 84 f., 88, 94, 98–101, 105, 111, 116, 150, 163
remembrance   1, 3–6, 8, 12, 17, 19, 39, 77–79, 90, 92–94, 99–102, 106 f., 109 f., 113 f.
- collective and individual remembrance   11
- collective remembrance   81
- process of remembrance   8, 92, 113
report   9, 32, 35, 45, 55, 58, 64, 84, 95, 112, 115, 131, 134 f., 143
rescue   11, 17, 25, 56, 68, 73
- rescuer   16 f., 42, 80, 106
resistance   48, 55 f., 80, 110, 113 f., 116
- armed resistance   14, 56
- Jewish resistance   3, 14, 48, 52, 55 f., 108, 110
responsibility   7, 12, 16, 48, 60, 77 f., 81, 86, 112, 114, 117
- responsible   4, 26, 29, 57, 73 f., 151
retribution   15, 29, 34, 113
return   3, 15–17, 21, 26, 28, 31, 35–37, 52, 54, 58–61, 63–66, 71, 76, 82–89, 95 f., 99, 103, 108, 110 f., 115, 131, 138 f., 150, 152–158
revenge   18, 32, 48, 90 f., 96, 142
revisionist   6 f., 11 f., 34 f., 102
revolver (see also: firearms, gun, pistol, weapon)   46, 62, 72
ritualize   5, 18, 73, 90, 109
rob   3, 14, 16, 19, 25 f., 28, 44, 59, 84–86, 88 f., 108, 113
- robbery   15, 19, 36, 41, 43 f., 63, 73 f., 85–87, 108, 130
round up   21, 38, 43, 55, 58–60, 133, 150
Russian   27, 67, 82, 85–88, 142, 148, 177

sacrifice   99, 109 f., 116, 170
second instance appeal   31
second instance court   31, 146
Second World War   1 f., 4, 6–9, 11, 14 f., 27, 34, 41, 79, 81, 90, 96, 98, 102, 110, 114, 116, 174
sentence   1, 31 f., 35, 42, 49, 69, 73 f., 78, 113, 115, 146
- sentenced   6, 13, 28 f., 35, 43, 73 f., 82, 95, 177

shooting   54, 59 f., 91, 149–151
– shot   13, 16, 39, 49, 51, 54 f., 58, 60–63, 76, 83, 85, 99, 138, 149 f., 154
– shot dead   38, 42, 48, 63, 138
silence   8, 10, 76, 79, 90, 101, 104, 106, 109, 112
silencing   19, 111, 113
– "communicative silencing"   111
site of memory   108
slaughter   54, 113
soldier   2, 9, 39, 46, 48 f., 51, 55, 60, 63, 66, 69, 72, 86, 113, 149, 153, 159
source   4–6, 10, 13–17, 19, 27 f., 32, 35, 39, 46, 55, 70 f., 79, 116, 128, 172
Soviet   12, 30, 33 f., 45, 57 f., 91, 110 f., 116
Sovietization   30, 35
Soviet occupation 7, 30, 35, 116
Soviet tribunals   33
Soviet Union   2, 30, 34
SS   26, 39–42, 53, 56, 66, 69, 72, 138, 148 f., 153
SS soldier   13, 37 f., 41–44, 46–49, 56, 61 f., 70, 72, 91, 101, 113, 133, 148–150, 152–155
Stalin   33
– Stalinist   33, 107, 114
standardize   89, 101, 106
steal   45, 60, 67, 72, 82 f., 86–88, 153, 157
– stolen assets   87 f.
– stolen goods   69, 82, 86, 94, 131
storage memory   106
suffer   80, 112, 114–116, 138, 153, 176
survive   21, 42, 49, 61, 63 f., 108
– surviving   35, 54, 63, 96
surviving memories   98
survivor   1, 4–6, 13 f., 16–19, 22 f., 26, 31, 35–38, 40, 47, 49, 53, 56 f., 61–63, 65, 73, 76–78, 88–90, 92, 96, 98–106, 108 f., 111–114, 117
suspend   33, 49, 133 f., 147
Svábhegy Sanatorium   27 f., 40, 55, 130, 133
Svábhegy (section of Gestapo)   26, 41, 43, 56, 64, 68, 70, 140 f., 155
Szálasi coup   55, 84
Szamocseta-files   74

Szamocseta trial   82, 89, 113, 145
SZEB   70, 144

take away   3, 39, 41–43, 47 f., 59 f., 63, 66, 74, 86, 97, 103, 130, 148 f., 152, 154, 156, 174
tenant   3, 5, 13, 16–18, 20–25, 36 f., 42, 44–46, 49, 53 f., 56–60, 64 f., 67 f., 71–75, 82–89, 94, 101–103, 110, 131, 141 f., 149–151, 153 f., 157, 159, 161 f., 164–171, 174
– Christian tenant   24, 103, 142, 148
tenant registry   21, 23, 45, 161
testify   54, 85, 94, 98
testimony   4, 13 f., 17 f., 23, 26–28, 33, 36–43, 45–48, 51, 53–73, 76, 83–88, 90, 94–96, 102–104, 107 f., 112, 117, 130–132, 138, 144 f., 148, 150 f., 153–156, 171 f.
– court testimony   37, 40, 46, 53, 96, 112, 161
theft   38, 42, 84
torture   37, 43, 51, 151
transitional justice   15, 29, 114
transmission of memory   106
transmitter of memory   81
transport   45, 49, 54, 67, 70, 91, 94, 150 f.
trauma   12, 17 f., 90, 106, 112, 116 f.
trial   3 f., 6, 9 f., 14, 17–19, 23, 26, 28–31, 33 f., 36–38, 40–43, 45 f., 49, 53–57, 60, 63, 65, 69 f., 73, 76, 80, 89 f., 94, 96, 98, 100, 102, 106, 112 f., 130–133, 136, 138, 143–145, 174
– "didactic trial"   112
– public trial   66, 73, 132, 145
troops   2, 41, 103
– Arrow Cross or SS troops   84
– German troops   14, 48
– Soviet troops   16, 105
– SS troops   138
truth   5, 10, 40, 66 f., 76–78, 90, 93 f., 103, 112, 114
– truth of law   93
– truth of memory (truth-memory)   93

uniform   16, 38–40, 43, 48 f., 58, 71 f.,
    104, 149
– black uniform   38 f., 43, 46
– German uniform   39
– SS uniform   72

verdict   17, 28, 30 f., 33 f., 46–48, 65,
    73–76, 82, 96, 100, 102, 115, 133 f.,
    137, 146
victim   3, 5, 7 f., 14, 19, 28, 35 f., 43,
    51–54, 60, 63, 76–78, 80, 91, 93, 99,
    104–109, 111–114, 117, 138, 161, 170–
    172, 174
violence   4, 6, 9, 16, 18, 40, 53, 93 f., 114
Volksbund-house   140

war crime   26, 28 f., 33 f., 66, 80, 146, 177
war criminal   1, 15, 29 f., 36, 65, 95, 112
wealth   17, 19, 25 f., 58, 81–85, 87, 96
weapon (see also: firearm, gun, pistol, re-
    volver)   46 f., 54 f., 56, 113, 138, 150,
    174
witness   5, 8, 10, 13 f., 17, 23, 26, 37, 39,
    44, 46 f., 49, 51, 53–55, 59 f., 62, 66 f.,
    70 f., 85, 89 f., 92, 94, 103 f., 115, 132 f.,
    145 f., 148, 150
– moral witness   92–94
– political witness   92 f.
woman   4, 6, 8–10, 13–15, 19, 26, 28,
    31 f., 35, 38–47, 49 f., 54 f., 61, 63,
    66–70, 83, 88, 90, 100 f., 103 f., 116,
    132, 134, 147–149, 151 f., 154 f., 167 f.,
    174
woman of the Arrow Cross   1, 4, 8, 15, 24,
    46, 112
woman perpetrator   32
– perpetrator research   4, 9, 76
– woman perpetrator   8, 26
wound   55, 61 f., 151, 154

yellow star   2 f., 44 f., 55, 141, 148
– yellow star house   2 f., 16, 19, 23, 25, 48,
    72, 83 f., 108, 150, 155
– yellow star houses   2, 20, 22

Zionism   56, 110
Zionist   56

www.ingramcontent.com/pod-product-compliance
Lightning Source LLC
Chambersburg PA
CBHW071741150426
43191CB00010B/1653